Fiona Watson is a medieval historian and writer specialising in medieval warfare in particular, and Scottish history more generally. Among her many publications are *Macbeth: A True Story* (2010), *A History of Scotland's Landscapes* (2018), *Traitor, Outlaw, King. Part One. The Making of Robert Bruce* (2018) and *Scotland's History* (2020). A former senior lecturer in History at the University of Stirling and presenter of the 2001 TV series *In Search of Scotland*, she is now venturing into historical fiction to make the most of the limited evidence for medieval Scotland. Her novel *Dark Hunter* is published by Polygon in Summer 2022.

UNDER
THE
HAMMER

Edward I
and Scotland

FIONA WATSON

BIRLINN

This edition first published in 2022 by
Birlinn Ltd,
West Newington House
10 Newington Road
Edinburgh

www.birlinn.co.uk

First published in Great Britain in 1998 by Tuckwell Press
Subsequently published by John Donald in 2005

ISBN 978 1 78027 689 2

British Library Cataloguing in Publication Data
A catalogue record for this book is available on
request from the British Library

Typeset by Hewer Text Ltd, Edinburgh

Printed and bound by Clays Ltd, Elcograf S.p.A.

To Mum and Dad
A small thank you for so very much

CONTENTS

ILLUSTRATIONS

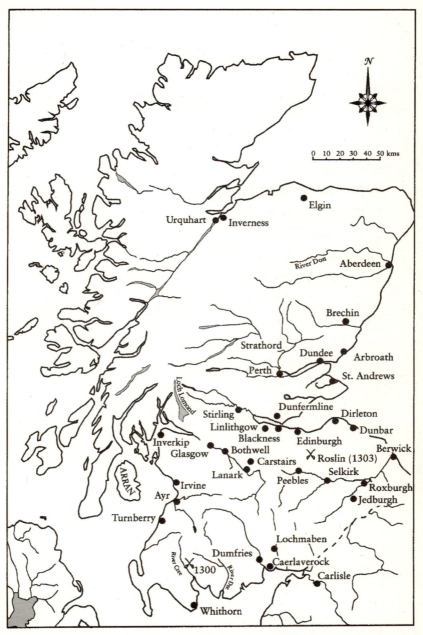

SCOTLAND IN THE TIME OF EDWARD I

TABLES

ACKNOWLEDGEMENTS

This book is largely based on the research I did at Glasgow University many moons ago for my Ph.D., updated with further research (my own and others') during the intervening decades. I was incredibly fortunate to have Archie Duncan as my Ph.D. supervisor. His iconoclastic approach to anything which lesser mortals might regard as cast in stone provided the ideal training for a young and far too biddable would-be historian. By treating my views with respect, but at the same time requiring always that such respect be earned through the use of firm evidence and a coherent argument, he essentially taught me to think. His great gift has been to inspire. I will always be profoundly grateful to him and deeply saddened by his death in 2017.

I have found my own generation of medieval historians to be most caring and supportive. My understanding of medieval history has been much improved by countless passionate discussions through the years, even if, having left academia now, they are much fewer than I might wish. I would still like to thank Steve Boardman, Dauvit Broun, Michael Brown, David Ditchburn, Theo van Heijnsbergen, Ally MacDonald, Richard Oram and Matthew Strickland for hours of endless disputation, even if increasing responsibilities, professional and personal, put that more in the past than the present. I would also like to acknowledge the influence of Norman MacDougall, who taught me as an undergraduate at St Andrews. His patience, good sense and canny intellect, combined with an unfailing enthusiasm for the later middle ages, has served as a quiet inspiration over the years. I am not sure what conclusion to draw from the fact that we are also Archie Duncan's first and last research students respectively.

There are a number of others who have been hugely influential on my own views on medieval history generally and this book in particular – Michael Prestwich, who has provided much of the example behind the approach to this period in history, Sandy Grant and Ted Cowan. I also owe a huge debt to John and Val Tuckwell, who originally published this book, patiently, firmly, but always with an infectious sense of fun, teasing the manuscript out of me. Please forgive me if I have missed anyone out.

Finally, this book is dedicated to my mum and dad who have given me a lifetime of love and support. Since my dad is no longer with us, I hope it also stands as a small memorial to all that he was and the many things he was not permitted to be, thanks to the times in which he lived. He certainly always believed I could be anything I wanted to be.

ABBREVIATIONS

APS	*The Acts of the Parliaments of Scotland*, ed. T. Thomson and C. Innes (Edinburgh, 1814–75). These are now to be found, re-edited, in the Records of the Parliaments of Scotland to 1707 at rps.ac.uk
Barrow, *Bruce*	G.W.S. Barrow, *Robert Bruce and the Community of the Realm of Scotland* (3rd edn, Edinburgh, 1992)
CCR	*Calendar of Close Rolls*, ed. H.C. Maxwell-Lyte (London, 1906–8)
CDS	*Calendar of Documents relating to Scotland*, ed. J. Bain *et al* (London, 1881–1986)
CPR	*Calendar of Patent Rolls*, ed. H.C. Maxwell-Lyte (London, 1906–8)
EHR	*English Historical Review*
Foedera	*Foedera, Conventiones, Litterae et Cuiuscunque Generis Acta publica*, ed. T. Rymer, Record Commission Edition (London, 1816–69)
Gough, *Scotland in 1298*	*Scotland in 1298: Documents relating to the campaign of Edward the First in that year, and especially to the Battle of Falkirk*, ed. H. Gough (Paisley, 1888)
Guisborough	*The Chronicle of Walter of Guisborough*, ed. H. Rothwell, Camden Society, 3rd Series, lxxxix (1957)
Hary's Wallace	[Blind Harry] *The Wallace*, ed. M.P. McDiarmid (STS, 1968)

HMSO	Her Majesty's Stationery Office
Itin.	*Itinerary of Edward I, Part ii: 1291–1307*, ed. E.W. Stafford, List and Index Society, vol. 132 (London, 1976)
Lanercost	*Chronicon de Lanercost, 1201–1346*, ed. J. Stevenson (Maitland Club, 1839)
Langtoft	*The chronicle of Pierre de Langtoft*, ed. T. Wright (Rolls Series, 1866)
Lib. Quot.	*Liber Quotidianus Contrarotulatoris Garderobae, 1299–1300*, ed. J. Topham *et al* (1787)
Melrose Liber	*Liber Sancte Marie de Melros* (Bannatyne Club, 1837)
Memo. de Parl.	*Memorandum de Parliamento, 1305*, ed. F.W. Maitland (Rolls Series, 1893)
Palgrave, *Documents*	*Documents and Records illustrating the History of Scotland*, ed. F. Palgrave (London, 1837)
Parl. Writs	*Parliamentary Writs and Writs of Military Summons*, ed. F. Palgrave (Record Commission, 1827–33)
Prestwich, *Documents*	*Documents Illustrative of the Crisis of 1297–8 in England*, ed. M. Prestwich, Camden Society, 4th ser. (London, 1980)
PSAS	*Proceedings of the Society of Antiquaries of Scotland* (1851–)
RCAHM	Royal Commission on the Ancient and Historic Monuments
RCAHMS	Royal Commission on the Ancient and Historic Monuments of Scotland
Rishanger	*Willelmi Rishanger, Chronica et Annales*, ed. H.T. Riley (Rolls Series, 1865)
Rot. Scot.	*Rotuli Scotiæ in Turri Londinensi et in Domo Capitulari Westmonasteriensi Asservati*, ed. D. Macpherson and others (London, 1814)

RRS ii	*Regesta Regum Scottorum*, ed. G.W.S. Barrow, vol. ii (Edinburgh, 1960)
RRS V	*Regesta Regum Scottorum*, ed. A.A.M. Duncan, vol. v (Edinburgh, 1988)
Scalachronica	*The Scalachronica by Sir Thomas Grey of Heton, Knight*, ed. J. Stevenson (Maitland Club, 1836)
SHR	*Scottish Historical Review*
SHS	Scottish History Society
SP	*The Scots' Peerage*, ed. Sir J. Balfour Paul (Edinburgh, 1904–14)
Stevenson, *Documents*	*Documents Illustrative of the History of Scotland, 1286–1306*, ed. J. Stevenson (Edinburgh, 1870)
Stevenson, *Wallace Docs.*	*Documents Illustrative of Sir William Wallace, His Life and Times*, ed. J. Stevenson (Maitland Club, 1841)
Stones, *Relations*	*Anglo-Scottish Relations, 1174–1328: Some Selected Documents*, ed. E.L.G. Stones, 2nd edn (Oxford, 1970)
STS	Scottish Text Society
TDGAS	Transactions of the Dumfriesshire and Galloway Natural History and Antiquarian Society
Trivet, Annales	*Annales Nicholai Triveti*, ed. T. Hog (London, 1845)
Wright, Political Songs	*Political Poems and Songs relating to English History*, ed. T. Wright (London, 1839)
Wyntoun	[Andrew of Wyntoun] *The Orygynale Cronykil of Scotland*, ed. D. Laing (Edinburgh, 1872–9)

DRAMATIS PERSONAE

Abernethy, Sir Alexander	Scot; warden from Forth to Grampians (1303–5)
Abingdon, Richard	royal officer; receiver of Cumberland (1297–1300); made baron of exchequer (1299)
Alard, Sir Gervase	of Winchelsea, Sussex; captain of the Cinque Ports; admiral of English fleet (1300–1)
Alexander II	king of Scots (1214–49)
Alexander III	king of Scots (1249–86)
Amersham, Walter	Edward I's chancellor of Scotland (1296–1304); also receiver of Northumberland; d. 1304
Angus, Gilbert d' Umfraville, earl of	lord of Redesdale & Coquetdale in Northumberland; d. 1307
Atholl, John de Strathbogie, earl of	Scottish sheriff of Aberdeen (c. 1300); brother-in-law of Robert Bruce, the future king; lieutenant & justiciar of Scotland beyond Forth (1304–5); d. 1306
Audley, Sir Hugh	Gloucestershire knight; keeper of Selkirk Forest (1301–c.1303); d. 1325
Balliol, Sir Alexander	lord of Cavers; sheriff of Selkirk (1301–c.1303)
Balliol, John	lord of Barnard Castle, co. Durham, & Galloway; claimant to Scottish throne; king of Scots (1292–1296/1304); d. 1313
Balmyle, Nicholas	'of St Andrews'; Scottish chancellor (c. 1301)

Bartholomew, Roger	burgess of Berwick; first to appeal from Scottish courts to Edward I (1291–2)
Barton, Robert	keeper of Abingdon's counter-roll (1297)
Beauchamp, Sir Walter	steward of Edward's household
Bek, Anthony	bishop of Durham (1283–1311)
Benstede, John	comptroller of the wardrobe
Bevercotes, William	royal officer; keeper of Edward's seal in Scotland (1296–7); chancellor of Scotland (1304–6)
Biset, William	?lord of Upsettlington, Berwickshire; sheriff of Clackmannan (1303–4) & Stirling (1304–5)
Bisset, Sir Hugh	lord of Antrim; captured Arran (1298)
Boniface VIII	pope; d. 1303
Botetourt, Sir John	lord of Mendlesham, Suffolk; given Dalswinton castle (1301); warden of western march (1302–4)
Brabazon, Roger	English royal adviser; involved in Great Cause; later chief justice of the King's Bench
Brampton, Stephen	English constable of Bothwell (1298–1300/1)
Bremesgrave, Richard	keeper of the Berwick store (1299– c. 1303)
Brittany, John of	Edward's nephew; governor of Aquitaine (1298–1305); appointed lieutenant of Scotland (1305)
Bruce, Robert, of Annandale 'the Competitor'	claimant to the Scottish throne; 5th lord of Annandale; d. 1295
Bruce, Robert, earl of Carrick	6th lord of Annandale; became earl through his wife, Marjorie; d. 1304 in England
Bruce, Robert, earl of Carrick	7th lord of Annandale; guardian of Scotland (1298–1300); king of Scots (1306–29)
Bunkle, Thomas	clerk of Dunkeld

Burdon, Sir John	Nottingham & Derbyshire knight; sheriff of Berwick & keeper of castle (1298–c. 1303)
Burghdon, Sir Walter	keeper of Carstairs castle & sheriff of Lanark (1301–3); justiciar of Galloway (1305)
Caen, John of	Edward's notary public; responsible for drawing up Great Roll (c. 1296)
Cantilupe, Sir Robert	Essex knight; keeper of Lochmaben and warden of Annandale (1298–9)
Carlisle, bishop of	*see* Halton
Cheyne, Henry	bishop of Aberdeen (1282–1328); brother of Sir Reginald
Cheyne, Sir Reginald, Sr.	lord of Inverugie & Duffus; sheriff of Inverness (1296–7); justiciar beyond the mountains (1305); brother of Henry, bishop of Aberdeen
Clifford, Sir Robert	lord of Appleby castle, Westmorland; given Caerlaverock castle; keeper of Carlisle castle (1297–9); warden of Galloway (1298–9); keeper of the bishopric of Durham (1300–6)
Comyn, Sir Alexander	brother of the earl of Buchan but on English side
Comyn, Sir Alexander	brother of Sir John Comyn of Badenoch, senior
Comyn, Sir Edmund	of Kilbride; head of third branch of Comyn family; member of Sir John Comyn of Badenoch, jr.'s council
Comyn, Sir John, of Badenoch, sr.	guardian (1286–92); brother-in-law of John Balliol; claimant to Scottish throne; d. ?1299
Comyn, Sir John, of Badenoch, jr.	son of Sir John Comyn of Badenoch; guardian (1298–1303; 1303); killed by Robert Bruce (1306)
Comyn, John, earl of Buchan	cousin of Comyn of Badenoch; often leader of Scottish army (1296–1303)

Convers, Alexander	royal clerk responsible for provisioning English garrisons in south-east Scotland (1298–c.1303)
Crambeth, Matthew	dean of Aberdeen; bishop of Dunkeld (1288–1309)
Cressingham, Hugh	treasurer of Scotland (1296–7); killed at battle of Stirling Bridge, 1297
Cunningham, Robert	nephew of James the Steward; Scottish constable of Caerlaverock (?1297–99)
Dalilegh, James	receiver in west; keeper of Carlisle store (1299–1303); escheator south of Forth (1303–5)
Dolive, Sir John	keeper of Dumfries castle (1300)
Douglas, Sir William	father of Sir James Douglas 'the Good'; d.c. 1299
Droxford, John	keeper of the wardrobe
Dunbar & March, Patrick, earl of	claimant to throne; consistent English supporter; keeper of Berwick town (1298); warden of eastern march (1298–9); keeper of Ayr (c. 1301)
Dunkeld, bishop of	*see* Crambeth
Dunwich, Peter	royal officer; escheator south of Forth & keeper of Yester castle (1296–7)
Durham, Sir William	knight of Essex & Hertfordshire; sheriff of Peebles (c. 1301); d. 1304
Durham, bishop of	*see* Bek
Edward I	king of England (1272–1307)
Edward 'of Caernarvon'	prince of Wales; future Edward II; d. 1327
Elaund, Sir Hugh	Yorkshire knight; keeper of Jedburgh castle & warden of Selkirk Forest (1296–7)
Felton, Sir Robert	Gloucestershire knight; constable of Lochmaben (1299–c.1300)
Felton, Sir William	Northamptonshire knight with Northumbrian connections; keeper of Linlithgow castle (1301–?)

FitzAlan, Sir Brian	lord of Bedale in Yorkshire
FitzMarmaduke, Sir John	custodian of earl of Lincoln's lands of Strathgryfe, forfeited from James the Steward
FitzRoger, Sir Robert	lord of Clavering, Essex; keeper of eastern Scottish march (1299–1300)
FitzWarin, Sir William	lord of Grimthorpe, Yorkshire; keeper of Urquhart castle; husband of Mary, countess of Strathearn and queen of Man; d. 1317
FitzWilliam, Sir Ralph	Northumberland knight; captain of Newcastle garrison (1297–9); captain of Yorkshire garrisons (1298); warden of Galloway (1299)
Fraser, Sir Simon	lord of Oliver castle; captured at Dunbar; made Edward's warden of Selkirk Forest (1297–c.1301); defected to Scots in 1301; d. 1306
Fraser, William	bishop of St Andrews (1279–97); guardian of Scotland (1286–92); great-uncle of Sir Simon Fraser
Fraunceys, Sir William	constable of Kirkintilloch castle (c. 1301)
Furnivall, Sir Thomas	knight of Nottingham, Derby & Yorkshire; captain of Nottingham and Derbyshire garrisons (1298)
Galloway, Thomas of	illegitimate son of Alan, lord of Galloway; prevented from succeeding his father by Alexander III
Gaveston, Piers	Gascon knight; close friend of Edward II
Glasgow, bishop of	*see* Wishart
Gloucester, Gilbert de Clare, earl of	his great-aunt, Isabel, was wife of Robert Bruce the Competitor; d. 1307
Gordon, Sir Adam	Scottish warden of western march (c. 1300); justiciar of Lothian (1305)
Graham, Sir David	son of Sir Patrick Graham of Airth

Halton, John	bishop of Carlisle (1292–1324)
Hastangs, Sir Richard	Staffordshire knight; keeper of Jedburgh castle (1298–?1305); brother of Sir Robert
Hastangs, Sir Robert	Staffordshire knight; sheriff of Roxburgh & keeper of castle (1296–c.1305); brother of Sir Richard
Hastings, Sir Edmund	sheriff of Ayr (1301); warden of Berwick town (1302)
Hastings, Sir John	claimant to Scottish throne
Henry I	king of England (1100–35)
Henry II	king of England (1154–89)
Henry III	king of England (1216–72)
Hereford, Humphrey de Bohun, earl of	constable of England; d. 1298
Hereford, Humphrey de Bohun, earl of	d. 1322
Heron, Robert	keeper of new customs at Berwick (1296–c.1304); keeper of counter-roll (1297–?1304); comptroller of chamberlain of Scotland (1305–6)
Hesilrig, Sir William	Northumberland knight; sheriff of Lanark killed by William Wallace in 1297
Hoddleston, Sir John	knight of Cumberland, Yorkshire & Lancashire; temporary warden of Galloway (1297); captain of Cumberland and Westmorland (1303); d. 1316
Holland, Florence, Count of	claimant to Scottish throne
Hunsingore, Master Thomas	King John's chancellor
Huntercumbe, Sir Walter	Oxfordshire knight; sheriff of Edinburgh (1296–7); keeper of Berwick town (1298); captain of Northumberland garrisons (1298–?1303); d. 1313
Huntingdon, Earl David of	Grandson of David I of Scotland; youngest son of Henry, earl of

	Northumberland; brother of Malcolm IV and William I; progenitor of Bruce, Balliol and Hastings; d. 1219
Jarum, John	royal clerk; keeper of Ayr store (1301)
Joneby, Sir Robert	Cumberland knight; sheriff of Dumfries (1296–7)
Keith, Edward	brother of Sir Robert; claimed to be hereditary sheriff of Selkirk through his wife
Keith, Sir Robert	Scottish warden of Selkirk Forest (1299–1300); justiciar north of the Forth (1306); brother of Edward
Kingston, Sir John	knight of Berkshire and Wiltshire; sheriff of Edinburgh (1298–1303)
Lamberton, William	archdeacon of Glasgow; bishop of St Andrews (1297–1328)
Langton, John	bishop of Chichester; chancellor of England
Langton, Walter	bishop of Coventry and Lichfield (also known as Chester); treasurer of England
Lathum, Sir Henry	knight of Lancashire; sheriff of Aberdeen (1296–c.1297)
Latimer, Sir William	Yorkshire knight; captain of eastern Scottish garrisons (1299); keeper of Berwick town & warden of eastern march (1300–1); in charge of chevauchées from Roxburgh (1302–3); d. 1304
Leeds, Sir Alexander	Yorkshire knight; sheriff of Dumbarton (1296–7)
Lennox, Malcolm, earl of	?1290–1333
Lincoln, Henry de Lacy, earl of	given James the Steward's lands; d. 1311
Lindsay, Sir Alexander	of Barnweill
Lindsay, Sir Simon	lord of Arthuret; captain in Esk Valley for Edward I (1298); keeper of Liddel and Hermitage castles

Livingston, Sir Archibald	sheriff of Linlithgow (1301–4?); sheriff of Stirling (before 1304)
Logan, Sir Walter	Scottish sheriff of Lanark
MacDonald, Alasdair	lord of Islay; 2nd line of descent from Somerled, king of Argyll; rival for power in north-west with the MacDougalls; d. ?1298
MacDougall, Alasdair	lord of Argyll & Lorn; senior line of descent from Somerled, king of Argyll; rival for power in the north-west with the MacDonalds; d. 1310
MacDougall, John	of Lorn; eldest son and heir of Alasdair MacDougall
MacDougall, Duncan	son of Alasdair MacDougall
MacQuillan, Malcolm	Antrim lord interested in western Isles
MacRuari, Lachlan	of Garmoran; 3rd line of descent from Somerled, king of Argyll; brother of Ruari & Christina, wife of Gartnait of Mar; married to daughter of Alasdair of Argyll
MacRuari, Ruari	brother of Lachlan & Christina
Malcolm III Canmore	king of Scots (1058–93)
Malherbe, Sir Gilbert	lord of Slamannan and Livilands; Scottish sheriff of Stirling, c. 1299
Manton, Ralph	king's cofferer; unofficial paymaster in Scotland
Mar, Donald, earl of	father-in-law of Robert Bruce, earl of Carrick (future king); ?d. 1298
Mar, Gartnait of	eldest son and heir of Donald, earl of Mar; husband of Christina MacRuari
March	*see* Dunbar
Margaret, 'Maid' of Norway	daughter of King Eric of Norway and Margaret, daughter of Alexander III; died 1290
Marshall, John	earl of Lincoln's baillie in barony of Renfrew forfeited from James the Steward

Maudley, Sir Robert	Yorkshire knight; English owner of Dirleton castle
Maule, Sir Thomas	Scottish constable of Brechin castle (1303)
Menteith, Alexander, earl of	captured at Dunbar; released 1297; d. 1306
Menteith, Sir John de	brother of earl Alexander; sheriff of Dumbarton & keeper of castle (1303–?9); d.c.1323
Moigne, Sir John le	keeper of Galloway and Nithsdale (1303)
Morham, Sir Herbert	son of Sir Thomas; leader of Scottish army besieging Stirling castle in 1299; captured & escaped; recaptured before 1304; d. 1306
Morham, Sir Thomas	father of Sir Herbert; served Edward
Mortimer, William	royal official; justiciar of Scotia (1296–7)
Moubray, Sir John	lord of Methven; member of Sir John Comyn of Badenoch junior's council
Mountz, Sir Ebulo	sheriff & constable of Edinburgh castle (1303–5)
Multon, Sir Thomas	lord of Lillesland, Cumberland; captain of Cumberland and Westmorland (1303); d. 1314
Murray, Andrew	son of Sir Andrew Murray of Petty; d. 1297
Murray, Sir William	lord of Tullibardine in earldom of Strathearn
Norfolk, Roger Bigod, earl of	marshal of England; d. 1306
Novelliano, Sir Montasini de	Gascon knight; constable of Ayr castle (c. 1301)
Ormesby, William	royal official; justiciar of Lothian (1296–7)
Pencaitland, John	keeper of Jedburgh castle for Scots (1297–8)
Percy, Sir Henry	Yorkshire knight; warden of Galloway & Ayrshire (1296–7); 1273–1314

Philip IV, 'the fair'	king of France (1268–1314)
Pilche, Alexander	leader of burgesses of Inverness
Redmayne, Sir Matthew	knight of Northumberland & Cumberland; sheriff of Dumfries (1304)
Ros, Sir Robert de	lord of Wark; struck first blow of the war for the Scots, supposedly because of his love for a Scottish lady
Ros, Sir William de	claimant to throne through illegitimate descent; brother of Robert de Ros, but on English side
Ross, William, earl of	remained in prison after Dunbar till 1303; lieutenant beyond the Spey (1303–5); d. 1323
Rue, William	royal clerk responsible for supplying Edinburgh, Dirleton & Stirling
Rye [Rithre], Henry	royal official, escheator north of the Forth & keeper of Elgin & Forres castles (1296–7)
St Andrews, bishop of	*see* Fraser; Lamberton
St George, Master James de	famous master carpenter from Savoy; worked on Linlithgow
St John, Sir John de, sen.	lord of Basing, Hampshire; warden of Galloway (1300–1302); effectively lieutenant of Scotland; d. 1302
Sampson, John	English constable of Stirling castle (1298–1300)
Sandale, John	chamberlain of Scotland (1305)
Segrave, Sir John	Oxfordshire knight; in charge of chevauchées from Berwick (1302–3); keeper of Berwick castle (1302–3); lieutenant in eastern Scotland (1303–4); lieutenant south of Forth & justiciar of Lothian (1304–5); d. 1325
Siward, Sir Richard	lord of Tibbers; captured at Dunbar; warden of Nithsdale (1299–); sheriff of Fife (1304)

Skoter, Roger	royal official; justiciar of Galloway (1296–7)
Spaldington, Osbert	Lincolnshire knight; sheriff of Berwick (?1296–8)
Soules, Sir John	guardian of Scotland (1301–3); died in exile in France, 1318
Soules, Sir Thomas	youngest brother of Sir John and Sir William
Soules, Sir William	lord of Liddesdale; butler of Scotland; elder brother of Sir John; d. 1293; succeeded by his brother, Nicholas
Soules, William	lord of Liddesdale; butler of Scotland; son of Nicholas; nephew of Sir John & Sir William
Steward, James the	guardian of Scotland (1286–92); close associate of Bruces; grandfather of future king, Robert II; d. 1309
Stewart, Sir John	of Jedburgh; brother of James; leader of the archers of Selkirk Forest; d. 1298
Strathearn, Master Alpin of	probably a son of the earl of Strathearn; archdeacon of St Andrews; King John Balliol's treasurer; ?bishop of Dunblane in 1296
Strathearn, Malise, earl of	captured at Dunbar; subsequently sided with Edward I; deputy of earl of Atholl as lieutenant north of the Forth (1305)
Surrey, John de Warenne, earl of	first post-conquest lieutenant in Scotland (1296–8); d. 1304
Sutherland, William, earl of	d.c.1307
Teye, Sir Walter	knight of Yorkshire and Bedfordshire; officer in Esk valley (1298–?); captain of Berwick town garrison (1300–1); d. 1324
Tilliol, Sir Robert	Cumberland knight; constable of Lochmaben (1301); d. 1321
Tweng, Sir Marmaduke	Yorkshire knight; d. 1323

Ulster, Richard de Burgh, earl of	father-in-law of Robert Bruce, earl of Carrick, the future king
Umfraville, Sir Ingram d'	Scottish sheriff of Roxburgh (1299–); guardian of Scotland (1300–1)
Umfraville, Thomas d'	younger son of Earl Gilbert of Angus; constable of Dundee, traditionally controlled by his family (1303–4)
Umfraville	see Angus
Valence, Sir Aymer de	later earl of Pembroke; given Murray castle of Bothwell; lieutenant in southern Scotland (1303)
Vernay, Sir Philip	keeper of Berwick town (1298–9)
Waldegrave, Sir Richard	Northamptonshire knight; sheriff of Stirling (1296–7)
Wallace, William	guardian of Scotland c. 1297–8; d. 1305
Warwick, Guy Beauchamp, earl of	d. 1315
Warwick, William, earl of	d. 1298
Weston, John	receiver and paymaster in south-east Scotland (1299–c. 1302)
William I 'the Conqueror'	duke of Normandy; king of England (1066–87)
William I 'the Lion'	king of Scots (1165–1214); captured and forced to concede Treaty of Falaise (1174)
Willoughby, Philip	former keeper of wardrobe; English treasurer's lieutenant
Wishart, Robert	bishop of Glasgow (1271–1316); staunch defender of Scotland's independence

Unless otherwise stated, all military/administrative offices were held by the above as part of Edward's government of Scotland.

*I venture to say no war can be long carried
on against the will of the people*
Edmund Burke

IN PRAISE OF FACT AND FICTION

The death of rulers is traditionally accompanied by much weeping and wailing and gnashing of teeth. Cynics might say that in many – most – cases, this should be interpreted as a display of political acumen in the face of changing political circumstances, or a rededication of adherence to the regime, rather than genuine emotion. The tears shed at the funeral of Alexander III of Scotland would no doubt have been similarly expedient had it not been for the dreadful shock of his untimely death and the knowledge that there was no male heir to succeed him. But Scotland's leaders were more than capable of guiding the ship of state for as long as necessary until the next monarch was ready to take the helm. They'd done it before, and would no doubt have to do it again. But in only a decade, when Edward I of England invaded and conquered his northern neighbour, it became clear that 19 March 1286 had ushered in a period of great misfortune for Scotland and the writers of history soon began to feel a profound nostalgia for Alexander and his reign. The traumas of the wars with England bit deep into the Scottish psyche, casting sweetness and light on to what came before:

> When Alexander our king was dead
> That Scotland led in love and security
> Departed was abundance of ale and bread
> Of wine and wax, of games and glee.[1]

Indeed, succeeding events have provided Scottish history not only with a supposed thirteenth-century Golden Age, but also advanced the cause of the later medieval Scottish kings – at least in their own propaganda – by rendering them essential to the survival of the nation itself; ironically, much later politicians of a Whiggish persuasion turned to the same period for evidence of a popular sovereignty restraining the monarchy.[2]

War is the natural environment of propaganda, whether to confound the enemy or to bolster morale. Periods of conflict between nations provide particularly fertile ground for polarised, black-and-white versions of events as governments seek to justify opposing military positions. As time passes, and such conflicts enter both history and folklore, new political agendas are given a wider context and legitimacy by harking back to an already simplified past. This is as true for the present as it is for the middle ages. In this way the past, or at least the currently acceptable version of it, is transformed to meet the needs of the moment, and crystallises to become a cast-iron truth. The results often have little to do with the beliefs and aspirations of the protagonists in the original conflict.

Having said that, there is no need to deny the importance of the late thirteenth and fourteenth centuries to the development of both a Scottish and an English national consciousness (albeit for slightly different reasons); nor does an acknowledgement of the role of propaganda and mythology in the creation of versions of the past undermine any general discussion of the prosecution of, or resistance to, a war of conquest. The history of the struggle between Edward I and the Scots is comparatively well-known at both an academic and a popular level. After all, the period produced two of Scotland's greatest heroes – William Wallace and Robert Bruce – and eventually earned King Edward the soubriquet of 'Hammer of the Scots'.[3]

However, the history of the middle ages, and of medieval Scotland in particular, remains stubbornly imprisoned in the popular mind as dark, dreary and violent, and, more importantly, as comparatively undocumented and therefore unknowable. Certainly, the fact that the history of this struggle must be constructed largely from English sources – mostly official government records and contemporary English chroniclers – has, understandably, given undue emphasis to Edward's government of Scotland. This is all the more unfortunate given that much of Scotland was not under English control between 1297 and 1303. Nevertheless, historians have already done much to illuminate this first phase of the Anglo-Scottish wars. Such studies fall into two main categories: to shed as much light as possible on the activities of the Scots, or to analyse the English war machine, but particularly the army, as part of studies of Edward I's government and military activity generally.[4] In both cases, the milestones on the way have tended to be the military 'highlights' – battles and sieges. This is natural; after all, there were campaigns every year during the period from 1296 to 1304, with the exceptions of 1299 and 1302, and battles will probably always fire the imagination to greater effect than descriptions of administration.

However, these explosions of military activity form, at best, only half the story. Since the success of any conquest does not rely ultimately on victory in battle, but on the ability of the occupying regime to transform such victories into an effective and accepted administrative system, it is of paramount importance that Edward's government of Scotland should be returned to centre stage. By shifting our attention on to the day-to-day activities of Edwardian officials, the process of conquest and attempted colonisation of one medieval kingdom by another can be brought more firmly into focus. Correspondingly – though still frustratingly inadequately – the means whereby the kingdom of Scotland was able to marshal its resources and create a coherent and cohesive national movement to deal with an enemy much more powerful than itself also become clearer.

I have taken the decision to end this book with Edward presiding over the final settlement of Scotland in September 1305, the point at which he surely believed he had succeeded in bringing his northernmost conquest under firm but fair control, rather than at his death two years later when it was clear that he had not. Within only a few months of that 1305 settlement, Robert Bruce killed John Comyn and seized the Scottish throne, precipitating the two nations back into conflict as well as starting a civil war within Scotland itself. But those hostilities continued, off and on, for another twenty-six years until the temporary respite brought about by the Anglo-Scottish peace treaty of 1328. It seemed wise, therefore, to focus on the period of warfare between 1296 and 1304, as well as the mopping-up period immediately thereafter, rather than opening a new can of worms that would have to be left largely unexamined.

As already mentioned, one of the most frustrating aspects of the study of this period of Anglo-Scottish warfare is the lack of surviving evidence from Scotland itself. This is particularly irritating when it comes to assessing the extent and effectiveness of the Scottish administration set up by Wallace and continued by a series of guardians after the latter's fall from power. It is not truly possible to gauge exactly what the English administration in Scotland was up against, especially in terms of the military and fiscal organisation of the enemy. Equally, we have no way of knowing what overall policies and specific military stratagems the various Scottish leaders attempted to implement over these years. Actions and results will largely have to speak for themselves.

In any case, even the comparatively full English sources provide only a very narrow focus. We are thus very well informed about the response of Edward's government and its various departments to the war, both at home and abroad; we also have the reactions of a number of monastic and other commentators to such activities at varying distances from them. However, we have few direct reactions from either the English or the Scots in general, though we know that its cost was disliked in England and that xenophobia rose up like a Hydra on both sides of the border within a short space of time.

But the problems posed by questions of evidence should not stop us trying to understand what happened by the criteria which contemporaries would themselves have applied both to their own actions and those of their political leaders, so far as we can uncover them. The kingdom of Scotland was certainly not isolated from the wider medieval world; indeed, the extent of its involvement – trade and diplomacy are only the most obvious elements – is one of the more striking features of this period. This was a complex society, which was neither monolithic at any one time, nor static.

Part of the historian's job is to understand how versions of the past have come about in order to separate fact from fiction, while acknowledging the role of both. Fact is, of course, multi-faceted – there is no one version of events even as they are occurring. Fiction, ironically, has a closer relationship to 'truth' than history ever can: its creators do not have to cover all the options or point out the difficulties with the sources as the historian does.

Then there is the twilight zone between the two; works such as Barbour's *Bruce* and Blind Harry's *Wallace*, and even the 1995 film *Braveheart*, which, while based on a modicum of fact, are primarily a reflection of the events and agendas of their own times. It is only recently, indeed, that historians have realised the extent to which our understanding of the Anglo-Scottish wars is a product of the comprehensive propaganda campaign conducted by King Robert Bruce against not only his predecessor, John Balliol, but also his arch-enemies, the Comyns, leaders of the Scottish political community before 1306. Analysis of the war has also been coloured by the commonly held and disparaging view of Scotland's medieval political system (still believed by some Scots), in contrast to that of England particularly. This has obscured the fact that that system was both sophisticated and appropriate to a kingdom that was not England; it has also made it more difficult to understand how resistance to Edward could have been so successful.

This whole spectrum of fact and fiction informs each generation's perceptions of the past and each of us must choose what makes most sense. We cannot alter what happened, nor know 'the truth' of it, but we can certainly be aware of what has brought us to our conclusions.

At the same time, if we did not believe that events of many hundreds of years ago had some resonance for our own times, we would surely take little interest in them. While the inhabitants of the middle ages certainly did things differently, we can still identify with the basic human motivations common to all eras – the desire to protect one's family, to live as normal a life as possible and, if we are honest, to strut on a wider stage from time to time than that allotted to us. It also seems to be human nature to subsequently portray decisions taken in accordance with these basic desires as noble and glorious, when – as we will see – they are more often mundane, contingent and myopic. That is perhaps the basic, symbiotic relationship between fact and fiction and, as Napoleon Bonaparte reputedly remarked: 'What is history but a fable agreed upon?'

CHAPTER ONE

THE LION AND THE LEOPARD

Where stood Scotland at the end of the thirteenth century? That is the question we must ask, so that we might better understand not only why Edward I went to such lengths to add his northern neighbour to his portfolio of acquisitions, but how resistance to his conquest proved so successful (up to a point).

Then, as now, Scotland was a land of formidable contrasts, ancient seismic forces having created great mountain barriers, particularly between Highlands and Lowlands. Soils were often poor for growing crops, but there was good arable land in the south and east and the uplands can sustain sheep and cattle and all manner of wild beasts. There was coal, lead, silver and gold in the ground, as well as valuable commodities like timber and salt above it. The short winter days were largely bereft of the sun's goodness and those with the power to entertain through the long nights must have been highly prized in the past when there was little to do at this unproductive time of year. Long before the Roman legions arrived in the first century AD, the tribes of northern Britain had become hierarchical and warlike, with architecture reflecting the power and authority of their chiefs.

Partly in, but mostly out of the Roman Empire, even tribes some distance away from the walls built to keep them at bay enjoyed the benefits of imperial trading networks. And once the Romans finally left in the fifth century, continental trade continued, though it looks as if there was a degree of social collapse even in areas not actually part of the Empire. Nevertheless, a number of kings (in Argyll in the west; Atholl in the central Highlands; and the area around Inverness in the north) soon emerged, consolidating their power and control of resources by military might and the attractive tenets of Christianity, which spread across these nascent kingdoms from the sixth century.

Scotland itself first comes on record in 900 AD. Sharing the Gaelic language with the inhabitants of Ireland, the Scots laboured under threats from the recently arrived Norse. But the new kingdom survived and even expanded into English territory beyond the River Forth which had marked the kingdom's original southern boundary.

After William of Normandy's conquest of England in 1066, Scottish kings copied what they fancied from the well-organised Normans, introducing innovation in agriculture, religious institutions, trading frameworks, royal administration and military organisation. But they were happy to keep traditional practices where it suited, the nation's story still bound up with an ancient connection to Ireland whose Gaelic language was spoken (along with Norman French) by many nobles and probably the king too. Scotland's racial make-up was 'complicated' (as is that of most nations), most obviously because its boundaries extended into other kingdoms, but also because its kings had encouraged a considerable influx of useful foreigners. Officially it encompassed Scots, Anglo-Saxons, Britons and Normans, the kingdom's social and political culture still tending to privilege local power structures and customs. Nevertheless, by 1200 Scotland had coalesced – according to its leaders at least – into a single Scottish people bound together by the comparatively undemanding, but nonetheless unifying, figure of their king.

It had certainly not all been plain sailing. Conflicts within the royal family and with powerful nobles, never mind outsiders, were a blight on political and cultural life almost from the moment Scotland was born, and continued into the thirteenth century. And by that century too, a fundamental divide had already opened up between Highlanders and Lowlanders. In part it was a recognition of the very different topographies of each region (broadly speaking), with settled peaceful farmers minding their own business in the Lowlands and lawless cowmen causing havoc in the Highlands. (This point of view was articulated from an unapologetically Lowland perspective and so must be treated with much caution.) But in the thirteenth century, royal authority started to become more forceful, more inclined to speak for the whole kingdom, even if the king himself ruled 'with the consent, testimony and acquiescence of my bishops, earls and barons.' He also worked hard, seeing and being seen regularly across the core of his kingdom from the Tweed to the Tay, collecting and disbursing royal revenues, giving justice and managing disputes.[1]

It no doubt helped that this was a time of general prosperity at the end of a comparatively warm period. A roaring trade in wool, bought up sometimes years in advance by the cloth-makers of Flanders in particular, brought wealth in the form of the great customs on trade into royal coffers and into the pockets of landowners great and small. Berwick, based on its peninsular site between the River Tweed and the North Sea and right on the border with England, grew into a port of great strategic and commercial importance. By the later thirteenth century, it was by far the most prosperous town in Scotland, primarily as the conduit through which the wool exported by the great Border abbeys flowed. Both the Germans and the Flemings probably had merchants' halls there.

This, then, was a time of peace and, so far as we can tell, prosperity. Though Alexander III had far less revenue at his disposal than the rulers of the more centralised kingdoms of England and France, he was easily the richest man in Scotland and, since his government was less intensive and his military activities negligible (give or take the tussle with the Norwegians in 1263), his outgoings were much less too.[2] It certainly helped that, despite perceptions to the contrary, the relationship between England and Scotland – the two kingdoms of the island of Great Britain – was, from the later thirteenth century, characterised by the very opposite of the fierce animosity that erupted after the outbreak of war in 1296. Indeed, war was one of the least likely scenarios that political pundits might have predicted in the aftermath of Alexander III's untimely death a decade earlier.

This is not meant to imply that there hadn't been problems in relations between the two kingdoms, up to and including the intermittent outbreak of overt hostilities; nor that racial taunting of the type well-known in modern sporting arenas was alien to thirteenth-century Scots and English.[3] Abuse and suspicion certainly existed, but among those whose responsibility it was to shape and steer the destinies of each kingdom – the lay and ecclesiastical élites – there was a deep-seated and fairly comfortable relationship based on shared kin, language (Norman French for the nobles and Latin for the churchmen), and values.

Indeed, it has been pointed out that a constant fixation on borders and distinct kingdoms 'can obscure as much as it illuminates. This was an age when local and trans-national political associations were often paramount, the national hesitant and fragile.'[4] Both in peace and in war, the interests of the thirteenth-century Scottish and English monarchies, together with the landholding class immediately beneath, flowed across and diluted the effects of the border; indeed, 'it has been calculated that, at some stage during the thirteenth century, nine out of thirteen Scottish earldoms had English property, while seven out of twenty-two English earldoms had Scottish interests'.[5] Intermarriage meant, to take only one example, that Edward I of England was brother-in-law to Alexander III of Scotland, and therefore great-uncle to the young Margaret of Norway, Alexander's granddaughter and heir presumptive to the Scottish throne from 1284; King John Balliol, who reigned from 1292, was son-in-law to John de Warenne, earl of Surrey, who defeated Balliol's army at Dunbar in 1296 and then became Edward's lieutenant in Scotland.

But there was one important bone of contention that had long threatened good relations between the two kingdoms and which consistently exposed the Scots as the aggressors. Scotland's kings had had a tendency to view Northumbria and Cumbria – parts of the once-powerful kingdoms of Northumbria (Anglo-Saxon) and Strathclyde (British) – as fair game for conquest. Indeed, they had acquired the northern tip of Northumbria from the River Forth to the River Tweed as early as the tenth century and saw no reason to stop there. They were often to be found south of the Solway or Tweed pursuing these claims as belligerently as possible, particularly in times of English weakness, such as the civil war following Henry I's death in 1135.

The English claim to overlordship was even more long-standing, becoming a consistent expression of the superiority of the West Saxon kings over all other rulers in the British Isles in the tenth century. With the Norman conquest, the concept of an overarching British kingship vested in the kings of England was readily inherited. In 1072 Malcolm III of Scotland became King William of England's man – the formal feudal method of accepting another's lordship – after the latter led an army deep into Scotland; this had only become necessary, however, because Malcolm had wrongly presumed that William's difficulties in the north of his kingdom in the aftermath of his conquest of England in 1066 provided an ideal opportunity for promoting his own ambitions in the area.

This encapsulates the basic relationship between the two crowns: English kings remained uninterested in Scotland so long as the border stayed where it was and peaceful; Scottish kings continued to exploit potential English weakness but were usually brought round to an understanding and acknowledgement of the military superiority of the English crown. A resolution of the problem was not forthcoming until 1237, when Alexander II of Scotland agreed to abandon his claims to Northumberland in the Treaty of York in return for lucrative English lands. Now that this long-standing issue had been resolved, there was little to hinder good relations.

Whatever the legal arguments, English claims to superiority were really a practical expression of the imbalance of power vested in the two crowns, given the resources available to each. Such an imbalance did not challenge the effective sovereignty of Scotland's kings or the independence of the northern kingdom, especially as most English kings had far more pressing issues to deal with when it came to their own extensive landed possessions in France. Even the Treaty of Falaise (1174), which permitted Henry II to garrison three Scottish border castles after the Scottish king, William I, managed to get himself captured in Northumberland, was not an attempt to interfere with Scottish government, but an extension of the usual (largely ineffectual) methods of guaranteeing Scottish good behaviour.

But times did change and centuries of acceptance of this big king/little king relationship (grudging or otherwise) became challenging after 1200. In the first instance, the loss of Normandy and Anjou loosened the English crown's connections with the continent (though they still held Gascony), prompting an increased interest in British affairs, particularly after 1259 when these losses were formally recognised. Secondly, developments in legal definitions of rights and jurisdictions were beginning to make it more difficult to maintain conflicting positions within the hierarchical structure of western European society.

By the mid-thirteenth century the kings of Scots had no problem with paying homage and fealty to the English king for their English lands. But they would no longer tolerate the idea that their kingship might be dependent in any sense on a greater *earthly* authority: kings were kings and sovereignty was not relative. The kings of England, of course, maintained the opposite view – the admissions of superiority which had accrued over the years could not be undone and might even acquire greater definition as legal rights became more refined. Technically speaking, the issue of holding land of another king and the implications for sovereignty were quite separate, but the two were often interlinked. The issue of the status of the kingdom of Scotland, for example, was only brought up when the king of Scots went to pay homage and fealty for his English lands. Both Alexander II and

Alexander III categorically refused to accept that they were bound to do so for the kingdom of Scotland; equally, Henry III and Edward I, while not pressing the point, reserved the right to demand acceptance of their overlordship in the future.

The clash of these conflicting interpretations of rights was not restricted to Scotland and England; indeed, the king of France, Philip IV (who came from a line of kings who pointedly 'upheld the doctrine that they themselves did homage to no man'[6]) energetically challenged Edward I's understanding of his own sovereignty by interfering in the latter's dukedom of Gascony. However, in the case of Scotland and England, no-one thought these technical difficulties would lead to war; indeed, both Henry and Edward had no desire to strain the relationship between the two kingdoms, however much they believed in their own rights. There was far too much to be gained from peace to warrant its deliberate sabotaging. But history is littered with moments when circumstances conspire to give one point of view a practical advantage over another and it would be an unusual leader indeed who failed to take advantage of them.[7]

And certainly the unthinkable did happen. In one of history's little ironies, Alexander III, aged only forty-four, brought his dynasty to an end by making a fatally romantic dash to attempt to perpetuate it with his new young second wife. All the children of his first marriage had already predeceased him, leaving as heir presumptive his granddaughter, a young Norwegian princess. The Scottish élites had only reluctantly accepted this Margaret as a potential ruler of Scotland in 1284, after the death of Alexander's two sons, no doubt agreeing primarily because choosing a male heir from the fringes of the dynasty was far too daunting a task; it was easier to assume that the king still had plenty of time to produce another boy. However, the Scottish political community's reaction to the latter's untimely death and the eventual arrangements made for the Maid and her future as queen of Scots (she was not formally accepted as heir till October 1286, when Alexander's queen probably gave birth to a posthumous stillborn child) reflected both the maturity of the Scottish political system, and the close relationship that England and Scotland now enjoyed.[8]

Margaret of Norway's great-uncle, Edward I of England, was in the prime of his life, and his reign. In his late forties, he had ruled the southern kingdom for nearly fifteen years and had already laid down the foundations of the conquest of Wales and the reformation of English finance, administration and law.[9] Ahead of him was still the final subjugation of Wales, the outbreak of a very serious quarrel with Philip of France, and the difficult years of domestic political wrangling which was both characteristic of English crown-magnate relations of the thirteenth century and a product of the dynamic and intensive style of government presided over by Edward himself. Despite the historical revisionism popular in our own time, he is still regarded as a great English king, if not on a par with Henry V or even his own grandson, Edward III. Though it is no longer fashionable to define a monarch's success by his contributions to expansionism and centralisation *per se*, it is still difficult not to be impressed; Edward's energy, his fierce intelligence, and even his ruthlessness did indeed provide him with remarkable success in these two areas. Scotland's bad luck lay not only in the failure of the dynastic line, but in having such a king as nearest neighbour.

However, we must not get carried away by hindsight. In the immediate aftermath of Alexander's death in March 1286, during the hiatus of his queen's pregnancy, Edward showed remarkably little interest in the northern kingdom, other than making conventional expressions of sympathy, until the Scottish guardians themselves approached him a few months later. That they should do so was also entirely conventional, given that the Scottish royal family was so closely related to Edward, that the Scots were quite accustomed to leaning on England's broad shoulders in times of difficulty (such as Alexander III's own minority),[10] and that Edward was regarded as one of western Europe's foremost statesmen. Indeed, it was mere courtesy to inform Britain's most dominant player of events which could have a potential impact on his kingdom, not least because Scotland's leaders already needed to take precautions against the nightmare of a civil war promoted by Robert Bruce of Annandale, an adult male alternative for the throne.

However, once the approach for advice had been made by the Scottish guardians – six nobles and senior churchmen appointed from within the political community to run the country – any search for an understanding of Edward's intentions immediately unleashes a hail of questions.[11] But there is no need to impute sinister motives to the English king to begin with, not least because his proposed solution to Scotland's problems – a marriage between Margaret and his own only surviving son Edward – won general approval in the northern kingdom even if the Maid's father, King Eric of Norway, was less overtly happy. That the union of the crowns of England and Scotland envisaged by the marriage did not happen is perhaps as much of a tragedy as the early death of King Alexander.

On the other hand, the fact that, among other things, Edward took control of the strategically vital Isle of Man[12] – in Scottish hands officially since 1266 – around the same time as he was promising to uphold the integrity of the Scottish crown suggests he was already happy to subordinate the northern kingdom's rights to his own advantage. But even he cannot have believed that such advantage was likely to be anything other than temporary. In any event, the Maid's own demise, perhaps from food poisoning, on her father's island of Orkney in the autumn of 1290 meant that the carefully formulated expressions of equality between the two kingdoms laid out in the Treaty of Birgham (July 1290) – as demanded by the Scots – became null and void; from then on, the quest for the peaceful accession of a new king moved Anglo-Scottish relations into uncharted and distinctly murky waters. And it is surely now that we can see Edward preparing to take advantage of leaderless Scotland to push a far more radical agenda of his own – to see if he could subordinate the northern kingdom to his own authority by means of a formally subservient Scottish king.

It is now much easier to understand how he manipulated the two-year court proceedings (1291-2) to identify Alexander's rightful heir to his own advantage, as well as using them as the legal basis for his direct takeover of the Scottish kingdom in 1296. This involved the rewriting, or deliberate suppression, of evidence so that the English king could show he was accepted as lord superior of Scotland by the Scottish political community as part of the process of choosing a new king, something Scotland's leaders did not think they had done, or at least not permanently.[13] Understanding this process – comparing what seems to have happened with the version presented a few years later – is a tortuous affair.

In the immediate aftermath of the Maid's death, there were only two claimants to the Scottish throne: John Balliol and Robert Bruce. Balliol was descended from the eldest daughter of David, earl of Huntingdon – grandson of King David I of Scotland – while Bruce was descended from the second daughter but was one generation older, that is a grandson rather than a great-grandson. The Scots knew they could not decide between them themselves, partly because this would imply their king could be subject to election by his nobility, but mostly because each candidate was supported by different factions within the kingdom. That was why they needed Edward, who had enough clout to make sure the decision on whether Bruce or Balliol should be king was upheld. However, the English king had already realised that the death of the Maid, though marking the slamming shut of one door, could open another. Edward now seized the initiative, summoning the Scots to a parliament to be held at Norham on the southern bank of the River Tweed on 6 May 1291 to deal with the thorny issue of who should be the next king in Scotland.

The Scots duly came south but remained at Upsetlington, just north of the border. Their intention was to have the king come to them – as Edward was required to do by the marriage treaty of Birgham if he was dealing with Scottish affairs, so that there would be no question of the Scots admitting his authority over them by going into England. However, they had not understood that there was now a new set of rules, though it soon became very clear that Edward was not budging from Norham. In an attempt to break the deadlock, a small group of Scots crossed the Tweed on 10 May. This deputation was treated to an extraordinary exposition from Edward through the mouth of his justice, Roger Brabazon. Though its main thrust related to the king's desire to see the vacant Scottish throne justly filled, it also contained two extremely portentous elements. The first was the most obvious: a demand for both assent to, and recognition of, Edward's overlordship as the prelude to his settlement of the succession. The second was a hint, for the first time, that that settlement was more than a simple adjudication between Bruce and Balliol.

The Scots, led by the bishop of Glasgow, Robert Wishart, reacted with shock and anger, but were then, according to Scottish sources, threatened with military action – the suggestion that Edward's temper was only just held in check would have been entirely believable. They thus had little choice but to return across the border to consult with their colleagues, having at least gained a three-week adjournment. It was apparently during this period that they attempted to wriggle out of the noose being prepared for them by denying their competence to comment on the status of the crown; the burden of defending Scotland's sovereign rights was thus placed firmly in the hands of their future king.

When the three weeks ran out on 1 June, the Scots rejected Edward's further exhortations to come south, delaying their response till the following day. They still seem to have thought it worthwhile appealing to his goodwill, hoping against hope that they could bring him north to arbitrate between the two claimants as they had always wanted and expected. But there was to be no change of plan, and there is even a suggestion that Edward used the following days to apply (further) pressure. Nevertheless, he had perhaps got what he wanted – as the Scots themselves admitted, Edward did not need to use force to gain acknowledgement of his overlordship. He merely needed to turn his attention to the men who would be king.

The difference between arbitration and judgement was crucial. The former, which implied, nay, demanded, neutrality on the part of the arbitrator, also required the participation of only two candidates. Judgement, on the other hand, implied certain rights, the most important of which was possession of the kingdom in order to execute the judgement on behalf of the successful candidate – a point which Edward seems to have grasped long before the Scots. It seems that the English king was not only the first to state that this was a question of judgement, rather than arbitration, but also that he was the one who covertly encouraged the assortment of claims to the throne that now emerged out of the woodwork.

There were fourteen candidates in total, including Edward himself, based – as the Scots apparently thought – on his position as judge requiring authority to execute judgement on behalf of the other claimants, a necessary legal evil but only for the duration of the court proceedings. The order of events between 3 and 12 June is absolutely crucial to our understanding of how Edward emerged with sasine (legal possession) of the kingdom and as overlord of Scotland. However, the fact that the English king required his notary, John of Caen, to rewrite what happened after the conquest of 1296 is evidence in itself that these events had not in fact gone entirely to plan.

According to the Great Roll which John of Caen doctored in 1296, the Scots had agreed that Edward should have sasine of the kingdom by 7 June 1291, at which point he was already also overlord. This was just not true. The key to this was Edward's own position as a claimant, a factor completely erased from the Great Roll. The reason for this 'error of commission' was fairly simple: after 1296 the king needed to show that the Scots had given him sasine of the kingdom *because of* his overlordship, rather than – as the Scots believed at the time – as a claimant representing the others until judgement was done. The letters of warrandice to the keepers of the Scottish royal castles absolving them for surrendering their charges to Edward on 12 June makes it clear that only the claimants themselves had thus far admitted the English king's overlordship, not the Scottish political community as a whole.

According to the Great Roll too, the process whereby all the candidates, including John Balliol, accepted his overlordship (called the award of Norham) was over by 3 June 1291. This implied that the king was then more or less at match point, leaving the Scots with little choice other than to solicit a few promises relating to the integrity of their laws and customs before the business of choosing a king who had already accepted English overlordship could finally begin. The award of sasine of the kingdom to Edward, accepted by all, was reckoned to have then occurred on 4 June.

The reality was, once again, far less agreeable than Edward could allow the written record to show. The Scots almost certainly remained north of the Tweed, having rejected Edward's continuing attempts to force an acknowledgement of his overlordship from them – something which was clearly very important to him. Edward then turned to the seven claimants actually at Norham (some, like himself, were more token gestures than real candidates),[14] and easily extracted both the acceptance of his overlordship and his right to sasine of the kingdom from Bruce, Count Florence of Holland, and John Hastings on 5 June, and the other four the following day. So far, so good.

However, one of the two original claimants had not yet done either of these things. John Balliol seems to have finally arrived at Norham on 10 June, still stressing his hope for *arbitration*, together with the strength of his own claim. Once more, Edward made it clear that he wanted an admission of overlordship, presumably alerting Balliol to the fact that the other candidates had done this and that it was, in fact, a condition of admission to the contest. After consultation with his council, Balliol conceded this point and, alone of the competitors, was made to repeat it in front of the king himself: this 'was the key that gave [Edward] entry to Scotland'.[15] Finally, John Comyn of Badenoch, the *de facto* leader of Scotland's political community, entered his own claim, one which he then put aside for his brother-in-law, Balliol.

This was indeed the turning point since it gave the rest of the Scots at Upsetlington no further reason to remain aloof from proceedings; their last chance to keep Edward to arbitration, vested in Balliol – the man regarded by a majority of the Scottish political community as the rightful heir – had failed, and their most important leader, Comyn, as one of Balliol's council, had seen this and accepted the inevitable. On 12 June the Scottish political community finally came to Norham and, though they did not themselves accept Edward's overlordship, sasine of the kingdom was granted.

This process of Norham, at least as important as the subsequent proceedings to choose the king (called the Great Cause), was effectively over; the king could now appoint various officers of state, 'the effect [of which] was to provide each Scottish sheriff with an English associate in charge of the seat and symbol of royal power'.[16] The four surviving guardians, Bishops Wishart of Glasgow and Fraser of St Andrews, John Comyn of Badenoch and James the Steward, continued in their office and were joined by a fifth guardian, the Englishman Sir Brian FitzAlan. Nevertheless, Edward 'did not get all he wanted from the Scots in the summer of 1291 ... recognition of his feudal suzerainty from the community of the realm of Scotland in its fullest, most solemn, most representative character'.[17] They did agree to recognise him as master of Scotland, but only for the duration of the search for a new king.

Although doctoring the evidence may appear immoral to us, the use and abuse of the written record was certainly not confined to Edward I and his clerks. Popes had for centuries provided the example to emperors and kings, and for the same reasons. They did so because hierarchy was defended by 'a reliance on tradition' and the papacy was quite used to creating 'a conservatism and a tradition by either antedating documents and ascribing them to earlier authors or by forging documents altogether and dating them in the far distant past in order to be safe enough to escape a check'.[18] They believed that, if the written record did not explicitly justify a particular claim, they were quite within their rights to 'adapt' it because their position of authority by definition entitled them to such rights, however unprecedented. Edward, then, was not alone in believing that altering a particular document could be done in order to bring it into line with the general principles belonging to his office as king, though of course there were those at the time who certainly did not agree.

The reference to the papacy is no accident and helps to explain why Edward found it so necessary, five years later, to doctor his own account of the process of Norham. The suppression of a recognised Christian kingdom was bound to provoke trouble abroad, not least because the Scottish church claimed special daughter status (no-one in between) in Scotland's relationship with the pope.[19] It was thus absolutely essential that Edward could show, as he would almost certainly be called upon to do, that he had become 'overlord without fear, by acceptance', since, under common law, a concession made in 'fear' was invalid. Alas:

> the threats of force, the resistance encountered, the concessions made, the fraud in the compromised solution, and, above all, the falsehoods told increasingly in the developing record, all show that Edward's lordship was built upon the temporary fears and weaknesses of the Scots, and not upon sound law and precedent.[20]

That Edward I was duplicitous is not really at issue, but we must be careful not to impose our own values on approaches to politics in the past. The king clearly knew that the events of 1291 would not, in their original version, guarantee his position in the eyes of

Christendom after the conquest of 1296, and he acted accordingly. But he himself was surely in no doubt that he had been within his rights, as a king of England who had inherited a long tradition of superiority vis-à-vis Scotland, to deal with the Scottish question in the way he did, including, in the end, the use of forfeiture, invasion and appropriation of the northern kingdom.

In the meantime, the conclusion of the process of Norham in June 1291 meant the commencement of the Great Cause.[21] Edward could now afford to be magnanimous: the court would sit on Scottish soil, at Berwick. One hundred and four auditors would hear the cases of the fourteen claimants – twenty-four from Edward's own council, and forty each on behalf of Balliol and Bruce. However, no sooner had the hearing got underway than it was abruptly halted when Count Florence V of Holland came out with the extraordinary assertion that Earl David of Huntingdon, through whom Balliol, Bruce and John Hastings all made their claim, had signed over his and his heirs' rights to the throne to his brother, King William, in return for the lands of the Garioch in north-east Scotland. Even more astonishingly, it was alleged that King William then named his sister Ada, wife of Florence's grandfather, as his heir, until the arrival of his son, the future Alexander II. The failure of the direct male line from King William, it was argued, meant that Ada's descendants were therefore the rightful heirs. Unfortunately Count Florence did not actually have any documentary proof of this claim but was given till 2 June 1292 to find it.

Count Florence's claim was certainly extraordinary, though more for its audacity in the face of extreme improbability than as a dramatic revelation.[22] The important question is why it was brought up at all. If, as seems likely, it was a delaying tactic, who wanted the delay? The most likely candidates were Robert Bruce of Annandale and Edward himself, both of whom seem to have had a hand in the Count's entry into the fray in the first place.[23]

Bruce's involvement suggests he believed Balliol probably had a better claim than him through a straightforward case of descent via the senior (eldest) line. As a result, the Competitor (as Bruce was called) was keen to adopt a contingency plan which might scupper Balliol's chances, even if Florence's claim also knocked out his own. The close relationship between the two and especially the agreement of 14 June 1292, whereby if either won the contest, one-third of royal lands and property would be given over to the other, makes this fairly clear: 'It seems hardly likely that the count was really anxious for the Scottish throne; if he used his claim in order to defeat Balliol, the Bruces would reward him well'.[24]

Edward also used these ten months to work on an alternative strategy. On 1 August 1291, immediately after the adjournment of the court, six Scottish magnates, including James the Steward, were offered lands in England 'if it happens that the realm of Scotland shall remain in the possession of the king and his heirs'.[25] This was probably an attempt to test the waters of Scottish public opinion for the use of the ultimate argument: that, in keeping with more general feudal law relating to land, Scotland should escheat to its overlord because of the failure of the male line. If so, it met with a stony response: Scotland was not any old estate, but an ancient and sovereign kingdom. The offers were cancelled and the Great Cause resumed. However, 'after a year of [Edward's] personal rule it would be difficult for any succeeding king to assert the independent tradition of Scottish monarchy'.[26] That too may have been part of the plan.

Given the eventual and unsurprising failure of Count Florence to find any relevant documents by the deadline, the reconvened court now agreed that its first task was to decide between the Bruce and Balliol claims. Yet again, the existence of the other competitors seems entirely peripheral to the search for a king. On 6 November, the court finally adjudicated in Balliol's favour. Bruce the Competitor was forced to accept this decision, but he had certainly not given up.

The court's decision that Balliol had a better legal right to the throne than Bruce was certainly not the end of the matter, for there were others with claims based on different legal arguments waiting in the wings. Next, the Competitor threw in his lot with John Hastings who, since November 1292, had argued that the kingdom should be divided among the three descendants of Earl David of Huntingdon, since his grandmother was David's youngest daughter. The adjudicators rejected this, deciding that the kingdom must remain intact. Count Florence's claim was then swiftly dealt with, for the simple reason that he still could not substantiate his assertions. When the latter withdrew, six others followed suit and three more were thrown out for having neglected to pursue their claims. Finally, on 17 November 1292, Edward judged John Balliol to be the rightful king of Scots, demanding an immediate admission of his overlordship; the new king was then enthroned at Scone at the end of the month. Within another month King John was ordered to swear homage and fealty for his kingdom yet again.[27]

Around this time – though he said he'd done it earlier, before the end of the Great Cause – Robert Bruce of Annandale transferred his claim to the throne to his heir, the earl of Carrick, who in turn tried to pass on his earldom to his own son, Robert (the future king). The end result of this careful legal manoeuvring was to ensure that the middle Bruce held no lands or title in Scotland. There was a very good reason for this apparent disinheritance: all Scottish landowners would soon be required to swear homage and fealty to Balliol. The Competitor's son, in whom the claim to the throne was now vested, would not need to make such an important and binding oath; he would therefore be free to pursue his claim to the throne when the time was right.[28]

The winter of 1292–3 did not augur well for the start of the new reign after six long years without a king. 'Much snow fell; the north wind came and pulled up the forests and withered the plants which it found; it unroofed houses, causing much loss, and violently threw some to the ground, thus accomplishing much devastation.[29] And yet, historians have been aware for some time that Balliol's reputation as king resulted in part from the very difficult circumstances of his reign, but more particularly from the effect on that reputation of the propaganda of the man who usurped his throne, Robert Bruce, and subsequent pro-Bruce writers like John Barbour. Nevertheless, the general impression that remains of unfortunate John is of 'Toom Tabard' [Empty Coat], the spineless monarch who did little or nothing to save either his kingdom or his good name from the rapacious Edward and had his coat with his royal regalia literally stripped off his back and torn apart. The reality of Balliol's reign is far less flattering to the Bruces, and rather more conventionally successful than will fit at all comfortably with the 'weak and incompetent' stamp usually placed upon it.

> Balliol set out to be no less a king than his predecessors: his family had had links with Scotland since the twelfth century; there was nothing to hinder the acclimatisation of the new dynasty, particularly since it was backed by the Comyns, not only the most powerful baronial family but one with the best claim to be regarded as 'patriotic' ... Between February 1293 and May 1294 at least four parliaments were held. On one occasion parliament was to be the seat of 'the dispensing of justice upon a scale which may have been unprecedented in Scotland' ... In general there is 'remarkable evidence that King John and his council were determined to secure the possessions and authority of the crown'.[30]

Within the domestic arena, therefore, John's style of kingship was fairly indistinguishable – if perhaps more energetic – from that of his predecessors as kings of Scots; his interest in the maintenance of royal authority through the bureaucratic machinery of government and the policy of assimilation of the newly acquired north-west Highlands and islands (sold to Alexander

III by the Norwegians in 1266) both underline this. Under normal circumstances, the creation of the sheriffdoms of Skye, Lorne and Kintyre in 1293 would have marked the final stage of the Scottish crown's acquisition of the region: 'the immediate consequence [of the creation of the sheriffdoms] – and one which the crown might well have desired to achieve – was destabilisation, even a localised civil war, as other important members of that community fought to maintain their own positions'.[31] However, the outbreak of war with England three years later, which initially eclipsed the Scottish crown and subsequently took up so much of royal time, largely stymied the process of assimilation, and sheriffdoms were not firmly established in the north-west Highlands until the later fifteenth century.[32]

But it was in his treatment of the Bruces that we see King John at his firmest, no doubt 'encouraged' by his relatives and backers, the Comyns. The first sign of trouble for his rivals for the crown came with summonses to Balliol's first parliament, to be held at Scone on 9 February 1293. By the end of that parliament, it became clear that, while Bruce the Competitor (Bruce 5) must have sworn homage and fealty for his lordship of Annandale, a number of other nobles, including his son, the earl of Carrick (Bruce 6), had not yet done so. The sheriffs were to deliver another summons – taking six men with them in case there was trouble – ordering these recalcitrants to appear before the king by 17 May.[33]

In fact, it was the youngest Bruce, nineteen-year-old Robert (Bruce 7), who finally turned up to the next parliament at Stirling on 2 August 1293, claiming that he, rather than his father, was now earl of Carrick. But King John was having none of it, for it was not for his subjects to swap earldoms amongst themselves, especially one acquired through a woman (Bruce 6 had married the heiress, Marjory). He ordered the sheriff of Ayr to seize Carrick, though he did promise that the Bruces could get it back if their paperwork was in order and if they paid the fee for the transfer. There is no evidence they ever did, strongly suggesting that, once the Competitor died in 1295, the family no longer held any land in Scotland (though they had estates in England), even if Bruce 6 continued to call himself earl of Carrick. Reduced to their admittedly less-than-shabby English estates, the English king offered them the best hope of a restoration of almost the entirety of their fortunes.

But it would be foolish to ignore the fact that, however promising his domestic achievements, King John's reign was overshadowed by Edward's determination, right from the start, to enforce a new definition of overlordship on the man he had made king. Overt English influence was noticeable at a number of levels. John's seal bore the style 'by God's grace king of Scots', instead of the traditional 'king of Scots under God's governance'. The new chancellor, Master Thomas of Hunsingore, was a Yorkshireman. Most likely to offend, however, was the fact that Master Alpin of Strathearn, the king's chief financial officer, was described as treasurer rather than chamberlain, conforming to English practice.

But such quibbles over words – possibly reflecting Balliol's own early career, which may have included a stint as a clerk in the English king's household[34] – were presumably of far less concern than what was going on elsewhere. At the beginning of January 1293,[35] King John was forced to release Edward from any possible implications of the Treaty of Birgham and his promises at Norham; nothing was to be allowed to stand in the English king's way of the widest possible interpretation of his rights as overlord. There had already been a test case within the judicial sphere: the speedy arrival of Roger Bartholomew's petition (7 December 1292, only one week after King John's enthronement), together with the remarkably prompt payment of his expenses (6 January 1293), makes it almost impossible to believe this was not a deliberate attempt by Edward to make the fundamental change in the relationship between the two crowns abundantly clear. Further cases underlined the fact that the Scottish king could, and would, be summoned to answer for the actions of his courts before Edward in England.[36] 'At every step he took, the new king would have to pause, examine its implications, and find out whether it could be allowed under the new régime … It was John's misfortune that he had succeeded to a kingdom which could not have been ruled by anyone forced to walk such a narrow tightrope'.[37]

Despite the strict legal noose tightening around Scotland, the Scottish political community were unlikely to take this unprecedented challenge to the independence of the northern kingdom lying down. Unfortunately, we'll probably never know whether Edward always intended to provoke a violent reaction from the Scots in order to justify getting rid of the kingship altogether and taking Scotland directly under his own control. It is not beyond the bounds of possibility, though he would certainly not have wanted a Scottish revolt by 1294, when he was planning a war with France. Ironically, however, the breakdown in Anglo-French relations provided exactly the catalyst the Scots needed to make their bid for freedom.

Edward's demand, as their feudal overlord, that the Scots perform military service for him in France was a powerful reminder not just to them, but also to the recently conquered Welsh, of Edward's success in extending and formalising English authority throughout the British Isles. The Welsh reacted first, seeking their independence under Madog ap Llewelyn, head of a junior branch of the royal house of Gwynedd. The failure of this revolt set the seal on Edward's conquest of Wales, begun in the 1280s.[38]

The Scots did not immediately follow suit, mostly because they meant to play a card denied to the principality – an alliance with France – which would take time. They may also have needed to overcome Balliol's reluctance to commit himself to an all-out war with England, adopting an extraordinary policy, given the essentially conservative nature of the Scottish political community. Side-lining King John, Scotland's political community may well have installed a caretaker government of twelve guardians or

Peers, supposedly on an ancient French model, or, at the very least, chosen a council to run the country. Perhaps this council, led still by the Comyns, was required to establish a broad base of support for a momentous step that would surely pitch the kingdom into war with England. These were extraordinary times, when normal procedures sometimes needed extraordinary modification.

We could blame Balliol for not having stood up to Edward earlier. However, events from 1291 onwards make it clear that nothing short of war would have been sufficient to stop the English king even temporarily in his tracks, and even conflict might not deter him. Unsurprisingly, the Scottish political community had, until now, also bowed to this implicit threat, primarily because to fight England alone, without a powerful ally like France, would have been almost suicidal. It was also unquestionably the case that such a war was likely to do serious damage to the nation's health and was therefore not a decision to be taken lightly, even with France on side. But at least by 1295 the Scots had also acquired a helpful absolution from Pope Celestine V of any oaths to Edward which they claimed had been made under duress.[39]

An embassy of four Scots – William Fraser, bishop of St Andrews, Matthew Crambeth, bishop of Dunkeld, Sir John Soules and Sir Ingram Umfraville – was despatched to Paris in July 1295. By 23 October, they had concluded a treaty with King Philip guaranteeing to maintain hostilities against England in return for military aid from the French should Scotland be invaded; a peace could only be made if both sides agreed. It was further stipulated that John's son and heir, Edward Balliol, should marry King Philip's niece, Jeanne de Valois. The Scottish king and a wide cross-section of his political community, including representatives of the burgesses, ratified this treaty on 23 February 1296; such an unusually broad acknowledgement of support suggests a need to impress on the country at large that the French alliance meant war. The army had already been ordered to muster on 11 March 1296 at Caddonlee, the traditional launching-pad for a Scottish invasion of England. There was no way back.[40]

Though Edward can't have known that the Scots had concluded a French treaty until after his own invasion of Scotland, he was well aware of the direction events were taking. His own preparations began as early as October 1295, when he ordered the lands of all Scotsmen living in England to be confiscated; two months later writs of summons for a muster at Newcastle on 1 March 1296 were issued. But it was the Scots who made the first move. Wark castle, just south of the Tweed, was surprised by a Scottish force, though soon recovered; another part of the Scottish army led by John Comyn, earl of Buchan, then crossed the border and ravaged the countryside round Carlisle – whose castle was technically held by Robert Bruce (6), the former earl of Carrick – on Easter Monday (26 March). Neither action gave the Scots any advantage, but it certainly provided the English king with more than enough excuse to order his own advance across the Tweed.

The army brought to Scotland for the first time in Edward's reign was intended to be overwhelming. Though the king's demands for 1,000 men-at-arms from among the landed classes and 60,000 infantry conscripted in set amounts from each English county were vastly over-inflated (the infantry certainly was at least half that number), it was still a hugely impressive show of military might by medieval standards.[41] The English army was one of the most advanced in western Europe, though Edward I's own contribution to transforming it 'from an old-fashioned and inefficient feudal force into a professional, paid army recruited by contracts and indentures' has been challenged effectively. In fact, the pace of change was slow and the king's cavalry forces were recruited on very mixed lines.[42]

The élite group of men from which the English cavalry could be drawn numbered between 1,250 and 3,000. But even that upper figure is still a tiny proportion (0.05%) of an English population of 5–6,000,000.[43] The problem was that, by the end of the thirteenth century, the quotas of knights owing the traditional feudal forty days' unpaid service to the crown had declined enormously. It has been reckoned that 'some 90 per cent had, in a word, evaporated . . .'.[44] This did not, of course, mean that knights no longer served enthusiastically in English armies, but the ways in which they were recruited had certainly changed from the Norman Conquest over two hundred years before.

Under Edward I the strict feudal element was certainly fairly small (perhaps around 20% of the total); most served for pay, including foreign mercenaries. However, a significant number of top-ranking nobles seem to have performed their service freely at their own expense, probably in order to maintain their independence. Many of these men were extremely experienced and had a strong personal association with the king, both as comrades-in-arms and through service in the royal household; they were thus ideally placed to serve Edward in a variety of military capacities, in the fleet, as constables of castles, as administrative officers.[45] However, as we will see, their zeal for royal service in general was not necessarily matched by an enthusiasm to serve in Scotland specifically.

Edward did overhaul the recruitment of footsoldiers, making it more efficient, though the effect of this on local communities was effectively an increase in taxation, which rarely goes down well. The commissioners of array were the main innovation: often royal clerks,[46] their main role was to make sure only the best were recruited into the royal army. These sturdy yeomen were then to be 'equipped with white tunics, swords and knives, all at the expense of the local communities'.[47] They certainly needed their strength: the long march into Scotland and the difficulties in keeping the army properly supplied with food and drink affected them first and hardest. It's fair to say that the difficulties involved in maintaining such large medieval armies (up to 25,000 infantry) in the field were almost too much even for Edward I; time and again he was unable to stop desertion from forcing him to head back home as winter approached. This, as we will see, provided the Scots with some respite and perhaps the opportunity to undo any gains Edward might have made in the previous campaigning season, ensuring that the war dragged on and on.

The composition and organisation of the Scottish army remains something of a mystery since there are no records relating to recruitment, pay or provisioning as there are for England. Indeed the historian – perhaps like the chronicler – is left to guess even rough working numbers by creating a proportion from English figures relative to the ratio of the two populations (generally reckoned to have been around 6:1).[48] That gives us a total of around 200 Scottish knights, with a pool of up to about 500, a paltry figure that would accord with the general lack of a role for cavalry in Scottish military strategy, which was focused – certainly when it came to battles – on the ability of Scottish spearmen to repulse horsemen.

As well as a basic numerical problem related to the size of the population and the resources of the kingdom (knights = land), Scotland's leaders also had a problem with their collective military experience. The last 'battle' on Scottish soil had taken place over thirty years earlier, in 1263, when the Norwegians invaded the west coast to protect their ownership of the Western Isles. Though the Scots ultimately won that contest, they did not do so as a result of the inconclusive skirmish at Largs, but through the death of King Haakon of Norway shortly afterwards.[49] Some Scottish nobles, including John Comyn of Badenoch and Robert Bruce of Annandale (5), had fought on the royalist side a year later during the English civil war between Henry III and Simon de Montfort. Unfortunately, they were on the losing side, initially at least, though Lewes was also the only battle in which Edward (still heir to the throne) took part and lost.[50]

That the Scottish crown had diverted its attention away from the military potential of the kingdom and sought to maximise its economic capabilities is a growing theme in thirteenth-century Scottish history. Indeed, the extent of 'feudalisation' in Scotland, in the sense of the holding of knights' fees in return for military service, is also questionable. For example,

> ... after the death of Alexander III, Earl Malise [of Stratheam] issued at least three – and doubtless more – discharges of extraordinary military service to tenants. As these discharges make clear, even Sir William Murray, an important member of the earl's inner circle, only owed traditional Scottish service for his lands, rather than a quota of knights. This, together with the clear evidence for the continued and increasing exploitation of the area's economic resources ... reflects a lack of concern over the exploitation of military resources which is evident throughout most of Scotland.[51]

Under William the Lion (1165–1214), the crown does seem to have tried to create more knights' fiefs beyond the 'Normanised' areas of Lothian and parts of the south-west. The king was particularly keen on more 'feudalisation' in the heartland of Scotland – north of the Forth – where the ancient Scottish earldoms, like Stratheam, were located. This policy, presumably motivated by the king's desire for a more modern military force to help him extend his kingdom's boundaries further south into Northumberland, was successful for a while. However, only a century later it is clear that the holding of land for knight's service was highly unusual; both blench-ferme and feu-ferme (token or monetary payments) were the norm.[52] If more proof was needed that the crowns of Scotland and England were growing closer, not further apart, during the thirteenth century, the fact that Scotland's kings deliberately chose to let the kingdom's military apparatus decline is surely a good indication of the confidence felt in their relationship with their southern neighbour.

Of course, when war did break out, Scotland was even more militarily unprepared than such a small kingdom would otherwise have been; on balance, the army might be better described as non-feudal in nature, rather than as a poorer version of the military machine it was about to face. The basic form of recruitment relied on 'free service' 'performed by free men – barons, thanes, knights, serjeants and other freeholders' who were equipped and mounted according to their rank; and 'Scottish service', demanded of the earldoms of the ancient kingdom north of the Forth, which demanded 'the attendance of able-bodied men from the "horseless classes"' under their lords. Despite attempts by previous kings to modernise the kingdom's military capacity along Norman lines, then, by c. 1300 the army was roughly what it must have been two centuries earlier, a truly national force diversified by its weaponry and military skills rather than by its method of recruitment.' And though the army which was defeated by Edward in 1296 was mostly cavalry, 'the speed with which Andrew Murray and William Wallace raised their infantry force in the following year suggests that the machinery for summoning and training the non-feudal "common army" still had life in it'.[53]

At the same time, the confidence shown by the Scots in 1296 is hard to square with the creaky old military machine with which they were about to try to defy that veteran commander, Edward I. Equally importantly for the prosecution of the war in the following years, the Scots seem to have had no siege weapons. It must also be said that the grip exerted by the Comyn family on the leadership of the Scottish political community meant that, initially at least, military command often devolved on the earl of Buchan, who certainly did not shine as a general. The contest between Scotland and England was always likely to have been of David and Goliath proportions but the Scottish army's backwardness and inexperience and their decision to fight anyway says much about the commitment of its leaders to the cause of independence. It also exposes their naïvety.

That commitment was perhaps given greater resolve by what happened immediately after Edward and his army crossed the border.[54] On 31 March 1296, the English arrived before the walls of Berwick-upon-Tweed, Scotland's most important burgh. A breakdown in communications caused the English fleet to launch an unsuccessful attack that resulted in the burning of a number of ships by the Scots, which in turn prompted Edward to unleash his army. The town, still defended only by a wooden palisade, offered little or no defence and the castle's commander, Sir William Douglas, promptly surrendered. Sadly, such alacrity did not save many of the town's menfolk, who were then butchered in great numbers.

King John was at Roxburgh, some twenty-five miles away, and now, having heard of the atrocity at Berwick, sent word to King Edward on 5 April that he was withdrawing his fealty, a some-what hypocritical act, given that he had already negotiated a treaty with England's greatest enemy. His army, still busy attacking the north-west of England to very little effect, quickly returned home and – free of even the veneer of loyalty to King Edward – promptly attacked Northumberland, causing the kind of devastation to which the region would soon become far too accustomed. A smaller force under the earls of Mar, Ross and Menteith seized the castle of Dunbar. Though the earl of Dunbar consistently supported Edward, his countess – the sister of John Comyn of Buchan – seems to have sided with her father against her husband and let them in. They were soon besieged by an English force under King John's father-in-law, John de Warenne, earl of Surrey, whom the rest of the Scottish army attempted to engage on 27 April. Foolishly misinterpreting English preparations for the engagement, the Scots rushed in too soon and were summarily defeated. The castle surrendered the following day.

Despite the fact that King John himself and, perhaps more importantly, the Comyns were not present at Dunbar,[55] Scottish resistance collapsed like a burst ball after the defeat. As castle after castle was handed over to Edward, Balliol and his allies moved north, but by midsummer they had accepted the inevitable. After some negotiation that initially promised fairly lenient terms to King John, Edward suddenly decided that he would be satisfied only with complete surrender – probably having found evidence of the Franco-Scottish treaty[56] – and Balliol was duly stripped of both his dignity and his kingship. The Scottish seal was broken in two and John, together with the symbols of Scottish independence, the stone of Scone and the Black Rood of St Margaret, was sent off to ignominious exile in London.

Meanwhile Edward enjoyed – or perhaps the word should be endured – nearly two months progressing through eastern and northern Scotland, accepting the homage and fealty of the vanquished Scottish nobility. He could not be accused of taking the conquest anything less than seriously, scorning the difficulties of travelling deep into the Grampian mountains, whose lofty passes are worth avoiding in bad weather even today. 'With kingly courage, [King Edward] pressed forward into the region of the unstable inhabitants of Moray, whither you will not find in the ancient records that anyone had penetrated since Arthur. His purpose was to explore with scattered troops the hills and woods and steep crags which the natives are accustomed to count on as strongholds.'[57] He was king of almost the entire country, not just the easily accessible bits of the south-east that might well have reminded him a little of home. Finally, in August, he called a parliament at Berwick and set about the business of constructing a suitable administration for his new acquisition.

It is hard not to marvel at the vast array of tactics which Edward I could and did employ in seeking to bring the Scottish kingdom under his control after 1290. Equally, it is easy to feel sympathy for the Scots, who had very little choice but to employ the unlikely longshot of the military option if they were to have any chance of extricating themselves from Edward's well-prepared web of powerful argument and legal half-truths, along with the threat of military action. It cannot, of course, be claimed that the English king had all the moves worked out long in advance, nor that the ultimate aim was always to suppress an independent Scottish kingship. However, it surely did not take very much involvement in Scottish affairs after the death of Alexander III to make Edward realise that such an outcome was perhaps on the cards if he played them shrewdly. The Scots certainly did not prove themselves unworthy or ignoble in the decade between Alexander's death and the conquest of 1296; on the contrary, the political community, as a group, generally acted with sense and a profound commitment to Scotland's sovereign rights. That they proved unable to prevent the takeover merely attests to the odds against them. Edward's success, on the other hand, was surely as much a result of his 'awareness of the potential for expanding royal power by cutting through an ambiguous, contradictory and ill-defined body of precedent and tradition which characterised most relationships, including that between Scotland and England' as on the rights he believed he had inherited.[58]

The collapse of John Balliol's government less than two months after the catastrophic defeat at Dunbar brought Scotland quickly and easily under King Edward's direct control. He and the triumphant English army were well-pleased with their efforts: the king himself allegedly remarked, with a believable air of crude over-confidence, that 'It's a good thing to be rid of a shit'.[59] But few, even among the vanquished Scots, can have been as thunderstruck as the Bruces when they discovered that Edward had not removed Balliol with the intention of replacing him with the earl of Carrick. Despite the latter's craven subservience, that was still too much trouble; from now on Scotland was to be ruled directly from England.

This was revolutionary. A kingdom on record since 900 AD had just been extinguished, though even Edward was unclear as to exactly what legal status he had now conferred on his new acquisition and his own position in relation to it. Leaving aside the defeated Scots for a moment, we must wonder what went through the minds of Robert Bruce, father and son (the Competitor died in 1295, so we're now down to just two), given the conspicuous lack of reward in 1296 for their loyalty to the English king even beyond their failure to acquire a throne. But there's not a peep of insubordination to be found from either of them in the record as they went about helping to extend Edward's grip on Scotland. Given his subsequent career, it is hard to imagine that the younger Robert felt anything other than fury, even if his father resolutely did not wish to rock the boat and he himself had to toe the line for the time being.[60]

What is perhaps harder to understand is Edward's apparent belief that the 'Scottish problem' had been sorted out once and for all, and much more quickly than Wales. He was certainly foolish to ignore the clear evidence for the depth of feeling towards the independence of the Scottish kingdom evident in the words and deeds of its political community – witness the anger expressed when Edward first brought up the overlordship question in May 1291 and the united front presented by the élites in the build-up to war from 1295 (apart from the earls of Dunbar and Angus and, of course, the Bruces, who by then were living entirely in England). Though we have the benefit of hindsight, the question political pundits should have been asking as 1296 drew to a close was not whether the Scots would seek to throw off England's rule, but if they would be able to bring together a form of resistance that would have any chance of success against the mighty Plantagenet.

CHAPTER TWO

THE RESISTIBLE RISE OF EDWARDIAN GOVERNMENT

Since the decision made by the Scots to go to war had been taken on the back of a broad spectrum of consent (for a medieval kingdom), the events of April to July 1296 must be seen as a defeat of the Scottish political community as a whole, and its Comyn leadership in particular.[1] The choice facing the Scottish nobility captured at Dunbar was stark: either accept Edward as overlord or remain *hors de combat* in prison. A number, such as William, earl of Ross, refused to give in for several years, before finally accepting that such a course, however honourable, was also futile.[2] Of course, once an oath of allegiance had been taken, the right course was to stick to it; a true knight would not merely pretend to swear it, then change sides the minute he was released. That many did choose to go back on their word was as much an issue of conscience as it was for those who did not. Obviously, what Edward had done was not regarded as honourable by the Scots either, but contemporary ethical codes made it difficult for the élites to always know which was the unquestionably 'right' course of action in these wars (a dilemma that may be applicable to more wars than we often admit). In addition, key members of the Scottish government not captured at Dunbar were required to go on extended hunting leave on their English estates.

The reticence of the Scottish nobility over the next year or so, which contrasts sharply with their assurance and assertiveness in 1295–6, is, on the one hand, a result of the simple fact that their leaders were now out of the country. But it surely also signifies a profound crisis of confidence caused by the ease with which the

English had brought about their defeat and submission. Unfortunately for Edward, this was only a temporary state of affairs.

Having progressed pointedly through an abject Scotland, Edward returned to Berwick in August to lay down ordinances for the future government of the conquered kingdom. The records bear out the assertion of the English chronicler, Walter of Guisborough, that the king ordained a new treasurer, seal and chancellor, appointed justices and commanded all to do homage to him. Though sufficient to provide for the establishment of the new regime, the king was a lot less clear about the constitutional position of his new acquisition: '. . . the kingdom was not abolished but remained in abeyance'. Nine years later, Edward would finally pronounce on Scotland's status but his silence in 1296 indicates just how ambivalent even he felt his legal position to be, a belief underlined by the doctoring of the record relating to the process of Norham.[3]

The most senior member of the new administration was the royal lieutenant, John de Warenne, earl of Surrey, the victor of Dunbar and father of Balliol's dead wife. As Edward's immediate representative in Scotland, his duties were almost as varied as those of the king himself, meaning he was – or should have been – crucial to the smooth running of the new regime. The temporalities of vacant sees (areas of ecclesiastical jurisdiction) were his to administer, as well as the patronage of benefices up to the value of forty marks,[4] which would have included most Scottish parishes in royal patronage.[5] However, apart from his military capacity, the earl's most important responsibility was to administer justice: he could either deal with petitions himself, or, if they had been submitted directly to Edward (in parliament), he was still obliged to investigate each case before the king made judgement.[6]

The best hope the new regime had of gaining acceptance from the vanquished Scots was surely to promote an effective judicial system for the redress of grievances, although the imposition of overtly English, in preference to Scottish, practices was a potential cause of resentment. In other words, Edward's government could have gone some way to offset the effects of being much more intensive and intrusive than the Scottish system by promoting the benefits of effective and efficient justice. But Surrey now made it clear that he was seriously underwhelmed by the honour of his new office and would expend the minimum amount of effort on it. This appointment was undoubtedly a serious error on Edward's part and is indicative of the lack of foresight which characterised the English king's treatment of his new acquisition in 1296. He would soon live to regret it.

The new chancellor was Walter Amersham, a royal clerk who did have previous experience of Scottish affairs, having served as an associate of Bishop Alan of Caithness, chancellor after Alexander III's death.[7] Amersham's primary responsibility was to oversee the issuing of royal writs. The other important official at the chancery was William Bevercotes, appointed on 5 October 1296 to 'keep, collect and deliver writs sealed with the seal used by the king in Scotland'. This was a new seal presumably struck in the same year as the conquest and a telling reminder to the Scots of just how much their relationship with England and its king had changed. Bevercotes was also to account for the issues of the seal[8] at the exchequer in Berwick.

However, the most important office turned out to be treasurer of Scotland, perhaps more by virtue of the zeal for his job exhibited by its incumbent, Hugh Cressingham, than through any deliberate royal policy. He was certainly extremely experienced, having served as justice in various English counties, most recently in Lancashire.[9] Unfortunately for Cressingham, being treasurer was in itself an offensive innovation, since the chief financial officer under the kings of Scots (before Balliol) had been the chamberlain.

In September 1296 rolls of parchment showing how the Scottish exchequer worked were sent from Edinburgh castle to Berwick, suggesting that there was at least the thought that

Scottish practice was to be followed. In March 1297, however, a transcript of regulations was despatched from London to establish the exchequer in Scotland along the same lines as the one at Westminster, together with various rolls from the early years of Edward's reign and a bundle of writs from the reign of Henry III, presumably for reference. Once again, King Edward proved unwilling or unable to pay attention to Scottish sensibilities, to the idea that Scottish ways of doing things might be different rather than intrinsically inferior to English practices. Such considerations probably didn't even cross his mind; his own needs came first, second and last. [10]

These three offices – royal lieutenant, chancellor and treasurer – formed the core of the English administration at Berwick. They were supplemented by three justiciars, who did follow the traditional Scottish format of 'a justiciar of Lothian, a justiciar beyond the sea of Scotland [i.e. north of the River Forth] and a justiciar of Galloway'. The appointees were William of Ormesby, William Mortimer and Roger Skoter respectively, [11] all Englishmen who cannot have been well versed in Scottish law or the Scottish legal system, surely a prerequisite for the job. Nevertheless, the office of justiciar was obsolete in England but not in Scotland, and so Edward was not completely insensitive to Scottish practices. [12] Finally, two Englishmen were appointed as escheators, whose task/role was to look after land that came into royal hands when there was no heir. Henry Rye was appointed north of the Forth and Peter Dunwich in the south. Rye was also granted custody of the royal castles of Elgin and Forres, while Dunwich was made keeper of the Gifford family castle of Yester in East Lothian. Edward was here conforming to English custom, since the office of escheator was normally performed by sheriffs in Scotland. [13]

The keepers of royal castles, who were often also sheriffs, were of great importance to the new administration. As the king's officers throughout the country, they were his most ubiquitous and obvious representatives and it was their behaviour – particularly if they were English – that was most likely to either persuade the Scots that their interests were still served by the new regime or that it was alien and repressive and therefore to be resisted.

After the conquest of 1296, several changes were introduced, providing the new administration with thirty sheriffdoms.[14] A number of appointments were made as early as May 1296,[15] strongly suggesting that Edward harboured no doubts that Scotland would soon be his after the battle of Dunbar; however, most were superseded in the autumn. Between September and October the sheriffdom of Roxburgh, with its impressive castle, was granted to Sir Robert Hastangs, junior; Sir Hugh Elaund took over the combined responsibility of the keepership of Jedburgh castle and the strategically vital Selkirk Forest; Sir Walter Huntercombe went to Edinburgh castle as sheriff of Edinburgh and its two constabularies, Linlithgow and Haddington; Dumbarton castle and sheriffdom were given to Sir Alexander Leeds; and Sir Richard Waldegrave was installed at Stirling.[16]

Most appointments do not survive in the official record, but a number can be added to the above from other evidence. Sir Robert Joneby was described as sheriff at Dumfries by August 1296; we can surely presume that the infamous William Heselrig (soon to die at William Wallace's hand) became sheriff of Lanark around this time; Sir William FitzWarin was certainly in residence at Urquhart castle in 1297, as was Sir Reginald Cheyne, senior, a Scotsman, at Inverness and Sir Henry Lathum at Aberdeen.[17]

The most important office after the lieutenant was the warden of the land of Galloway – part of which had been inherited by King John from his mother – and of the county [*comitatum*] of Ayr, awarded to Surrey's nephew, Sir Henry Percy, on 8 September, nearly three weeks before Surrey's appointment. The castles of Ayr, Wigtown, Cruggleton and Buittle were also committed to Percy's custody. The first two were royal castles controlling sheriffdoms; however, Buittle and Cruggleton[18] were King John's own castles (though the latter had been given to John Comyn, earl of

Buchan) and permanently confiscated from him, along with the rest of his lands, in 1296.[19] With Surrey (supposedly) based in Berwick in the east and Percy in the west, King Edward could be reassured that the border was effectively controlled. But this arrangement meant that the centre of Scottish government was located in the far south of the country, a very different power-base from the Edinburgh-Stirling-Forfar axis favoured by thirteenth-century kings of Scots.

On balance, the men appointed to office in Scotland (and those who held such positions in the following years) came from a wide range of geographical backgrounds. This stands in stark contrast to the composition of the armies, which tended to be dominated by the northern English counties who turned out to have most to lose in this war. However, as the war dragged on, it became harder to find noblemen inclined to take up such appointments, presumably because any potential financial gains had often evaporated.

There was one other wardenship created in 1296, though its role and significance were rather different from that held by either Surrey or Percy. In order to extend English control into the north-west highlands and islands – just as King John had tried to do – and to counteract the influence of the pro-Comyn/Balliol west highland magnate, Alastair MacDougall of Argyll, Edward had initially made use of MacDougall's main regional rival, Alastair MacDonald of Islay. Macdonald had been with the Bruces in Edward's army in March 1296.[20] However, on 10 September 1296, the earl of Menteith, who had been captured in Dunbar castle in April, was appointed as warden of an enormous area of the western seaboard stretching from Ross to Rutherglen. As such, he was given authority over the men of important Scots such as James the Steward and Sir John Comyn of Badenoch and Lochaber, who had their own ambitions in the area. It is not at all clear what exactly prompted such munificence towards Menteith, but perhaps Edward was looking for someone less completely enmeshed in west highland politics than MacDonald, though the earl had considerable interests in the area himself. However, this was clearly one region where the English king needed Scottish support to even attempt to rule it.[21]

Arrangements for the payment of all Edward's officials in Scotland were made between September and November 1296. Surrey was to receive 2,000 marks per year; Sir Henry Percy, 1,000 marks; Amersham, 200 marks, plus the income from the church of Kinross, which he was given in September 1296; the three justiciars, 60 marks each. No records survive for the fee to be paid to either Cressingham or the two escheators.[22]

Payments to the keepers of castles, and the constables who were usually in day-to-day charge,[23] varied considerably, depending on the size of the garrison and whether their duties included those of sheriff. Such payment often took the form of a fixed annual fee, or *certum*, agreed with the keeper, for himself and a set number of men-at-arms. Footsoldiers were always paid by the day, as were the various tradesmen and officers required for the welfare of the garrison, such as smiths, masons and watchmen, not to mention chaplains. All annual, as opposed to daily, fees were to be paid in two instalments in the Trinity and Michaelmas terms (around Easter and at the end of September respectively), supposedly from the issues of Scotland at the Berwick exchequer.[24]

The last and potentially most impressive indication of Edward's confidence in the finality of his conquest was the town-planning programme he envisaged for Berwick, along the same lines as that implemented at Kingston-upon-Hull a few years earlier. This busy, wealthy port was a prize worth having but Edward, typically, believed there was room for improvement, including 'the displacement of the Scottish population and the assignment of their homes to English settlers, to attract whom a new constitution was clearly necessary'.[25]

Various representatives from England's major boroughs were summoned to a general parliament held at Bury St Edmunds from 3 November 1296. London, for example, was to choose 'four wise men of the most knowing and most sufficient to know best how to devise, order and array a new town to the most profit of the king and of the merchants.' Twenty-three other cities and boroughs were each to elect two representatives with similar qualifications.

This first meeting achieved little and another group of advisors was ordered to consult with the king on 2 January 1297. It was only at this point that Edward intimated that Berwick-upon-Tweed was the object of his attention. Perhaps this 'transparent veil of secrecy' was adopted merely for its own sake. However, the English king may have realised that his enthusiasm for transforming the northern town, so recently the subject of a brutal assault, might not have been shared by his subjects. Certainly, he now dropped the idea of elected representatives and sent writs to his own nominees, who included Henry le Waleys, mayor of London and 'sometime joint-planner of Winchelsea', and Thomas Alard, warden of Winchelsea.

Yet again, nothing happened, presumably because the frozen north was still of little or no interest to these southerners. A third set of summonses called for nominees from certain north-eastern towns to meet at Berwick itself in April 1297. This assembly finally managed to arrange for a number of Englishmen to be resettled there, but little was done to change the actual plan of the town.[31] Issues of far greater urgency were to occupy Edward's mind for the next five years and so only Berwick's military and defensive needs were attended to during that period. Now, with the conquest of Scotland completed in record time, King Edward could turn to far more pressing and important matters: wresting back control of his duchy of Gascony, seized by its superior lord, Philip IV of France, in 1295.

To what extent was the regime imposed on the Scots by Edward I likely to be seen as oppressive, antagonistic and/or overtly alien? With regard to the last element, it is stating the obvious to say that almost all appointments made in 1296 were to Englishmen, and the key offices exclusively so. While this may have been convenient for Edward and certainly echoed his treatment of Wales after its conquest in the 1280s, it was also risky. Whether he realised it or not, he had just given the Scottish political community – who were used to running the kingdom on behalf of their kings – nothing to do and no reason to feel any real loyalty to their new master. It was the king's job to distribute patronage and they were effectively being told they weren't going to get any. That exclusion from government also made it crystal clear that Edward had little respect for the nuances of the Scottish system, in which the new appointees can have had almost no experience.

Obviously, the fact that there was no longer a resident king made change inevitable, but it was perhaps at a local level that the 'alien' nature of the new regime had most impact. The new sheriffs of 1296 no longer had any connection with the areas in which they served (with the exception, for a few months at least, of Sir Reginald Crawford at Ayr and Sir Walter Twynham at Wigtown, as well as the longer-lasting Sir Reginald Cheyne at Inverness).[26] Throughout the kingdom, therefore, the local community was obliged to deal with men who were foreign in every sense – strangers to both county and kingdom and perhaps not even able to speak the local language.[27] It is true that the earl of Menteith was given an important office but, to be honest, the government of the north-west highlands and islands was not really part of the mainstream administration, given that the area had only recently become part of the Scottish kingdom. In any case, there is no evidence he actually took up the job.

It's highly likely that Edward did regard the Scottish system as backward and, at worst, worthy of contempt; he had, after all found, parts of English government in need of reform, to curb – as he saw it – the power-hungry instincts of his own nobility, as well as the citizens of London.[28] But such an attitude, given that he was dealing with a well-established kingdom which had developed an administrative system to suit its own needs, was likely to arouse considerable resentment. Scotland was certainly not as sophisticated as England when it came to the mechanisms of central administration but, equally it was not Ireland or Wales with little prior history of unified government. On the one hand, it could be argued that what was imposed on Scotland in 1296 was far less of an innovation than that which English rulers attempted to introduce to Ireland and Wales; there was no need to introduce shires, for example, simply because they had already been adopted into the Scottish system, even if there were significant differences. On the other hand, perhaps those Scots normally involved in the administration of the kingdom felt that 'anglicisation' had taken place for its own sake, heightening their appreciation of the 'Scottishness' of the original system. Moreover, the example of Ireland, which was fairly effectively milked of large sums of money and goods by Edward I,[29] not to mention Wales, so recently and so violently subdued, now stood before the Scots as a fate to which they had once regarded themselves as too superior to succumb.[30]

It took a while for Edward even to consider that his easy conquest of Scotland might have given him a rather false picture of the Scots' ability to challenge his annexation of the northern kingdom. He may also have failed to realise that, constitutionally speaking, Scotland was actually remarkably sophisticated when it came to managing without a king, now that John Balliol was in the Tower of London, even if the system of guardians heading a caretaker government must always be a temporary arrangement. The first hint of revolt may not have caused too much consternation in Berwick since it was focused on the north-west highlands, which had resisted rule by the kings of Scots, never mind Edward I. Despite the appointment of the earl of Menteith as lieutenant there, Alasdair MacDonald of Islay – a good friend of Robert Bruce 6 – was named as Edward's baillie of Lorn and Ross and the Isles, much of which had previously been under MacDougall control, on 9 April 1297.[31]

MacDonald's appointment may well have been made in anticipation of trouble, since it was certainly not long in coming. Part of the problem lay in the fact that, even though the region's most important player, Alasdair MacDougall of Argyll, had submitted to Edward and was currently in prison at Berwick, many of the *nobiles* of Argyll, including MacDougall's sons (Iain and Duncan), together with the MacRuaris of Garmoran (Lachlan and Ruari), were still at large. Alasdair Macdonald claimed in a letter to Edward, probably of late April 1297, that these gentlemen had now performed homage but the MacRuaris were soon on the rampage, killing Edward's officials (probably Alasdair's own men) and seizing their ships, as well as invading royal lands in Skye and Lewis.[32]

MacDonald moved in force against Lachlan and Ruari MacRuari, who both nearly submitted in April. However, Lachlan changed his mind and it was rumoured he was looking for support from the men of his father-in-law, Alasdair Macdougall, lord of Argyll, who were commanded by the latter's son Duncan. Even more worryingly, Lochaber, which belonged to Sir John Comyn of Badenoch, was on the verge of rebellion. Certainly, Comyn's men in Inverlochy castle, which guarded the western entrance to the Great Glen, soon refused to co-operate with MacDonald, whose authority, and Edward's with it, was looking increasingly ineffective.[33]

To add to these difficulties, Alasdair MacDonald also reported his suspicions – whether rightly or for his own ends – of James the Steward and had seized, on Edward's behalf, the castle and barony of Glasrog (Glassary) which the Steward apparently held.[34] To cap it all, Alasdair claimed he was prevented from fulfilling his duties by a lack of funding, either from royal issues from the areas supposedly under his control, or directly from England.[35] The government did, at last, make some attempt to control the situation, freeing Alasdair MacDougall from Berwick castle on 24 May 1297 in a belated acknowledgement that he alone could bring his son Duncan to heel, and also, perhaps, restore a degree of stability to the area. This was highly unlikely to bring relief to his long-standing enemy, Alasdair MacDonald, however, and in fact the lord of Argyll soon joined his sons and MacRuari relatives in devastating MacDonald lands.[36]

It is usual to dismiss this rebellion as a local civil war – the quarrel between the MacDonalds and the MacDougalls was partly over the disputed lands of Lismore and does represent the resumption of long-standing hostilities among key members of north-west highland society, which were far more important to them than the relationship between the kingdoms of Scotland and England. However, this rebellion can also 'be seen as the response of representatives of the Scottish government'. MacDougall of Argyll, like King John himself, was brother-in-law to John Comyn of Badenoch.[37] Although the latter was still in exile in England, we can read this revolt as the reaction of those who had lost power and influence after 1296, having been intimately connected with the Comyn-dominated Balliol government.

Meanwhile, on 3 May 1297, William Wallace began his brief but remarkable career with the murder of the English sheriff of Lanark. He then raised the nearby men of Clydesdale and headed south.[38] The northern counties of England scrambled to defend themselves. The sheriff of Westmorland excused his failure to make an assessment for the lay twelfth (a tax on noble property) in that county, as he was ordered to do in a writ dated 26 April 1297, because 'all the knights and free tenants are in Cumberland to defend the march between England and Scotland against the coming of the Scots'.[39]

Whether or not Wallace and his men crossed the border, he almost certainly led a remarkably successful foray into Dumfriesshire. A letter from the king dated 13 June thanked Sir Donald MacCan, Gillemichael MacGeche, Maurice Stubhille and others in the company of Sir Thomas Staunford 'for their late ready and willing service in repelling disturbers of the peace and recapturing for the king castles which had been taken by those in those parts'.[40] MacCan, MacGeche and Stubhille were all Dumfriesshire men, while Staunford was one of Sir Henry Percy's retinue.[41] Though it is tempting to attribute the reduction of castles to the 'aristocratic' rebellion of Robert Wishart, bishop of Glasgow, the Steward and the young Robert Bruce 7, now officially earl of Carrick, that rebellion was not launched until at least the end of May, which is not early enough for Dumfriesshire to have been lost and won by the time the king heard about it in the south of England a couple of weeks later.

William Wallace, now joined by the Lanarkshire knight, Sir William Douglas, may have decided that discretion was the better part of valour in the face of resistance from Staunford and the rest. He certainly now headed north to Scone, where the justiciar, William Ormesby, was holding a court. Ormesby may have attracted Wallace's ire because he '... prosecuted all those who did not wish to swear fealty to the king of England without making distinction of person'. Though the justiciar escaped, word of this uprising was now circulating and Wallace soon received certain messengers at Perth who arrived 'in great haste on behalf of certain magnates of the kingdom of Scotland'. These were almost certainly sent by James the Steward, the bishop of Glasgow, and the earl of Carrick, who were about to launch their own rebellion and may have wished to establish William's intentions and perhaps to coordinate their attacks.[42] While Wallace himself seemed to prefer to keep out of noble politics, the essential point here is that, with the Comyns and other members of Balliol's government *hors de combat* in England, this was the perfect time for a new Scottish political faction to rise to leadership, one intimately connected with the Bruces, or at least its youngest generation.

Carrick, Wishart and the Steward were not – or so they soon claimed – challenging Edward's right to rule Scotland at this point. Rather, they were objecting to the heavy-handed nature of his government, most particularly the fear of military service overseas on the part of 'the middling folk' of Scotland.

Fifty-seven Scottish nobles were certainly summoned to serve in Flanders on 24 May;[43] in addition, any Scot still imprisoned in England after Dunbar could go with Edward in return for his freedom. It may also have been believed north of the border that the kind of conscription of footsoldiers that went on in each English county with the approach of a campaign (and also, on occasions, in Ireland and Wales) would happen in Scotland, though there is no evidence that this was Edward's intention in 1297. In the end, very few Scots actually went overseas and all who did so travelled straight from English prisons. But it would have surprised few in the northern kingdom if their new master had made exactly this kind of unprecedented and deeply controversial demand.

It is not clear exactly when Wishart, the Steward and the young earl came out in open rebellion, though the catalyst may well have been the demands for military service sent out at the end of May. A month later, on 24 June, Sir Henry Percy, the warden of Galloway, and the Westmorland knight, Sir Robert Clifford were given powers to 'arrest, imprison and otherwise do justice on persons making meetings, conventicles and conspiracies against the king's peace in divers parts of Scotland'. Dumfries and Nithsdale were mentioned specifically, as well as the north-western English counties; the danger was sufficient for the people of Cumberland and Westmorland to make a 'voluntary' offer of service on an expedition against the Scots, although they required reassurance that this would not be used as a precedent in the future.[44] It may well have been that, after the discussions with Wallace at Perth, Wishart, the Steward and Carrick decided to continue his good work in the south-west, an area that included the Bruce family's lordship of Annandale now held by Carrick's father who remained entirely loyal to Edward.

Clifford and Percy forced the Scots back north and entered into negotiations with their leaders soon after, concluding a surrender agreement at Irvine on 7 July 1297. It was suspected in England, however, that these Scottish nobles, who demanded a return to the ancient laws and customs of their land, 'took so long in discussing the concessions with frivolous points, so that Wallace could gather more people to him'.[45] There was clearly no appetite as yet for a military showdown with even a much smaller English army than the one that had categorically defeated the Scots at Dunbar. And yet there is no doubt that Wishart et al kept Clifford and Percy occupied in the west, deliberately or otherwise, thereby allowing Wallace and his men to make their way into Selkirk Forest in the more strongly English-held south-east, reputedly reducing several castles on the way.[46]

The murder of a sheriff, followed by the attack on the justiciar, together with the rhetoric used during the 'aristocratic' revolt, makes it clear there was fierce revulsion throughout Scotland towards intensive and high-handed Edwardian government. That this was more than just an outbreak of patriotic emotion is given substance by the fact that 1297 witnessed the peak of opposition to Edward I's regime within England itself. As well as unpopular demands for military service overseas (which was bound to prove expensive for the participants), preparations for the war with France had unleashed all manner of deeply resented forms of taxation, including the compulsory seizure and sale of wool. Scotland was not exempted from such treatment: both Sweetheart and Melrose abbeys later petitioned Edward for compensation for eight and a half and fourteen sacks of wool respectively, seized in 1297.[47] The Scots, quite unused to this level of governmental demand, were bound to view it as highly oppressive, compounded by the fact that many of them viewed the regime itself as foreign and illegal.

But, despite what Sir Henry Percy and Sir Robert Clifford chose to believe, Scotland was far from pacified by the time they rode back to Berwick from Irvine. Nor was Wallace the only man still prepared to challenge Edward's authority. In terms of achievement, the most significant rebellion was arguably that of young Andrew Murray in the north-east. Beginning – so far as we can tell – in late May (around the same time as the aristocratic one in the south-west), the first objective of Murray's force, which included the enigmatic Alexander Pilche and other burgesses of Inverness, was the castle of Urquhart, guarding the eastern end of the Great Glen. Urquhart belonged to William Soules, nephew of John Comyn, earl of Buchan, but, because he was still a child, the castle had been granted by Edward I to Sir William FitzWarin in 1296.[48] Andrew Murray was himself a nephew of Comyn of Badenoch and these family ties, together with the disaffection of Comyn's men at Inverlochy at the western end of the Great Glen mentioned above, provide a potential connection between the two northern rebellions, and with the former government of Scotland.[49]

Having survived the first attack, Urquhart was nevertheless extremely vulnerable. On 11 June, a group of Scottish nobles, including Sir John Comyn of Badenoch and his cousin, the earl of Buchan, were granted safe conducts to return home, presumably for much the same reason as Alasdair Macdougall of Argyll had been let out of prison in Berwick – they were by far the best people to restore calm. King Edward may have made a mistake, but he was prepared to learn from it. Buchan was to join Henry Cheyne, bishop of Aberdeen, and Gartnait, son of the earl of Mar, who were already in the north, in going to FitzWarin's aid.[50] English opinion, albeit with the benefit of hindsight, was very scathing about Buchan's efforts, claiming that he '... at first pretended to repress certain bold people, but in the end turned perversely from us'. Certainly Buchan's excuse that Murray and his army '... took themselves into a very great stronghold of bog and wood, where no horseman could be of service ...' sounds rather lame coming from a man whose family had gained huge swathes of land, including an earldom, in the north by subduing the men of Moray only a few generations earlier. Cressingham, who seems to have had a nose for these things, certainly didn't believe it.[51]

Without effective reinforcements, the fall of Urquhart and the surrounding castles, including Inverness, was only a matter of time. FitzWarin survived to fight another day, since he was with the English army at the battle of Stirling Bridge in September and had the misfortune of joining the garrison of Stirling castle on the same day.[52] However, Sir Reginald Cheyne, the sheriff of Inverness, later claimed that he had been '... thrice burned and destroyed and thrice imprisoned for his faith of his liege lord the King of England'.[53] It would seem likely that one of those occasions was in 1297.

Aberdeen was also lost during the summer of 1297, though the exact motivation of its sheriff, the Lancashire knight, Henry Lathum, whom Surrey accused of 'making a great lord of himself', is hard to determine.[54] It is possible that, by the time they joined Wallace at Dundee or Perth, probably in August, Andrew Murray and his men had effectively recovered control of the north-east of Scotland and re-established some form of Scottish administration over it, including sheriffs.[55]

Despite Cressingham's best efforts, this catalogue of military reversals was reflected in the slow but inexorable attrition of Edwardian government. As early as May 1297, Sir Henry Percy, warden of Galloway, was complaining to the king that he hadn't been paid for the Trinity term; the £2,000 which Cressingham received from the English exchequer in the following month was almost certainly used primarily to pay overdue wages.[56] Walter Amersham, the chancellor, doesn't seem to have been able to extract any income from the church of Kinross, granted to him the previous September, judging by the fact that Surrey was ordered to present him to another living 'in Scotland or Galloway' on 3 July 1297.[57] This would strongly suggest that, after an initial shocked acquiescence, the Scots *en masse* were now able to deny their new government the revenues which ordinarily should have sustained it, and that within nine months of its establishment. They also seem to have discovered that they didn't need the Comyns in Scotland to lead them in making their feelings known.

Problems were not restricted to those holding office at a distance from the central administration; even those in Berwick were finding it difficult to establish and maintain their authority. Amersham is described as chancellor for the last time in August 1297. Crisis then completely overwhelmed the Edwardian government and, from then until 1302, he is described only as receiver of royal revenues in Northumberland, an office to which he was appointed on 12 July 1297. This appointment in itself underlines the need to subsidise Scotland's government from south of the border, which was definitely not supposed to happen. William Bevercotes, the keeper of the seal, also seems to have become redundant, though he returned as chancellor in 1304 after Amersham's death; the seal appears to have gone into retirement for the same period.[58]

The treasurer's basic function should have been to receive and audit Scotland's revenues through the exchequer at Berwick, and to use the same to pay for its administration. Credit and debit were thus, in theory, intended to cancel each other out. Initially Hugh Cressingham and his officials appear to have been very successful in raising revenue – in June 1297 the considerable sum, by Scottish standards, of £5,188 was used to pay a subsidy to the Count of Bar (now in north-east France but then an independent duchy), whom Edward was cultivating as an ally in his imminent war against France.[59] But as already noted, a month before the Count's subsidy was accounted for in London, the revenues of Scotland were starting to become uncollectable. In some ways Cressingham may have been a victim of his own success in raising such an unprecedented amount from the Scots in such a short time. He was certainly notorious for his rapaciousness: the English chronicler, Walter of Guisborough, remarked, with an unusual hint of sympathy for the Scots, that the treasurer 'loved money' '. . . and robbed too much and they did not call him treasurer but treacherer to the king, and they believed this as the truth'.[60]

Initially it was expected that the £2,000 sent up to cover arrears of wages would be paid back out of the issues of Scotland by 1 August 1297. However, Cressingham soon had to admit to Sir Philip Willoughby at the Westminster exchequer that this would not be possible since the king had ordered that all (any) revenues received at Berwick were to be handed over to Surrey, suggesting that the latter's fee was also in arrears.[61] By the end of July, the treasurer was forced to tell the king that the flow of cash to the Berwick exchequer from north of the border had well and truly dried up:

> ... from the time when I left you, not a penny could be raised in your [realm of Scotland by any means] until my lord the earl of Warenne [Surrey] shall enter your land and compel the people of your country by force and sentences of law.

Cressingham, unlike Amersham, still had plenty to do as the system began to collapse around him, but now he was responsible for auditing and disbursing large sums direct from the English exchequer. After his death at Stirling Bridge, his office as Treasurer was not officially refilled and control of Scottish finances was taken over by two receivers, Amersham at Berwick and the other, Richard Abingdon, at Carlisle.

References to escheators and justiciars also peter out in 1297. William Ormesby, perhaps as a result of his close encounter with William Wallace and Sir William Douglas in June of that year,[62] was transferred to England in August on the king's business. William Mortimer and Henry Rye both came with Edward on campaign in the summer of 1298. Roger Skoter was still in Scotland in July 1297, but there is then no further mention of him. By December 1297 Peter Dunwich had given up his office of escheator and been sent to Lancashire with William Dacre to choose footsoldiers for the winter expedition planned by the regency government in the aftermath of Stirling Bridge. This was his last appearance in official records before he was released from Scottish prison in April 1299, presumably having been captured during that expedition.[63] These officials had surely not reckoned that serving in Scotland would prove so dangerous.

However, the most illuminating illustration – and cause – of the instability of the Edwardian administration is Surrey himself. Soon after his appointment in September 1296 there were serious doubts about his commitment.

> The earl of Warenne, to whom our king committed the care and custody of the kingdom of Scotland, because of the awful weather, said that he could not stay there and keep his health. He stayed in England, but in the northern part and sluggishly pursued the exiling [of the] enemy, which was the root of our later difficulty.[64]

This accusation seems to have been largely true. In June 1297, during the uprising of Wishart, Carrick and the Steward, Surrey wrote to the king, blaming the postponement of his arrival in Scotland on the need for more troops and promising the delay would cause no harm.[65] Nevertheless, when news of the Scottish lords' capitulation at Irvine was conveyed to Cressingham and his force gathered at Roxburgh, a decision as to whether or not they should move against 'the enemies on the other side of the Scottish sea' (Andrew Murray) or upon Wallace in Selkirk forest had to be put off until the earl's arrival. 'And thus', as Cressingham so eloquently informed his master, 'matters have gone to sleep.'[66]

Perhaps we can understand Surrey's lack of enthusiasm for his office – he was pushing seventy and had served his king, and the king's father before him, long and well, but such a heavy administrative burden was unlikely to have been his cup of tea. On 4 August 1297 a letter was sent to Edward from Berwick, perhaps from Osbert Spaldington, the sheriff there, stating that the earl had offered the lieutenancy to someone else, as the king had ordered. The importance of the need for firm government in the north – and further evidence that Surrey had indeed been remiss in his duties – is illustrated by the writer's advice that the Scots, who, despite Irvine, were still extremely restless, would 'be obedient ... if the lieutenant frequently oversees that no-one does harm to them or mistreats them'.[67] This clearly implies – with greater significance since it comes from an English official – that the regime had been unable to enforce the rule of law effectively and suggests that some of Edward's officers may have been responsible for treating the Scots badly.

Presumably, then, Surrey had petitioned the king to be relieved of his duties so that, according to the writer of the above letter, he and his nephew, Sir Henry Percy, the warden of Galloway, could go with the king to Flanders. The fight against France was surely much more to the taste of both men. Surrey and Percy were soldiers, with little inclination, it seems, for the burden of administration that was supposed to form a significant part of their work in Scotland until the Scots began to resist; and even then it probably wasn't the kind of 'proper' campaigning they hoped to experience on the continent. The extent to which service in the northern kingdom was unpopular among those whom the king sought to appoint there is extremely important to our understanding of the difficulties faced by Edward I in trying to hold down his conquest. At the same time, the regime was far less likely to endear itself to the native population if it was served by men who didn't want to be there.

The person to whom Surrey had, in fact, offered the job of lieutenant was Sir Brian FitzAlan of Bedale, 'an English baron of more reputation than fortune', who had been added as an extra guardian to the four Scots already in that position in 1291–2.[68] Most recently, in July 1297, he had been appointed captain of royal fortifications in Northumberland, with responsibility for overseeing expenditure there. From the government's point of view, he was an eminently suitable choice. But FitzAlan was no fool. On 5 August 1297, he wrote to the king declining the offer (or perhaps trying to squeeze more money out of him):

... due to insufficient skill and ability to take on such a great thing, unless I had the wherewithal to support it to your honour ... My resources, however stretched, are too small to sustain the land to your honour (they do not extend to more than £1,000) and to keep fifty armed horses. Thus I would not be able to keep the land in peace to your honour when such a nobleman as the earl cannot well keep it in peace from what he received from you. Nor do I know how I could do it with less than he receives.[69]

Sir Brian had clearly understood one of the main difficulties facing those who took up office in Scotland. Though an appropriate income was allocated to each position, it was often not enough to maintain men and equipment *and* allow the holder to make a profit in what was fast becoming an all-out war situation; not only that, but the difficulties faced by the English government in actually making wage payments often meant that retinues had to be sustained for long periods of time from their leaders' own pockets. FitzAlan was being offered £1,128 per year, compared with the 2,000 marks (£1,333 13s.4d.) granted to Surrey. While this reflected the different social status of each man, it still had to pay for the retinue necessary and appropriate to a royal lieutenant. The contract was to last, initially at least, for six months, to begin when Surrey had brought Scotland to a peaceful state, something of an optimistic prospect in itself.[70] In refusing, FitzAlan seems to have had a far more realistic grasp of the situation in the north than Edward, not least because the king's attention was currently directed firmly towards Flanders and his upcoming war with France.

However, by 18 August 1297 the matter was regarded in the south as settled, since on that date the chancellor was ordered to issue letters patent to FitzAlan as lieutenant similar to those previously given to Surrey. Ten days later custody of Galloway was entrusted to Sir John Hoddleston, presumably because Sir Henry Percy was required elsewhere. (In fact, he seems to have become a member of the king's regency government remaining in England rather than going to Flanders[71]). On the same date, writs were sent out to all sheriffs north of the Trent, ordering them to help 'Brian FitzAlan, keeper of the realm and land of Scotland, whom the king is sending to the parts of Scotland to do justice on the rebels who are wandering about there committing murders and other crimes and to repress their malice'.[72] However, there is no definite evidence that he left Northumberland, despite the fact that he authorised the issue of £200 as 'keeper of said kingdom [Scotland]'.[73]

The reality of the situation in the north meant that Surrey was unable either to join the king in Flanders, or, in effect, to relinquish his position as lieutenant. On 12 September 1297, shortly after Edward's arrival on the continent, rumours of continuing and increasing unrest in Scotland had reached the king and he ordered the earl to remain in Scotland until the country was pacified.[74] Such rumours came rather too late: Surrey's army had been routed at Stirling Bridge the previous day.

The increasing inability of the Edwardian administration to fulfil its functions was, of course, primarily a result of the growing threat of rebellion throughout almost the whole of Scotland as 1297 progressed. One of the most revealing pieces of evidence relating to the success of the Scots in challenging their new government comes, yet again, from Hugh Cressingham, who informed Edward on 24 July that:

> ... by far the greater part of your counties of the realm of Scotland are still unprovided with keepers, as well by death, sieges or imprisonment; and some have given up their bailliwicks and others neither will nor dare return; and in some counties the Scots have established and placed bailiffs and ministers so that no county is in its proper order excepting Berwick and Roxburgh, and this only lately.[75]

While the Treasurer may have been exaggerating, in order to shock Edward into taking the threat seriously, it is difficult to see the English presence in Scotland by this point as much more than a highly circumscribed military occupation that was almost entirely defensive in nature. Equally – and perhaps more importantly – the Scots were already able to set up and operate an alternative administrative system, despite the fact that their ostensible leaders had resubmitted to Edward's officers at Irvine a few weeks before Cressingham wrote the above letter.

But Edward either could not, or would not, believe that the Scots posed a sufficient threat to postpone or cancel his departure abroad. While this is understandable, given that Scotland was not as important to him as Gascony, his presence in the north would surely have provided a different outcome to the year's events. Nevertheless, he did recognise a degree of danger and ordered measures to be taken to provide for the safety of the border. On 12 July – news of the negotiations with Wishart, the Steward and Carrick at Irvine presumably not yet having reached the south – Sir Ralph FitzWilliam and Sir Brian FitzAlan were appointed captains of fortifications in Northumberland and Sir Robert Clifford, one of the Irvine negotiators, in Cumberland.[76]

In the meantime, Cressingham, at least, was taking things seriously, going personally to Northumberland to raise troops. The muster organised for 17 July at Roxburgh produced, according to the Treasurer's own letter to the king, a considerable force of three hundred covered horse and ten thousand foot but its northerly progress was forestalled by the arrival at Berwick of Sir Henry Percy and Sir Robert Clifford on the same evening. Their good news from Irvine, together with the assurance of hostages to be taken from the leaders of the revolt, convinced the Scottish government – with the inevitable exception of Cressingham – that 'their enemies of Scotland were dispersed and frightened from their foolish enterprise'. In any case, they now had to wait for Surrey.[77]

The Treasurer was right, of course: the situation was about to get much worse. William Wallace had now left the sanctuary of Selkirk Forest, probably having gathered men to him and given them a few weeks basic training. He was busy besieging Dundee castle when he received word that the Treasurer had brought in a fresh army from England. Reputedly ordering the burgesses to 'kepe that castell rycht stratly' ('keep that castle most rigorously'), he and his men set off south again.[78] Murray was also on his way and the two forces probably met up in August, perhaps at Perth, the most obvious crossing-point of land routes from Inverness and Dundee. Surrey had also finally arrived in Scotland and, as we've seen, was firmly told by the king on 7 September, some two weeks after Edward's departure for Flanders, to stay there. However, a mere week later he was recalled to London as civil war threatened to engulf England, led by the earls who had refused to go to Flanders.[79] This was the biggest crisis of Edward Longshank's reign and he wasn't there to deal with it.

Surrey, for once, was bent on action and had already gone to meet the Scots. His army, which was presumably composed of those he'd brought north himself, those raised by Cressingham in mid-July, and those brought back to Berwick by Clifford and Percy from Irvine, was certainly not the one thousand cavalry and fifty thousand foot claimed by chroniclers, notoriously unable to calculate the size of large crowds. However, it may well have been a respectable force perhaps one-fifth of that size. A similar reduction would give Murray and Wallace thirty-six horse and eight thousand foot.[80] Presumably, whatever cavalry belonged to the Scottish side came with Murray, the nobleman.

The two armies met at Stirling, where both needed to cross the River Forth on its singular bridge. The Scots took up position on the high ground to the north, while the English, controlling the castle and burgh, remained on the south bank. Negotiations, apparently conducted for the English by the recently submitted James the Steward, along with the earl of Lennox, brought nothing more than Wallace and Murray's defiant arowal to fight for the liberty of their country. Cressingham, reputedly driven to distraction by Surrey's late rising the next morning, 11 September, finally urged an immediate advance over the narrow bridge in preference to using the less suicidal ford upstream. He died a brutal death at the head of the army, the true leader of the Edwardian administration, albeit its most hated representative; Surrey, at the back, was able to flee.[81]

The news of the massacre reached London by 26 September. The only fortunate outcome for the English government was that the ensuing crisis finally united the discontented English nobility behind the absent king. Writs were immediately directed to the sheriff of York, fifteen northern lords and thirteen Scottish magnates, including Comyn of Badenoch and the earls of Dunbar, Angus, Strathearn, Menteith, Lennox, Buchan and Sutherland (but, interestingly, not Carrick who, despite the agreement he'd signed up to at Irvine, never handed over his daughter Marjorie as hostage for his good behaviour). Sir Brian FitzAlan, effectively still keeper of the Northumberland fortresses, would lead this force against the 'rebels'; Surrey was ordered to London to give a personal account of these terrible events.[82]

In the immediate aftermath of Stirling Bridge, with Cressingham dead and Surrey discredited, the most important members of what was left of the English administration were Master Richard Abingdon, the receiver of Cumberland, based at Carlisle, and Master Walter Amersham, receiver of Northumberland and erstwhile chancellor, still at Berwick. They had been appointed to replace a single receiver, Robert Beaufey, on 12 July 1297, the need for two yet another indication of the increased flow of resources from England to Scotland by that date. Each was assigned a keeper of the counter-roll (comptroller) to work with him – Master Robert Heron, who had also been keeper of the new customs at Berwick since 1296, was to work with Amersham, and Robert Barton with Abingdon.[83] For some reason, perhaps associated with the turmoil of the summer months, Abingdon and Amersham do not actually seem to have taken up their offices until November.[84] We should not underestimate their role, however, since their rise to prominence is a clear indication of the state of the English administration of Scotland. In the same month the various documents sent north in March 1297 to act as examples to be followed in Cressingham's Berwick exchequer were all returned to Westminster; there was no further need for them because the Edwardian administration had collapsed.[85]

In the aftermath of their victory at Stirling Bridge, the Scots were naturally eager to expel English garrisons across the kingdom. They had some temporary success in the south-east over the winter of 1297/8 and more permanent success in parts of the south-west. But most importantly, Scotland north of the Forth was cleared of English officials and remained under the authority of the Scottish government – soon headed by a series of guardians – from then until early 1304. By the spring of 1298 (but no doubt long before) Wallace was no longer merely leader of the army of Scotland but had become both a knight and guardian of the kingdom in the name of King John. This remarkable transformation must have appalled many of those who thought of themselves as Scotland's natural leaders, especially after the death of the more palatably noble Andrew Murray shortly after Stirling Bridge.[86] But they just had to get on with it. At the same time, Sir William's elevation placed far greater resources at his disposal and brought him wider responsibilities.

According to one of the charges laid against Wallace at his trial, he had been audacious enough to issue writs in the name of King John, which carried sovereign authority – something that King Edward believed only he wielded in Scotland. This included the letter sent in the names of both Murray and Wallace on 11 October 1297 to the mayors and communes of Lübeck and Hamburg, re-establishing trading links between these ports and the newly liberated kingdom of Scotland.[87] The confidence exhibited by the Scots, and the inference that an administrative structure, including the re-institution of a chancery to issue these writs, had been revived by Wallace shortly after Stirling Bridge, attests to his success. But he was also ably advised on administrative matters by men like Bishop Wishart of Glasgow and, soon, William Lamberton, bishop of St Andrews, implying that the new guardian could take advice as well as issue orders.

Militarily, Wallace extended his repertoire, rather than adopting fundamentally new tactics. Roxburgh and Berwick castles were besieged and survived only through the intervention of an English army in February 1298; Jedburgh was successfully reduced and a Scottish garrison installed under John Pencaitland; Stirling castle, 'the gateway to the north' – despite a last-minute rescue bid by Sir William FitzWarin, Sir Marmaduke Tweng and Sir William Ros after Stirling Bridge – succumbed not long after; and there is firm evidence of Scottish control of Dumbarton.[88] Given the lack of references to English garrisons in the west, and Edward's activities after the battle of Falkirk in 1298, it would seem likely that the Scots secured control of southern Scotland west of Edinburgh in the aftermath of Stirling Bridge. The English garrisons in the south-east were none too secure either.

The Scots did not confine their activities to home, however. On 11 December 1297, Sir Robert Clifford, captain of the Carlisle garrison, in collaboration with other knights of the area, and the bishop of Carlisle, keeper of the castle, made arrangements to strengthen the town's defences. According to Guisborough, Wallace and his men had already unsuccessfully attacked the town, but clearly it was believed that he, or others, would be back; Newcastle was similarly subjected to Scottish attentions and in effect the entire border needed to defend itself.[89] The actual numbers subsequently staying at Carlisle did not quite reach the stipulated figure of thirty covered horses and one hundred footsoldiers; this may reflect the fact that those in charge of the defence of the northern counties had to be very careful, when dividing their manpower between the garrisons and expeditionary forces against the Scots, that neither was left vulnerable to attack. This was a problem faced by the English garrisons within Scotland too.

Another problem faced by both sides was the deteriorating climate, bringing with it failed harvests and food shortages. Wallace's raids into northern England were motivated in part by the need to feed his men without putting undue pressure on his own people, which was bound to be hugely unpopular. A few months later, the English on the western border employed exactly the same tactics. Demoralising the enemy through the crude but crowd-pleasing destruction or removal of basic foodstuffs was a constant theme of this war, inflicting untold misery on both sides of the border, but particularly the counties either side of it.

One expedition against the Scots left at Christmas for Annandale, led by Robert Clifford himself. It was a risky strategy since a force totalling 460 footsoldiers under five constables – presumably raised specially – as well as Clifford's own retinue of seven knights and sixteen esquires, was withdrawn from the defence of the Carlisle area. When it returned a couple of weeks later, a group of one hundred footsoldiers was left north of the Solway 'as they believed the Scots were coming'.[90] Those living immediately south of the border doubtless came to the conclusion during those months that William Wallace could give Edward I a lesson or two in oppression; the vitriol reserved for the Scottish leader by the chronicler based at Lanercost priory only twenty miles south of the border shows that xenophobia was not restricted to the Scots even as the inhabitants of the north of England felt abandoned by their own government in the face of these costly attacks.[91]

So far as the regency government – nominally led by thirteen-year-old Prince Edward, the king's only surviving son – in London was concerned, Stirling Bridge – disaster that it undoubtedly was – did wonders to halt the drift towards civil war as England united in outrage and consternation at this unthinkable defeat. Prince Edward and his advisers were also keen to undo some of the damage inflicted on the English in Scotland before the king's return.

Their first reaction was to set about organising a winter campaign, which it was initially thought would be led by the thirteen-year-old prince but ended up, unimaginatively, under the earl of Surrey. Writs for service on the expedition were issued on 26 October 1297 for a muster at Newcastle on 6 December. The numbers summoned, which totalled nearly thirty thousand, bore little relation to the numbers that actually arrived, perhaps reflecting the turmoil currently sweeping through the northern counties, for though they were supposed to contribute twenty thousand, Wales actually provided the greatest number of men (5,157). Indeed, the North Wales contingent missed fulfilling its quota of 2,000 by only 61 men, a high turnout for any winter campaign.[92] Doubtless, and quite naturally, the men of the northern counties preferred to stay and defend their families and property from Scottish attack.

By 24 December a dilatory twenty constables and nineteen hundred men had arrived at Newcastle from various English counties. A note attached to the wages account for the period 18 December to 31 January made to Sir Ralph FitzWilliam, captain of the Newcastle garrison and temporarily also commander of this paltry army, states that they were – typically – waiting for Surrey.[93]

Since so few English magnates had accompanied Edward to Flanders, this at least meant they were available to ride against the Scots. Five hundred horsemen, divided into six groups ranging in size from thirty to one hundred and thirty and led by the earls of Surrey, Norfolk, Gloucester, Hereford, Warwick and Sir Henry Percy, were paid for by the £7,691 16s.8d. contributed primarily by the archbishop and clergy of Canterbury.[94] Given the anger, vocally expressed earlier in the year against Edward I's various financial impositions, such a sum represented a considerable change of heart in England so as – from their point of view – to reverse the defeat at Stirling Bridge and re-establish their rightful hegemony over the rebellious Scots as quickly as possible.

The activities of the receivers, Sir Walter Amersham at Berwick and Sir Richard Abingdon at Carlisle, underpinned this whole exercise since the collection and distribution of hard cash for wages was crucial to the maintenance of the army over this difficult winter period. Nevertheless, by late March, Surrey and Percy, the two most heavily involved in Scottish affairs, had again not been properly paid and money was desperately sought from the clerical tenth in the bishopric of Lincoln.[95] The archbishop of York and his clergy also contributed to the war effort with a grant of a fifteenth of clerical property in November 1297. This was to be used '... when necessary for the defence of the kingdom against our enemies and for the sustenance of Brian FitzAlan, captain of our garrisons of Northumberland and the same garrisons against the Scots rebels'. Wallace's attacks on the border counties were indeed hitting the English where it hurt most – their purses.[96]

By 12 February 1298 the English army had reached Roxburgh, forcing the Scots to abandon their siege of the castle there, and moving on to Berwick only three days later.[97] The town, captured by the Scots a few months previously, was duly restored to English control, rendering the castle less of an English oasis in a Scottish desert. The army reached its maximum size, an impressive sixteen thousand men, while at Berwick, but by mid-March the numbers had dropped dramatically to just over three thousand. There was nothing sinister about this, for fresh orders had just arrived from the king ordering Surrey to postpone the campaign until Edward returned from Flanders to lead the army personally. Such a decision is hardly surprising; campaigning during the winter season was unlikely to be either popular or successful, victuals were low and Surrey's qualities of leadership were by now distinctly questionable.[98]

Edward had done less badly than he is often accused of on the continent, a degree of stalemate prompting Philip of France to open up negotiations on the return of the English king's duchy of Gascony, which is what it was all about. Nevertheless, the carefully constructed network of alliances which included the emperor-elect, Adolf of Nassau, the duke of Brabant and the counts of Bar and Savoy, at a cost of one million pounds, proved difficult to coordinate and Edward himself arrived too late to stop the defeat of some of his allies at Furnes (between Bruges and Dunkirk) in Flanders.

His own army, largely as a result of the domestic discontent over taxation in particular, was far too small. The Flemish towns, who often did not see eye-to-eye with their count, proved troublesome and Count Guy of Flanders found his English ally of far less use than he'd hoped and earlier promises had suggested. All rested on the appearance of Adolf of Nassau, and when that failed to happen there was little more Edward could do. Thankfully, his forces in Gascony itself proved more effective. The English king began talks with King Philip, culminating in the truce of Vyre-Saint-Baron on 9 October 1297. Alas, Edward was not yet free of his continental obligations – that could only happen when at least some of his allies had been paid, which took until the following March. 1297 had not been a particularly good year for Edward I.[99]

Curiously, as a postscript to all this continental hyperactivity, the fate of one particular noble prisoner captured by the French at Furnes almost had a curious knock-on effect on the Scottish wars. After the truce of Vyre-Saint-Baron, which included provision for the release of prisoners on both sides, the count of Flanders and his sons lobbied hard for the liberation of the lord of Blâmont (whose castle lies now in the north-eastern French province of Meurthe-et-Moselle). King Philip responded by saying that he would not let him go since Edward I still held the king of Scotland, to which the Flemings replied that Balliol had never been mentioned before and the general conditions agreed in the truce could not possibly apply to such a great and notable party. There is no reason to imagine that Edward I was ever consulted on the matter, or that he would ever have agreed to a swap – Philip was just being obstreperous. John Balliol – not to mention the Sieur de Blâmont – would have to wait a little while longer for freedom.[100]

Given that most, if not all, of the victuals required by what little was left of the English administration in Scotland and the troops on campaign there had to come from England, Wales and/or Ireland, the acquisition of enough food for both men and horses played a vital role in the success or failure of their operations in Scotland.

On 26 October 1297 various towns, including York and Newcastle, were ordered to issue proclamations stating that those with victuals for sale for the forthcoming expedition should have them carried by land or sea for purchase at Holy Island (off the Northumbrian coast) or Newcastle. With an eye to the current and vociferous grievances concerning prise – the compulsory seizure of goods for royal activities for less than their market value – prompt payment was promised. On 5 November 1297 further purveyance was ordered in Lincolnshire, Yorkshire, Cambridge and Huntingdon, and Nottingham.[101]

The accounts for the purchase and collection of supplies in this regnal year[102] are incomplete but the evidence strongly suggests that most of the purveyance came from Yorkshire; as a county greatly affected by events in Scotland, but perhaps not as subject to the full impact of Wallace's devastating raids as those counties immediately south of the border, this makes sense. As with the muster itself, however, the purveyance did not occur on time and by early December William Fraunk of Grimsby was appointed to hurry proceedings up. The provisions from Yorkshire did not, in fact, reach the store at Berwick from Hull until 1 March 1298, implying that the army, which was in Scotland by mid-February, faced a lack of supplies for at least two weeks.[103]

Not surprisingly, the accounts of the two receivers, Abingdon and Amersham, dealt almost exclusively with the defence of the border and the winter/spring campaign led by Surrey. Abingdon's account was not particularly large, involving a total of just £900. His sources of revenue were those sums collected from the lay ninth (a tax on landed property, excluding that owned by the church) levied in Cumberland, Lancashire and Westmorland. His greatest expense was the wages for the garrison at Carlisle, which totalled about £400.[104]

Amersham, by contrast, was responsible for over ten times the amount of money which passed through the hands of his colleague in the west. The main sources of his income were again the various taxes – the clerical fifth and the lay ninth – granted to the king in response to the threat to the kingdom, primarily from Yorkshire, but also from Northumberland, Staffordshire, Derbyshire and Warwickshire. On this occasion he also received the impressive sum of £252 from the customs at Berwick, suggesting that trade had by no means completely dried up in this difficult year, and, in contrast, the pathetic figure of £17 from the rest of its issues.[105] It is clear, therefore, that almost all the king's revenue in the north of England was required either for the defence of these areas or to support operations within Scotland itself.

The major problem for those accounting for Scotland was simply that of raising any revenue at all to set against the large sums of money sent north. At least the English Crown, having acquired supplies effectively at cost price, could recoup some of its expenditure by hiking up the price on these same goods even when selling to other government departments. In the summer of 1298, for example, one quarter of wheat cost around 2s. 4d. when bought by the government; it was then sold on to Amersham at Berwick for a staggering 15s. per quarter, only some of which was needed to cover transport costs.[106]

All the same, since wages were so often in arrears, credit had to be allowed for the purchase of supplies by those on active service and such credit was not always easily recovered. In addition, the *certums* and wages paid to Scottish garrison commanders often had to be paid for and then written off by the English exchequer, except for amounts deducted for victuals, since it was still impossible to collect any of the issues of the areas nominally under their control. It must have been painfully obvious that England was now saddled with an expensive project which was showing no immediate signs of even partially paying for itself. Amersham's account already showed a deficit of £108 16s. 8d, which was eventually deducted from his fee as chancellor in 1303.[107] The attractions of royal service are sometimes to be wondered at.

The collapse of the Edwardian administration in 1297 was almost as swift and unexpected as the conquest itself had been. However, as already said, Edward had been unwise to assume that the capitulation of the Scottish government after the humiliating defeat at Dunbar would be the end of the story; equally, he exhibited a considerable lack of foresight in assuming that the draconian financial measures which he instituted throughout his domains in preparation for the war with France would be construed in the northern kingdom as anything other than the oppressiveness of an illegal regime. It was but a short step to transform that general feeling of resentment into patriotic fervour. The very effectiveness of Cressingham and Ormesby, in particular, in implementing Edward's demands, together with the lack of commitment to maintaining an impartial and effective judicial system that might have benefited the Scots, meant that the new regime had done very little by the spring of 1297 to make itself at all attractive to most sections of Scottish society, but particularly its more prosperous and influential.

It would also be fair to say that there were weaknesses within the English administration which, once pressure was applied, began to look very serious indeed. Its top lay officials clearly did not relish serving in the north and there can be little doubt that Surrey's reluctance to even come to Scotland allowed the situation to degenerate rapidly; it was frankly impossible to keep on top of things from Yorkshire. The decision to release from prison those Scots, like Alasdair of Argyll and Comyn of Badenoch, who might prove more effective in restoring order was made only once it was clear that the actions of Edwardian officials had generally failed to do so; this can only have underlined to these Scottish nobles how important they were to the government of their country, along with a corresponding understanding of the limitations of England's ability to win the peace, despite English prowess at waging war. They might yet have accepted positions of authority from Edward, but the king had neither the time nor the inclination to bother about Scottish sensibilities over the summer of 1297.

To begin with, most of the Scottish nobility were either in prison or unwilling to come out in open revolt, thanks to their military failures in 1296. But once Andrew Murray and William Wallace had shown what could be achieved when less orthodox military tactics were employed, the rising tide of Scottish success, particularly after Stirling Bridge, began to look convincing. It must also be said that, with the brief assumption of political/ military leadership by what might be termed the Bruce faction in June and July of 1297, together with the return of the Comyns and other members of their affiliation to Scotland around the same time, the stage was set for a potentially debilitating split within the Scottish political community. To add to that was the unavoidable fact that Edward I was now heading back to England and, with his full attention and still considerable resources directed against the Scots, he promised to be a quite different proposition in the field to Cressingham and Surrey. Both sides, then, had their strengths and weaknesses.

The success or failure of English activities in Scotland now fundamentally depended on the effectiveness of the two receivers – Walter Amersham and Richard Abingdon – and their superiors in the English government and their subordinates focused on Scotland. Their task was a difficult and thankless one, with resources and credit, not to mention their royal master's patience, often stretched to the limit. The financial threat to any military strategy employed in Scotland was no idle one either: to give but one example, by mid-February 1298 the earls and barons on campaign informed Surrey that they could not remain in the north any longer unless the footsoldiers were paid their wages, without which they could not, of course, buy food. The royal clerks immediately sought to avert the crisis by buying 1,000 marks-worth of victuals and other merchandise from English merchants. Although they succeeded, they soon found them-selves being sued by the merchants for payment for these goods. It was essential that such men were paid, in order to encourage them to sell to future campaigns, and they soon got their money.[108] Nevertheless, the incident illustrates just how hand-to-mouth the whole system might rapidly become. The battle for Scotland had only now begun.

CHAPTER THREE

A KINGDOM DIVIDED

Both sides seem to have done very little between Surrey's aborted winter campaign and the arrival of Edward and his army in June 1298. No doubt the relieved English garrisons of south-east Scotland made good use of this hiatus to restock their supplies and check their defences. Fortunately, they remained safe from attack even once the English army headed south in March because the earls of Surrey, Norfolk, Gloucester, Hereford and Angus stayed behind at Berwick with their companies. Edward returned from Flanders on 14 March 1298 and on 8 April summoned these senior noblemen to a royal council to be held in York on 24 May. That the danger was far from over is attested by the fact that they were ordered to come from Berwick as secretly as possible, leaving behind enough men to defend the town.[1] The English were now taking the threat from the Scots very seriously.

The writs of summons for the summer campaign also went out on 8 April 1298. A total of twelve thousand six hundred Welsh footsoldiers, along with one thousand from Lancashire, were ordered to arrive at Carlisle by 17 June, later postponed to 25 June.[2] According to the exchequer accounts recording the payment of these troops, the total numbers of Welsh who actually mustered reached an astonishing twelve thousand seven hundred and seventy-nine. A further four thousand and forty-seven footsoldiers came from Ireland, Shropshire and Staffordshire, serving together under Sir John Segrave, two thousand and fifty-seven were gathered from various English counties, one thousand and twenty-seven were withdrawn from the Berwick garrison and twenty-nine crossbowmen arrived from all over the country. Most of the English soldiers, along with the king, came north along the traditional eastern route. Edward's army thus reached a magnificent twenty-one thousand five hundred and thirty-nine footsoldiers, sixty per cent of whom, it should be noted, were Welsh. The army continued to increase in numbers right up until two days before the battle of Falkirk on 24 June, when twenty-five thousand seven hundred and eighty-one footsoldiers were paid their wages; since the additions came mostly from England, this lowered the overall Welsh total to around 50 per cent which was still a remarkable contribution.[3]

Two hundred and ninety-three personal summonses were sent out to various nobles, though in many cases there is no evidence, either from safe-conducts or horse-evaluation rolls, for their presence on campaign, which is frustrating since they may well have been there. On the other hand, we can trace a grand total of about fifteen hundred men-at-arms serving in the four English battalions at the battle through, for example, safe-conducts issued to them and payment for horses lost by them. Edward also ordered twenty or thirty carpenters and around two hundred of the best diggers to come to him at Alnwick, perhaps to take back castles, though it's not clear which ones.[4]

Almost all of those with Edward in Flanders, including Sir Aymer de Valence with the largest retinue, Guy de Beauchamp, about to succeed to the earldom of Warwick on the death of his father, the Scot Sir Alexander Balliol of Cavers, and the bishop of Durham, continued in the king's service over the summer. Even more impressive was the service performed by the North Welsh over 1297–8. Gruffydd ap Rhys, their captain, served under Surrey from 8 December 1297 until 29 January 1298. He then seems to have taken a Welsh contingent briefly to Flanders since a safe-conduct was issued to him and his men on their return from the continent on 15 March. Ap Rhys did not himself serve on the Falkirk campaign, though five constables from

North Wales who had been with Surrey in December 1297 returned to Scotland in July 1298. The other Welsh contingents do not seem to have served quite so devotedly, though a further thirteen Welsh constables were present on both the winter and the summer campaigns.[5] It's worth remembering the reality of this Welsh service, given the stories about their lack of loyalty on this campaign that soon circulated via English writers.

If provisioning had been important – and difficult – for the winter campaign, it was crucial to the maintenance of the huge army Edward took north in 1298. John Sheffield, who had overseen the collection of victuals in Yorkshire for Surrey's campaign, continued to be responsible for purveyance for the rest of the regnal year. Given the resentment already caused by the cost of Edward's war efforts, the king was very keen to ensure that all taxation came in quickly and efficiently so that payment for provisions could be made as swiftly as possible.[6] Those being asked for contributions required constant reassurance, however. The sheriff of Gloucester told the king that the men of his county were still worried they would not be paid for what was taken from them; Edward soothingly replied that purveyance would be made 'in the best way and to the least grievance' of those from whom it was exacted. However, payment was not to be made until the goods had been received by the king, implying a delay in recouping the costs of a good few weeks.[7]

The counties of Lancashire, Cornwall, Devon, Gloucester, Somerset and Dorset, as well as Ireland, were also ordered to purvey victuals and send them to Carlisle, where the Welsh footsoldiers were assembling before presumably marching to meet the rest of the army that was mustering in the east. Unfortunately, there is no evidence for the arrival of these provisions, except for sixty barrels of wine which came from Bristol in July, rather late in the day. Though Edward appears to have been trying to spread the burden of payment for the Scottish wars across England, rather than relying so heavily on the northern counties, the practical difficulties involved in transporting goods from the far south usually meant that very little was sent from these areas. But it was obviously in the interests of the southern counties to make the government think it was not worth asking for contributions.

Since Scotland was easily accessible from the ports on the east coast of Ireland, large amounts of purveyance were demanded from the lordship in every year of Edward's Scottish wars. On 15 April 1298 the request for provisions did not even specify the exact amounts, as was the case for the English counties; basically, as much as possible was to be sent to Carlisle. In the end, the Irish treasurer paid out more than £4,000, an enormous sum considering that the total receipts at the Irish exchequer for this year amounted to only £5,671.[8]

Purveyance was not confined to foodstuffs, of course. On 12 June 1298, a few weeks before the army was due to muster, the sheriff of Northumberland was ordered to buy as many horses and carts as possible to be sent to Newcastle by 17 June. Iron was also to be acquired for shoes and nails for the king's horses.[9] The army could certainly not get very far without such mundane but necessary equipment.

The logistics of this whole operation, which involved the proclamation throughout each county of the demand for purveyance, and the setting-up of collection points followed by the transfer of goods to a port ready for transportation north, rarely went smoothly and certainly not smoothly enough for Edward himself. On this campaign, the sheriff of Lincoln, Peter Draycote, and the clerk assigned to help him collect victuals, Peter Mollington, attracted the king's particular wrath. Edward may have had a point, however, since the pair seem to have arbitrarily detained three ships from Sandwich, en route to Berwick laden with corn, despite the production of royal protections. A week later, on 7 July, the king was complaining more generally about the negligence of officials in Yorkshire and Lincolnshire in getting victuals to Berwick and demanding punishment as a warning to others of the harm they could cause to the campaign. Edward then wrote directly to Peter Mollington, complaining of the delay and ordering him to send the grain northwards immediately, on pain of the utmost penalties.[10]

On 21 July 1298 a ship containing one hundred and six quarters of wheat and eighty-nine quarters of malt at last arrived in Berwick from Lincolnshire rather too late to provision the army – which had passed through the area nearly three weeks earlier – before the battle of Falkirk on 22 July. The next recorded arrivals were not until September, when two ships reached Berwick on the 2nd and the 11th respectively.[11] To conclude that this was unsatisfactory is something of an understatement.

As well as the goods sent up from England through purveyance, English merchants followed the army, bringing their merchandise with them to sell in this captive market. But this was not a risk-free enterprise, to judge from the fact that, as the army prepared to march to meet the Scots immediately prior to the battle, the king '... with his own mouth spoke to those who sold merchandise, so that they should carefully bring their bundles and follow him without fear'. The surnames of those mentioned in the records suggest they were English, rather than local, merchants.[12] Profits were presumably high but so were the dangers as the army advanced into what was effectively enemy territory.

Details of provisioning are nevertheless of very little use unless we have some idea how much was needed to keep Edward's army from starvation. It's not easy, but with a few assumptions (please see the footnote if you really want to know how I did it) we reach a figure of approximately one hundred and twelve quarters of wheat per day to feed twenty thousand footsoldiers.[13] Other evidence hints that this is about right. For example, it is recorded that three bushels (eight bushels = one quarter) of wheat were intended to feed seventy-six men for one day,[14] meaning that approximately one hundred quarters per day would be needed to feed twenty thousand men. These are only rough estimates – and admittedly the footsoldiers may well have supplemented their diet with things like beans and peas – but they serve to give us an idea of how far the amounts of foodstuffs transported to Scotland would go, presuming they arrived in time. Given that the ship-load from Lincolnshire mentioned above brought only one hundred and six quarters of wheat, this was enough to feed the army for a grand total of one day.

If these rough calculations hint at the uphill struggle the English king faced, there is at least no doubt that Edward intended to pursue his goal of subjugation thoroughly and whole-heartedly this time. He even ordered the exchequer and the common law courts to move north from London to York, where they remained for the next six years.[15] The royal council meeting planned for 24 May, to which those nobles still holding out in Berwick were to come secretly, also had in attendance two repre-sentatives from each English shire and burgh.[16] The Scottish nobility were apparently summoned, on pain of outlawry (though there is no official record of these summonses); not surprisingly, none of them turned up. This gave the king the legal justification he needed to pass sentences of forfeiture on them, paving the way for the granting out of Scottish lands to his own supporters after the campaign. The army then set off north and Edward arrived in Scotland for the second time in two years, on 3 July 1298, prob-ably crossing the border via the ford at Coldstream.[17]

Food, or, more accurately, the lack of it, was a dominant theme in the initial stages of the Falkirk campaign, according to the chron-iclers. One writes that the king camped with his army at Kirkliston, just south of the Firth of Forth and west of Edinburgh, between 15 and 20 July, in order to receive provisions from ships coming up from Berwick. Unfortunately, contrary winds prevented the arrival of these ships and many in the army died of starvation. At the same time, a force under the bishop of Durham was sent to recapture Dirleton and two other castles (probably Yester and Hailes) in East Lothian.[18]

Another writer tells a similar story, stating that the bishop of Durham was only able to win the siege of Dirleton because '... three ships came laden with victuals ... While these things were going on, for almost a month the king's supplies failed. Ships had not come by the 'eastern sea' (North Sea) [as the king had fore-ordained] 'because of contrary winds, but some came with 200 barrels of wine and a few provisions', causing the Welsh to get drunk and start fighting their English comrades-in-arms. According to the chronicler, this did not faze Edward, who declared that he couldn't care less even if the Welsh were to join the Scots. Given the huge numbers of Welsh in the English army, Edward should certainly have been perturbed by the possibility of their rebellion. Indeed, this disparaging story might even be termed ungrateful, considering the service performed by the North Welsh in particular in these years.

The lack of victuals, however, did cause him much concern and he was seriously considering a retreat to Edinburgh to see if he could get some there. The evidence for food supplies supports the assertions of the chroniclers that the army suffered from an acute lack of provisions as it marched through Lothian. Of the seventeen ships that reached Berwick in July, only five arrived in time to supply the army before the battle of Falkirk (22 July), presuming the winds were favourable in taking these supplies further north to catch up with the army. These five ships brought between them 63 quarters of malt, 7 meat carcasses, 250 quarters of oats and 725 quarters of wheat, enough to supply twenty thousand footsoldiers for about a week.[20]

To make matters worse, the English had no idea where the Scottish army was hiding out, nor what Wallace, the Scottish guardian's intentions might be. Indeed, on 19 July (only three days before the two sides met at Falkirk), the treasurer's lieutenant at York wrote to the sheriffs of the northern counties ordering them to investigate, 'as secretly and circumspectly as possible', whether the Scots were planning an expedition across the border. If this looked likely, the sheriffs were to send a messenger, 'riding day and night', to York, so that orders could be given to resist the invaders. This would prompt a call-up of men with horses and arms, the preparation of wood and turf for making beacon fires and the imprisoning of all Scotsmen living in these counties.[21]

King Edward discovered the enemy's whereabouts in the nick of time, informed by two Scottish earls still loyal to him. He immediately called everyone to arms and they marched straight from Kirkliston for Wallace's army at Falkirk, stopping overnight at Linlithgow.[19] The battle came just in time, both for those starving in the royal army and those panicking at the thought of another of Wallace's raids across the border.

The Scottish guardian, no doubt heartened by news of the famine sweeping through the enemy army, decided to seize the opportunity to defeat Edward and, so he no doubt hoped, expel the English once and for all. There may also have been a degree of peer pressure on Wallace, whose incredible ascendancy had come about entirely because of his early military success, from those nobles who believed he occupied an office to which his status did not entitle him and which, moreover, was rightfully theirs. Wallace's decision to risk his troops in battle against a very large and experienced English army led by the king himself – who in fact had sustained injuries after being stood on by his horse at Linlithgow – becomes rather more understandable, if risky.

Despite accusations that he was caught by surprise, the Scottish guardian had prepared his ground well, positioning his spearmen in their *schiltroms* – semi-circular or hedgehog-like formations – interspersed with archers, who in turn were protected, theoretically at least, by the Scottish cavalry. They were defending a hill, with a loch 'of pitch' (perhaps a description of a rather wet peat bog) separating them from the English army. Though accounts are far from clear, the battle may not have begun well for the English, thanks to an ill-disciplined charge of two of the cavalry divisions. However, once the Scottish cavalry had fled, leading to the annihilation of the Scottish archers under Sir John Stewart, the English archers were able to employ their deadly skill against the helpless schiltroms.[22]

Edward and his army had re-established English military supremacy over the Scots, restoring a more usual martial order to proceedings. Scottish casualties must have been catastrophic but we have no way of ascertaining a realistic number; one estimate runs to between eighty and one hundred thousand dead, the writer smugly noting that '. . . there were no noble men killed on the English side except the Master of the Templars and five or six esquires'.[23] In fact, there were many fatalities on the English side: the wages payments to footsoldiers for the period covering the battle decrease by over three thousand.[24] We are left to draw the inevitable conclusion that these men fell at Falkirk. Wallace himself left the field on horseback, no doubt hoping to fight another day. But he no longer had a mandate to lead the Scots. Whether he left office of his own volition or was pushed, he was soon no longer guardian, a position he had earned through military success alone. His place was taken by two rivals for power within the Scottish political community, though Sir William continued to plough what often looks like his own lonely furrow in opposing the English at home and abroad in the coming years.[25]

In the aftermath of his victory, Edward was under no illusions this time that Scotland had necessarily been subdued. Though he sent his footsoldiers back over the border to wait at Carlisle, the cavalry stayed at his side in the north, for there was more work to be done. His main priority was to re-establish control over southern Scotland and to ensure that all his garrisons were capable of defending themselves against future attacks. His first target was that most strategic of castles, Stirling, which had been in Scottish hands since shortly after Stirling Bridge. The siege lasted about two weeks, the castle surrendering around 8 August, on which date it was supplied and the king left for his next appointment.[26]

Once again, it's not entirely clear what exactly Edward and his cavalry got up to after Falkirk, with a number of accounts giving different versions. Piecing the evidence together, it looks as if a separate force led by the Earl of Lincoln was despatched north immediately after the battle, recapturing the royal castle at Cupar in Fife before the end of July before laying waste to Perth and St Andrews. The main force, led by the king, moved west after the fall of Stirling. Their next target was Ayr castle, which the earl of Carrick – who had probably never fulfilled the terms of his surrender at Irvine a year earlier and now unequivocally nailed his colours to the Scottish mast – had recently set alight and left empty.

This outrage then sent Edward down through Annandale, despite the fact that its lord – Carrick's father, Bruce 6 – remained staunchly loyal to the English king and may even have been with him. They stopped off at Tibbers, about twenty miles north of Dumfries, to inspect a 'stone' house being constructed there by its owner, Sir Richard Siward, which was deemed sufficiently impressive to earn Sir Richard a role in building upgrades planned for the following year. The plan was probably then to make an expedition further west into the difficult country of Galloway, but once again Edward and his men faced food short-ages due to the non-arrival of ships to support their activities. After fifteen days of severe famine (*fames valida*), the king turned back through Annandale and reduced its main stronghold at Lochmaben.[27]

On 8 September Edward and his men-at-arms rejoined the rest of his army at Carlisle. The earls of Hereford and Norfolk, with their retinues, then seem to have left the army because they were upset at the granting of Arran to Sir Hugh[28] Bisset of Antrim. This Irish opportunist had landed on the island with a large force, intending to support the Scots; hearing of the English victory at Falkirk, however, he promptly offered his allegiance, and his conquest, to Edward and was duly rewarded. The earls took exception to this because the king had 'forgotten' his promise to take their advice when making any land grants, a source of noble resentment that had been one of many elements underpinning the grumbling towards civil war in England in 1297.[29]

Edward was, in fact, now ready to make extensive grants from estates forfeited from the recalcitrant Scottish nobility back in May. These included James the Steward's barony of Renfrew, given to the earl of Lincoln, the fairly new Maxwell castle of Caerlaverock, given to Sir Robert Clifford, and certain lands belonging to the tiny Andrew Murray, posthumous son of the victor of Stirling Bridge, which went to Sir Robert Tony.[30] However, the extent to which these grants were worth more than the parchment they were written on remained to be seen. But they surely encouraged many an Englishman to join in the war effort in the hope of securing Scottish lands.

Despite the defection of the senior earls and the approach of autumn, Edward still had one last piece of business to finish off. The king could not rest easy, so far as the security of the south-east was concerned, until Jedburgh castle – a lone Scottish outpost in the region – had been neutralised. An English force – surely a small fraction of the original army – recrossed the border from Carlisle and headed back east. The siege lasted for the first eighteen days of October and, despite orders for coal, iron and steel to be sent from Berwick for the siege engines, a payment of 100s. to John Pencaitland, the Scottish constable, suggests that the garrison submitted after negotiation. Their compatriots probably tried to save the castle, however, skirmishing with the company of Sir Simon Fraser, Edward's warden of nearby Selkirk Forest.

Jedburgh was now given a new garrison under the command of Sir Richard Hastangs, whose brother, Sir Robert, was already in charge of Roxburgh twelve miles to the north. As a final precaution, a 'great engine' was to be sent up from Carlisle castle.[31] Edward could finally go home, though his officials in Scotland still had work to do. Throughout October and November, the other south-eastern castles of Edinburgh, Berwick and Roxburgh were resupplied and a check made that the men inside were sufficient to protect them from attack now that there was no English army nearby to provide relief.

As **Table 1** indicates, the numbers allocated to the south-eastern garrisons were fairly substantial, particularly in terms of footsoldiers. This was not the full complement either because, as well as the garrison in Berwick castle shown in the table, a significant force of sixty men-at-arms and one thousand footsoldiers was ordered to take up residence in Berwick town. This impressive total was almost reached by the end of October 1298 when up to fifty-six men-at-arms and nine hundred and ninety-nine footsoldiers were either encamped in the town or on their way there.[32]

In order to put these figures in some kind of context, it is interesting to compare them with the size of the garrisons placed in Wales by Henry IV one hundred years later during the revolt of Owain Glyn Dŵr. During the years of crisis for the English (1402–6), many of the huge Welsh castles built by Edward I were manned by little more than thirty men. On the other hand, in south Wales particularly, forces of up to five hundred men served under the command of important magnates like the Duke of York. The difference in size was a reflection of what was expected of them; the smaller garrisons were just supposed to hang on until the situation got better, while the larger forces were usually put in place when things had improved, often after a royal campaign. Though they were certainly intended to defend their hinterland, these larger garrisons were also expected to play a more active role in bringing the local population to peace.[33] It was a similar situation in Scotland after 1297. In 1298, after an intensive campaign, the south-east was to be defended by one hundred and seventy-five men-at-arms and nearly thirteen hundred footsoldiers; this was effectively a small standing army and it speaks volumes about the extent to which the English still had work to do to pacify the local population even in the heartland of their occupation.

Table 1: *Edinburgh, Roxburgh, Jedburgh and Stirling garrisons, 1298–1303*[34]

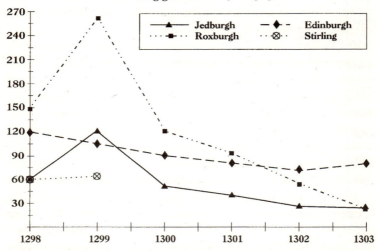

But as well as the sheer numbers deployed in the south-east, other precautions were taken to guard against potential mishaps. It was made absolutely clear that no-one in Berwick town was to venture out against the enemy unless in the company of thirty men-at-arms and five hundred footsoldiers from the garrison. The keeper of Berwick town, Sir Philip Vernay, and his opposite number in the castle, Sir John Burdon, were ordered to take turns as leaders of these expeditions so that one was always left in charge of Berwick itself. Such prudence implies a recognition of the fact that, in contrast to 1296 and despite winning the battle of Falkirk,[35] there was to be no let-up in the Scottish war effort. Edward had learned from the failures of 1296–7, but it remained to be seen if it was already too late to persuade the Scots that Edwardian government could ever have their interests at heart.

Edward also bowed to the inevitable when it came to the chain of command to be established over English forces in

Table 2: *Linlithgow, Selkirk and Peebles garrisons, 1301–1303*

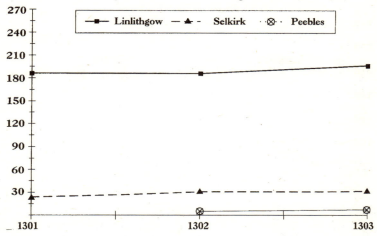

Scotland. Surrey had finally made his point regarding his unsuitability for the job as lieutenant and no-one else seems to have been either willing or able to take it on.[35] In keeping with the provisional and proscribed nature of the reconquest, Edward made a series of lesser appointments of a predominantly military, rather than administrative, nature. Patrick, earl of Dunbar, captain of the Berwick town garrison since 28 May 1298, was promoted to captain of all fortifications and troops in the eastern march on 19 November 1298.[36]

Similar ordinances were made for the English garrisons in the south-west. Sir Robert Clifford replaced Sir Henry Percy as captain of the western march six days after Dunbar's appointment. Clifford was ordered to receive the men of Nithsdale to the king's peace, though we have no way of knowing whether this was based on a firm expectation of Scottish submissions or was merely the triumph of a natural English optimism.[37] Another Scot, Sir Simon Lindsay, was appointed as captain of Eskdale on 20 November; Sir Ingram de Guines, Sir Walter Teye and other English officials holding unidentified posts in the area were

Table 3: *Carstairs, Kirkintilloch, Strathgryfe and Ayr garrisons, 1301–1303*

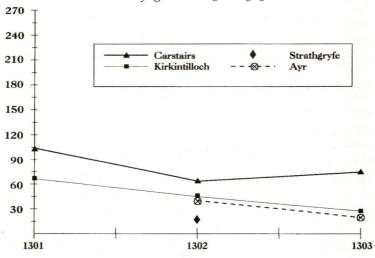

ordered to obey him.[38] De Guines was a nephew of Alexander II's queen, Marie de Coucy, and had married Christian Lindsay, an heiress to extensive estates particularly in Clydesdale; he was presumably being asked to put his private castles and garrisons at the new captain's disposal. These were all key appointments in the hills and dales of the upland border region, which could afford Edward's enemies ample opportunity to slip across country and threaten even relatively secure garrisons. The fact that Scots who knew the lie of the land in more ways than one were given these positions of authority within the English military establishment is an interesting development that perhaps indicates a growing pragmatism on Edward's part, given the general lack of enthusiasm for Scottish office among his own nobility. And clearly some Scots, however few at this point, saw the benefits of English service.

The recent campaign through the south-west had at least created the illusion of English control in that garrisons were

Table 4: *Berwick*

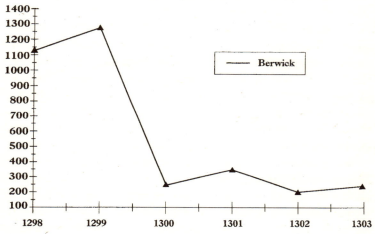

established in Dumfries and Lochmaben. As already mentioned, this last castle had not been forfeited by its owner, Bruce of Annandale, and Edward thus technically had no right to occupy it, despite the rebellious behaviour of Bruce's son, the earl of Carrick. However, Lochmaben was of major strategic importance to the English administration. Served by the wharf at Annan twelve miles to the south, it was easily reached from Carlisle and was therefore ideal, from Edward's point of view, for controlling the south-west. To all intents and purposes, it had become a royal castle along with the rest of Annandale, though presumably Edward was forced to explain the exigencies of war to its bewildered lord.

Lochmaben's new keeper was Sir Robert Cantilupe, who was also made warden of Annandale. Cantilupe was the only officer explicitly given authority to hold courts and pleas, with the assistance of the bishop of Carlisle and Master Richard Abingdon, the receiver, under him. It is possible that Sir Robert Clifford held overall administrative responsibility for the south-west but, given his obvious interest in military matters, it is more likely that Cantilupe, with his two associates, were key figures in any 'normal' government in the area.

Dumfries, which came directly under Clifford's jurisdiction, was given a garrison of twenty-six crossbowmen and six footsoldiers, together with a total of ten miscellaneous carpenters, engineers, smiths and masons, implying that some renovation of its physical structure was required. This was a comparatively small force and, though we have no figures for the Lochmaben garrison at this point, the evidence for succeeding years suggests that it, not Dumfries, was the main English base in the south-west.

It's tempting to imagine that any concern with firmly establishing the rule of law through English officials, both as a laudable end in itself and as a means of promoting acceptance of Edward's regime, might be construed as a recognition of the failure of the first attempt. This may well be the case, but we should not forget that English control in the south-west after Falkirk was only really effective in the areas immediately surrounding the castles of Dumfries and Lochmaben, covering Nithsdale and Annandale at best. And even that control was by no means total since Caerlaverock castle, situated between the two garrisons, was still held by the Scots and proved a thorn in their sides until its capture in 1300. In other words, the injunction to Sir Robert Cantilupe at Lochmaben to hold courts by no means implies that he could do so and there is no evidence for Edwardian judicial activity in the south-west before 1303. For all we know, the Scots may themselves have maintained some kind of administrative control there, though there is, as usual, no way of proving it.

Far from reverting to the dejected submissiveness of 1296 after their defeat at Falkirk, the Scots continued to harass Edwardian positions in Scotland and to take the war south of the border, or at least to threaten to do so. Once again, the sheriff of Cumberland, Sir William Mulcastre, excused himself from turning up at the exchequer in York to render his accounts on 30 October 1298, claiming that:

... during the present war between the king and the Scots, who lately invaded the said parts and caused much damage and put them in much danger ... the county could not be without its sheriff, and so he could not come to render his account.

Obviously, it was in the interests of the sheriff to try to gain a rebate on the issues which he was expected to collect for the Crown's coffers, but that's not what he was asking (on this occasion) and his excuse for not turning up at all does strongly suggest that Scottish incursions across the border were continuing even in the autumn. It was certainly accepted by the central government and he was ordered to come when he could. This he did on 16 November '... and returned to those parts to save them from damage or danger from the Scots'.[39] The threat was still not over.

And having been made aware of problems in the north, Edward took action. Further appointments were made, putting the northern counties on the same war footing as the English-held areas of southern Scotland. Three captains – Sir Walter Huntercumbe, Sir Ralph FitzWilliam and Sir Thomas Furnivall – were to take charge of the defence of Northumberland, Yorkshire, and Nottinghamshire and Derbyshire respectively, with Sir William Latimer given ultimate charge over them as captain-general. Furnivall's appointment so far south implies that Scottish activities were biting deep into the English Midlands; even if the raids themselves did not extend so far, these counties were still expected to defend the north.

Such precautions were made to ensure that a mobile force could defend the border over the winter months. All the captains were ordered to assemble the men-at-arms of northern England and the western marches of Scotland at Carlisle. Those owning land worth £30 were to provide one *barded*, or lightly armoured, horse (and rider), those having £60 worth of land to provide two, and so on.[40]

However, although these English preparations look impressive, the reality was far less so. Once again, the problem was provisioning. Huntercumbe, the captain of Northumberland, now wrote desperately to the king, seeking an allowance for the corn and cattle which he had been forced to take for his men 'as Northumberland was in the greatest danger from the Scots, for his own means were exhausted and if he had left his ward, the county would have been ruined'. Like any royal official, Huntercumbe could have been exaggerating the situation and Edward certainly had no sympathy for him, denying the petition.[41] However, this incident once again illustrates that those thinking about taking on royal office required a significant private income if they were to have any chance of fulfilling their duties – even if they eventually got back what they were supposed to pay out (and hopefully more!), there was almost certainly bound to be a significant period of time in between.

The threat to the northern counties may have remained just that, however real it seemed to those on the front line – it is not at all clear that the Scots did actually cross the border after the battle of Falkirk. Nevertheless, the English in Scotland certainly had reason to fear an enemy attack. On 25 November 1298, Sir Simon Fraser in Selkirk Forest was ordered by the king, who was still at Newcastle, to join an expedition currently being organised by Sir John Kingston, the sheriff of Edinburgh. Edward was very keen that this raid should be a success and did not think Kingston's men would be enough. Five days later the remaining garrisons of the south-east were also ordered to join in and it turned out that the object of the expedition – and one which the king was clearly determined to keep as secret as possible – was Stirling castle, already under serious threat from the Scots only four months after the English recovered it. At a meeting held in Berwick, Huntercumbe, Fraser, Sir Robert Hastangs and Sir Philip Vernay agreed to pass on to Kingston any information about Scottish activities so that he could decide by 14 December whether they should come to Edinburgh castle. One hundred and ninety horsemen were to be gathered from the garrisons of Jedburgh, Roxburgh, Berwick town, Edinburgh, Northumberland and even Norham castle (which belonged to the bishop of Durham), as well as quotas from Sir Simon Fraser, Sir Alexander Balliol of Cavers and, as a special request, the earl of March, the most high-ranking nobleman in south-east Scotland.[42]

This was not the end of the preparations, however. On 2 December 1298 a clerk, William Rue, was sent to Berwick to oversee the despatch of provisions to Edinburgh. It was hoped that Sir Philip Vernay, the keeper of Berwick town, could buy them locally and pay any 'small expenses' from the Berwick revenues (predominantly customs duties), but, in the final resort, they would be sent from England. A ship was to be kept ready at all times to carry goods up to Edinburgh until the following Easter (9 April 1299). Vernay does seem to have had some success in procuring goods himself, suggesting that the local population was prepared, willingly or otherwise, to co-operate with the English regime. At the same time, sixty quarters of wheat, sixty quarters of barley and sixty quarters of oats were set aside to be taken on to Stirling.[43] This was almost eight months' supplies for the 63-strong garrison.

By the end of December preparations were in full swing. Sir Alexander Convers, the royal clerk responsible for provisioning the south-east as a whole, was sent instructions by the king, who was still taking a close interest in proceedings. Six hundred men-at-arms were now being sent to Edinburgh, and Convers was to accompany them with money from the wardrobe (the accounting department of the royal household) to pay their wages, 'for it seems to us that the money can be best kept in Edinburgh castle as anywhere else in these parts'. The clerk was not allowed to return south until Stirling had been successfully relieved, 'which expedition is to be done as hastily as you can but in such a good way and surely'.[44]

From the tone of these royal letters, it is easy to imagine the king at Newcastle, frustrated at his inability to involve himself personally in Scotland because he had not been able to keep his army together beyond the autumn, and worried that the effects of the 1298 campaign in general, and the battle of Falkirk in particular, would come to nothing. It had been an expensive year: most of the £76,549 4s. 6d. spent through the wardrobe had gone on the Scottish war.[45]

Despite the lack of evidence for the activities of the Scottish administration, we must still remember that, in the years after Falkirk, English control did not extend beyond the Forth in the south-east, and was limited to a small patch of the south-west. In neither case was that control absolute, as illustrated by the ability of the Scots to target Stirling castle so soon after its recapture. Some areas on the edge of English and Scottish control were probably not administered effectively by either side, and local communities were effectively left to get on with it. But we can surely presume that north of the Forth in general – and the Comyn-dominated north-east in particular – acted as the heartland of a reasonably cohesive Scottish administration, even if we know precious little about it.

There's no doubt that, almost immediately after Stirling Bridge, Wallace and his advisers knew how essential it was to re-establish as full an administrative system as possible in the name of King John. The main office of state – the Scottish chancery – was up and running again within a month of the battle, issuing charters and restoring the diplomatic links vital to Scotland's economic and political wellbeing.[46] Scotland was fortunate in having men of long administrative experience, such as the former guardian, Robert Wishart, bishop of Glasgow, active in the cause of wresting the kingdom out of English control. Their activities were complementary to, and just as important as, the work of the military men, in the same way as Edward's clerks were vital to the survival of the English administration in Scotland. Already the Scots, led by churchmen like Matthew Crambeth, bishop of Dunkeld, were exerting constant diplomatic pressure on both the king of France and the pope, Boniface VIII. Their first major achievement was not long in coming: in 1299 King John, forcibly resident in London since 1296, was transferred into papal custody. At the same time, Edward, desperate to recover full control of Gascony, could not afford to completely ignore all the requests of his new brother-in-law, Philip of France, who still found it useful to encourage the Scots to keep up the good work in resisting the English.[47]

Despite his belligerent and overbearing attitude towards the Scots, Edward was no fool; he recognised that, notwithstanding the victory at Falkirk, his grip on Scotland remained most unsatisfactory. In the first instance, he was determined to return north as soon as possible but had to ensure that next year's campaign would not suffer from a lack of supplies. His first priority was therefore to refill his coffers. On 27 December 1298 he sent an urgent message to his sheriffs requiring money from any possible source – arrears, issues – except that put by for the 'purveyance recently made for Scotland [i.e. for the next campaign]'.[48]

Not surprisingly, Edward's financial situation required the constant juggling of the Crown's various sources of income to keep ahead of his creditors: on 25 May 1299, for example, he granted the citizens of Bayonne in Gascony all the customs on wool, hides and woolfells in England, Ireland and Scotland 'after that land is in good peace' to pay off his debts to them.[49] This was very much robbing Peter to pay Paul and it was a moot point just how long he could continue to do so without finding he had nothing left to juggle with. The annual return from the customs between 1278 and 1287 has been estimated at an average of £8,800, increasing to about £13,000 for the last four years of the reign.[50] Though Edward had little choice but to pay the Bayonne merchants, not least to ensure continued credit, the loss of this vital revenue even for one year was likely to have an important knock-on effect on his ability to prosecute the war in Scotland over the longer term.

Preparations for the 1299 campaign began almost immediately. The orders for purveyance sent to various English officials and also the sheriff of Berwick on 12 December 1298 included detailed instructions as to how grain should be stored properly so that it remained in a fit state not only to survive the long and difficult journey north, but also for a year or so thereafter.[51] Lessons were learned the hard way in Edward's garrisons: they hadn't received regular supplies for their stores over the previous eighteen months either because they were cut off by the enemy, or because there just wasn't enough available. Edward also seems to have thought carefully about the organisation of his fleet after the non-appearance of ships carrying victuals almost brought disaster to his army before Falkirk. This led to more clear-cut definitions of what service was owed and by whom, though it did not take effect until 1300, since there turned out to be no campaign in 1299.[52] Instead, King Edward took a new wife some forty-five years his junior, the sister of King Philip of France. This formed part of the ongoing negotiations over Gascony, though Edward would prove as devoted to Queen Margaret as he had to his first wife, Eleanor of Castile.

Despite the considerable preparations made at the end of 1298 to preserve Stirling castle, the Scots were able to upgrade their activities from attacks on Stirling's supply line to a full-scale siege during the spring of 1299. Without proper siege equipment, this was more of an attempt to starve or bore the English garrison into submission, rather than a significant bombardment. It's likely too that the Scots were neither willing or even able to spare enough men to cut the castle off completely for the necessary duration of the siege, and there is evidence for the conclusion of at least one truce made with the English garrison in the first few months. The usual period for unpaid military service in Scotland, as in England, was only forty days and thus large sums of money were surely necessary, as the siege dragged on, to pay those remaining with the besieging force.

Nevertheless, we should be wary about presuming that the Scottish military effort at Stirling lacked commitment. Nor should we suppose that all members of the local community were desperately waiting to be rescued from the evil English garrison. One Eva of Stirling fell foul of the besieging army when it was discovered she had been supplying the English garrison with grain purchased from the surrounding area. After a ten-week spell in prison, she was finally exiled from 'the land of Scotland' and didn't dare return until at least 1304, when Edward once more commanded the entire kingdom. In the following year she was finally able to petition the English king to be restored to the messuage[53] and three acres of land she once held in the burgh, though it is not known if she was successful.

Sir Herbert Morham, an East Lothian man whose father, Sir Thomas, was in fact currently in Edward's service in the Edinburgh garrison, seems to have had command of the Scottish army at Stirling to begin with.[54] It is not clear whether he was acting in conjunction with the Scottish government which, since at least December 1298, had been in the hands of two guardians, Sir John Comyn of Badenoch, junior, and Robert Bruce, earl of Carrick.[55] Presumably there was some collaboration, or at least authorisation, between the government and those engaged in military operations but much of the impetus behind activities of this kind undoubtedly lay with individuals or communities acting on their own initiative.

However, Sir Herbert seems to have overestimated the potential for private enterprise in this war, proving unable to resist abducting Joan de Clare, widow of Duncan, earl of Fife, when she tried to leave the insecurity of Stirling castle for England, presumably during a truce. By 22 April 1299 Morham had himself been captured and imprisoned in Edinburgh castle (putting his father in an interesting position). Meanwhile, command of the Scottish army at Stirling had devolved on someone else, most probably Morham's kinsman and local landowner, Sir Gilbert Malherbe of Slamannan and Livilands, who was named as sheriff of Stirling around this time and received the eventual submission of the castle towards the end of the year.[56]

The dependence on local interest groups to engage the enemy in their own areas may imply a lack of co-ordination in the Scottish war effort. However, since it did not require huge numbers of men to make life difficult for many an English garrison, such an approach may well have been the most effective; this was especially true in terms of cost, not least because the Scots could take advantage of that large part of the year which was generally free of English armies during winter conditions. Such a devolution of military authority may have been more usual in medieval warfare than the traditional concentration on large national enterprises led by kings and princes with the intention of provoking battles or sieges might lead us to believe.[57]

The resources available to the Scottish government were certainly risible compared to those flowing in to even Edward I's depleted coffers, partly because the population was much smaller, but also because the Scottish state was smaller and took less of a share of the kingdom's wealth.[58] The outbreak of war, with the subsequent occupation of much of southern Scotland, hardly improved the situation but the Scots were still able to launch attacks on English garrisons even in the south-east. On 28 January 1299, the sheriff of Northumberland was ordered to take a sum of money without delay to Berwick 'safely and securely, taking heed of the danger'.[59] At some point in the following month, the threat was considered so serious that an ordinance was made for the town's security. All defences (Berwick was still surrounded by a timber, rather than a stone, wall[60]) were to be checked twice a week and any damage was to be repaired immediately. All military personnel were to be examined to ensure they were 'sufficient' and the footsoldiers were to be quartered near their guard. If anything untoward was found, the king's council at York was to be notified via the sheriff of Northumberland.[61]

The imposing castle on its rocky bluff above the River Teviot at Roxburgh was also causing concern. Sir Robert Hastangs, the constable, had begun building walls there (it's unclear whether in stone or timber) but he needed reinforcements to man them and also to defend the nearby town. Provision was made for one hundred men to be sent from Berwick, but only if they were available and if an attack on Roxburgh was imminent.[62] The danger to these castles, which had been the only two to survive the Scottish onslaught after Stirling Bridge, was clearly a very real one, while the borrowing of soldiers by one garrison from another suggests there were not enough of them to defend them all adequately. If this was the situation in the south-east, the isolated English garrisons of the south-west were surely even more vulnerable.

Lochmaben was also undergoing refurbishment, including the construction of a pele, or palisaded area. Although the presence of twenty-seven crossbowmen to protect the builders highlights the constant fear of Scottish attack, the most pressing problem early in 1299 was the lack of supplies at a time of continuing unreliable harvests. Sir Robert Clifford, captain of the south-western garrisons, wrote to Master Richard Abingdon, the receiver at Carlisle, requesting that the crossbowmen be paid fifteen days' wages in advance, ostensibly because 'at present no supplies can be got here', but knowing full well that otherwise they would not stay.[63]

The royal castle on a bend of the River Nith at Dumfries proves something of a mystery in this period. A garrison was paid to stay there between 20 November 1298 and 30 June 1299,[64] but none of the purveyance which arrived at Carlisle from Ireland in May 1299 was sent to replenish their supplies and there is no direct mention of the castle at all. It is quite possible that Dumfries fell temporarily into Scottish hands – nearby Caerlaverock was already held by the enemy. This might also explain why Clifford found it impossible to find supplies: Lochmaben was surrounded by a hostile countryside and could only be supplied with difficulty via the road south to Annan and the river-link with Carlisle.

The spring of 1299 also heralded yet another revamp of English military personnel: on 25 May the earl of March was replaced as captain of the eastern garrisons by Sir William Latimer, who brought one hundred men-at-arms to his new job.[65] At the same time, Sir Robert FitzRoger seems to have volunteered to take on the keepership of the eastern march, a post that was kept separate from control of the garrisons, unlike the west. Both these men were extremely experienced, having served in similar positions in the northern counties of England; in both cases, also, they were allowed to forget (temporarily) about their debts to the English exchequer, which was presumably the carrot that persuaded them to serve in Scotland.

Clifford staggered on as captain of the western march throughout the summer, supported by Sir Simon Lindsay, captain of Eskdale, and, from 23 April onwards, Sir Richard Siward, the great house builder of Tibbers, as warden of Nithsdale.[66] Their job was becoming increasingly difficult, given not only the garrisons' vulnerability to attack, but increasing problems with the supply line through enemy activity. By July 1299 the situation was pretty grim indeed: on the 31st of that month, Clifford again wrote to Abingdon at Carlisle requesting payment in either money or victuals for Richard le Bret, an Irish hobelar at Lochmaben employed to spy on the Scots 'by night and day, who has been on duty for six weeks and three days, lest he takes himself off for lack of sustenance'.[67] Admittedly the Irish serving in Edward's armies (excluding nobles, of course) tended to be bottom of the list for payment but le Bret's situation was far from untypical: only a few weeks later the entire Lochmaben garrison apparently threatened to leave if they did not receive their full wages.[68] Clifford had soon had enough, writing to the king asking to be relieved of his wardenship.

The Scots were ultimately responsible for this situation. At the beginning of July, the south-eastern garrisons were expecting an attack. However, Sir William Latimer, their captain, was soon busy organising a large expedition to Galloway, perhaps in response to the deteriorating situation in the south-west hinted at in Clifford's letters; a force of forty-three men-at-arms and three hundred and twenty-two footsoldiers had thus mustered at Carlisle by 18 July.[69] Unfortunately, this is the last reference to payment for these troops and the expedition probably did not take place. The threat had not disappeared, however, and preparations were made at Lochmaben to repel an expected attack by the earl of Carrick (whose father's castle it was) as late as 14 August.[70]

The fact that Latimer had charge of this expedition is extremely revealing, since Clifford should certainly have been responsible for any English activity in Galloway. Though his letter to Abingdon of 31 July indicates that he was at Lochmaben on that date, Sir Robert was probably away for the rest of the month, perhaps having gone to petition the king personally. Unfortunately, he could not be released from his duties immediately, because Edward wanted to wait until his own arrival in Scotland to make a new appointment. However, by 19 August Sir Ralph FitzWilliam, another stalwart of the defence of the north of England and a member of Latimer's aborted expedition, had finally been given the job of lieutenant in the west.[71]

The military situation was perhaps also affected by the fact that on 18 July 1299 King John was released into papal custody from the Tower of London, where he had been lodged since 1296. This was a very positive sign of Pope Boniface VIII's favour towards the Scots and lobbied for by a Scottish embassy led by William Lamberton, who had gone to Rome to be confirmed as bishop of St Andrews in 1298.[72] Indeed, it was construed as such a categorical change in Balliol's fortunes that Robert Bruce of Annandale was moved to send a letter to the pope via the bishop of Vicenza, who received the exiled king on Boniface VIII's behalf; despite the fact that the earl of Carrick remained a guardian, the elder Bruce had certainly not given up his claim to the Scottish throne (subordinated to that of England, of course) and took a dim view of papal support for Balliol.[73] So, of course, did King Edward.

The English government continued to take the situation north of the border very seriously, calling a meeting to be held at York on 1 August 1299 between the bishop of Durham, Sir Henry Percy, and the earl of Lincoln, as Edward's representatives, and those most immediately involved in Scottish affairs on both sides of the border. Yet again, however, events overtook these plans and the meeting was almost certainly cancelled; those on the 'front line' doubtless had no time for discussions in York as they were constantly required at their posts. Sir John Kingston, constable of Edinburgh castle, indicated in a letter of 9 August to the English treasurer at York, Walter Langton, that he was unable to come to him: the Scots, including John Comyn, earl of Buchan and cousin of the guardian, William Lamberton, bishop of St Andrews, 'and other earls and great lords' who had been north of the Forth, had reached Glasgow on that same day [9 August], 'and they intend to go towards the border, as is reported among them and their people who are in the Forest [Selkirk]'.

Kingston also had a warning for Langton about the keeper of Selkirk Forest, Sir Simon Fraser. This Scotsman had been captured at Dunbar but redeemed himself in Edward's eyes by exemplary service on the 1297 campaign in Flanders. On his return to Scotland, Fraser had been restored to his lands and appointed keeper of Selkirk Forest, an office traditionally held by his family under the kings of Scots.[74] He was apparently now on his way to York with news of the enemy's approach, an unnecessary dereliction of duty, according to Kingston, since the southeastern garrisons could certainly prevent any incursions if they had sufficient warning. However, 'it was reported that there was a treaty between [the Scots] and Sir Simon'; it was further implied that Fraser had attempted to draw men away from the Edinburgh garrison, whereupon the Scots had surprised the castle, capturing one of its knights. With classic understatement,

Kingston remarked: 'Wherefore I fear that he is not of such good faith as he ought to be'.[75]

Fraser certainly felt the need to procure a letter dated 31 July 1299 from an official at Berwick, vouching for his diligence and loyalty in the discharge of his duties.[76] It is impossible to know exactly what game he was playing – perhaps he was a double agent, or merely uncomfortable in Edward's administration, particularly if the English grip on the south-east was looking less than firm. Kingston certainly noted 'rebel' activity as near to his own castle of Edinburgh as Penicuik, ten miles away. The support of the local populace was vital to the English garrisons. However, this support would have been largely dependent on the latter's effectiveness in persuading the Scots within their jurisdiction that they were both willing and able to allow them to live their lives as normally as possible without undue imposition or harassment.

Kingston's letter to Langton probably provoked the latter to write to English officials along both sides of the border on 19 August. It was impossible to tell where the Scots would attack, but it was known that they were targeting unharvested crops, prompting the Treasurer to order the immediate collection of all unreaped grain for safe keeping. The threat was apparently so dire that 'our people cannot resist since they have nothing to eat'.[77] Of course, the Scottish inhabitants of these areas were equally affected by this scorched-earth policy though it is harder to tell who they would ultimately blame – King John's men for inflicting it or King Edward's men for failing to prevent it.

A letter from Sir Robert Hastangs at Roxburgh on 20 August 1299 finally provided a clearer picture of the enemy's movements. On 13 August[78] Sir Ingram d'Umfraville and others harried Fraser in Selkirk Forest. They then awaited the arrival of 'the great lords of Scotland', namely Bishop Lamberton, the earls of Carrick, Buchan, Atholl and Menteith, Sir John Comyn, 'the son', and James the Steward.[79] Conflicting rumours continued to circulate, however, since the Lochmaben garrison expected Carrick to descend on them around the same time.

There was some cheer for the English garrisons, though. The Scottish leaders, gathered in apparent safety in Selkirk Forest in the heart of English-held Scotland, had intended to launch an attack on Roxburgh. On discovering the strength of the town's defences, however, they decided 'that they could make no exploit without great loss of their troops'. The various measures taken throughout the year to secure the south-eastern garrisons, however hand to mouth, had done their job. The Scots then 'kept quiet' until the following Wednesday (19 August), when they held a meeting at Peebles, by which time Hastangs had a spy among them.

The spy's news was most uplifting from an English point-of-view, depicting in graphic detail the deep rifts within the Scottish political community. Though the ostensible reason for the fracas that broke out was Sir William Wallace's intended trip to the continent without the permission of one of the guardians, Sir John Comyn the younger, this was really an eruption of the Bruce/Comyn feud which the appointment of a representative from each family to lead Scotland's government had not diminished. The earl of Carrick had tried hard, as guardian, to avoid describing himself as acting in the name of King John, while Comyn worked equally hard to ensure that he did. Comyn' suspicions of Wallace, whose brother was now a member of Carrick's retinue, were almost certainly fuelled by a belief that the former guardian was going abroad to lobby for a Bruce kingship. In truth, Sir William seems to have kept out of noble politics, perhaps realising that any question marks over the kingship was a can of worms the Scots really couldn't afford to open. But that didn't stop the two current guardians from coming to blows.[80]

As is so often the case, it took an external threat to bring these militant factions to heel. News arrived that Lachlan MacRuari and Sir Alexander Comyn, brother of the earl of Buchan, who, for reasons that will probably remain forever obscure, fought for

King Edward, were busy devastating the north of Scotland. It was quickly agreed that the bishop of St Andrews should become chief guardian, with control of Scottish castles, to keep the peace, while Comyn and Carrick remained uneasily in office with him. However, while the problems caused by this political divide are certainly significant, it is important not to overstate their effects. The Peebles council ultimately displayed a degree of confidence which contrasts markedly with the despondency shown by Edward's officials and they could certainly act together when they had to.

Indeed, the Scots were bold enough to appoint Sir Ingram d'Umfraville as sheriff of Roxburgh and Sir Robert Keith as warden of Selkirk Forest, offices currently held for Edward by Sir Robert Hastangs and Sir Simon Fraser respectively. Keith and Umfraville were reportedly to have command of a force numbering one hundred men-at-arms and fifteen hundred footsoldiers, excluding the men of the Forest – a huge standing force by Scottish standards – to cause havoc along the border. Hastangs assured the king that this was no idle threat 'because each great lord has left a part of his troops [*gentz*] in the company of the said Sir Ingram'.[81] Roxburgh castle may have provided sufficient protection for the English garrison but this intelligence seriously calls into question the sheriff's ability to function with any degree of confidence beyond its walls.

Sir Robert Keith was certainly no mere token keeper of Selkirk Forest, given that Sir Simon Fraser – his counterpart in Edward's administration – spent from 4 September 1299 until 12 June 1300 in a Scottish prison, though the circumstances of his capture are unknown. Of course, this could have been an attempt by the Scots to avert suspicion in order to maintain a friend on both sides in the strategically important forest; however, such a conspiracy theory is rendered less likely by the fact that Keith's brother, Edward, claimed to be heritable sheriff of Selkirk through his wife, Isabella Sinton, challenging Sir Simon's own position in the area.

After the close of the Peebles meeting, the Scottish nobility departed for their own estates, though Lamberton remained at his episcopal house at Stobo near Peebles, again underlining the limited nature of English control even in the south-east. The danger from the Scots was again far from over. On 21 August 1299, John Sampson, constable of Stirling castle, lost a horse 'when William Wallace came to take away our supplies'. Though Sampson does not state the year, describing it as taking place on 'a St Bartholomew's day [21 August],' this is unlikely to have been 21 August 1298 since Stirling castle had been reprovisioned only a couple of weeks earlier, while Wallace was abroad by the end of 1299.[82]

Meanwhile, Sir Ralph FitzWilliam was en route to relieve Sir Robert Clifford, arriving at Carlisle on 30 August with his contingent of two knights and ten esquires, a clerk and nine foot-soldiers.[83] However, FitzWilliam had even less stamina for the office than the previous incumbents. Despite organising another expedition into Galloway during September (which, again, probably didn't happen), the orders for his recall had been issued by 12 November 1299.[84] Though there is no evidence that FitzWilliam followed the time-honoured tradition of begging to be relieved of his office, it is likely that he simply could not afford to fulfil his duties properly. He certainly had an impressive record of service, mostly in northern England, both before and after his brief stint as lieutenant. Unfortunately for the stability of the English position in the south-west, no replacement was appointed until 5 January 1300.

At a time when there was no governor of Scotland as a whole, the two lieutenants of the eastern and western marches, the former based at Berwick and the latter at Carlisle or Lochmaben, in conjunction with the receivers, Amersham and Abingdon, formed the backbone of the English administration of Scotland. Sir Robert Clifford, despite his continuing commitment to Scottish affairs, obviously did not relish this responsibility. However, his resignation in July/August 1299, and the uncertainty which this caused at a time when the Scots were intensifying their activities, was unfortunate, to put it mildly. This was certainly not improved by FitzWilliam's two-month stint in the job. It was surely no coincidence that both expeditions planned for Galloway failed to take place, suggesting that the area was still an English no-go zone and would continue to be so for the time being.

The Scottish garrison at Caerlaverock remained a constant threat despite the death of its constable, James the Steward's nephew Robert Cunningham, during an attack on Lochmaben; accounts indicate that the English garrison there lost one hundred and sixty-two footsoldiers during the period from 28 September to 19 October; a further hundred then 'disappeared' between 20 October and 19 November. This left only forty men, excluding the men-at-arms. The Scots can't be given all the credit – lack of resources must also have contributed to the decrease. However, by the time FitzWilliam departed, Lochmaben was little more than an impotent English outpost. Despite his claim to have the Scots under control, and the cheering news of Cunningham's death, Sir Robert Felton, the constable, was finally forced to admit the need for an English army to subdue the area, begging the king 'to turn his face to Scotland and they will be discomfited'.[85] What was also desperately needed was a man with the taste, ability and resources for both administration and warfare to be warden of the south-west. It was another year before Edward finally got one.

An English campaign was still on the cards, despite the lateness of the season and the attractions of Edward's new wife. However, the garrisons couldn't wait much longer to take further precautions. Three new siege engines, perhaps intended for use against Caerlaverock, were ordered to be built at Carlisle in September.[86] On 15 November Sir Richard Siward was ordered to investigate what needed to be done to further strengthen the new pele at Lochmaben after Christmas; the receiver, Master Richard Abingdon, was to go with him so that he could oversee the work once Siward had gone to join the king on campaign.[87]

The more high-profile activities of Edward's military officials should not obscure the fact that the two receivers, Sir Walter Amersham, still ostensibly chancellor of Scotland, and Abingdon, were at least as busy supporting those activities. Indeed, Amersham was so overworked that he soon required the services of an associate, Sir John Weston, as receiver. The 'chancellor', who received and accounted for all the money coming to Berwick from the exchequer at York, might thus be better described as treasurer of Scotland. Weston, on the other hand, was put in charge of the disbursement and delivery of money and goods within Scotland, primarily in support of the eastern garrisons, together with Sir Robert Heron, the comptroller. Another royal clerk, Sir Richard Bremesgrave, had charge of the store at Berwick.[88]

The flow of money trundling north was alarmingly regular from the English exchequer's point-of-view. On 2 May 1299 £400 for the Berwick garrisons (town and castle), £150 for the Roxburgh garrison and £36 13s. 4d. for the Jedburgh garrison was handed over to the sheriff of York. This money was then transported to Newcastle, where it was delivered to the various constables. It is not clear whether the latter travelled by sea or overland, though all but the Berwick constables would have had to make part of their journey by road. A further £400 for the Berwick garrisons made the same journey two weeks later.[89] The task of transporting large amounts of coin across the border was undoubtedly both dangerous and time-consuming; it is not difficult to envisage the potential for long delays between wage payments and the muttering in the ranks as a result. As ever with government records, pages of statistics should not obscure the fact that the fates of real men[90] are concealed within them. The one bright spot was the comparative plenty in the Berwick store, which had been supplied by purveyance collected from English counties for Edward's planned expedition. On the downside, it was noted that, despite the careful instructions for its safe keeping, all the wheat was either putrefied or desiccated.[91]

The Carlisle store was similarly flush, again due to purveyance but this time from Ireland. As usual, the total brought in fell short of that demanded by the king; but it was still a substantial amount, including over 10,000 quarters of grain (wheat and oats) and 551 barrels of wine. This revictualling took place just in time, given some of the paltry amounts remaining in the store.[92] Even once some of the provisions had been passed on to English officials in south-west Scotland, the store was comparatively well-supplied at the end of this year's account. The ultimate postponement of Edward's campaign until 1300 managed to reverse the situation of 1298 when the English army and garrisons had the military capacity to maintain lines of supply, but insufficient victuals to feed such large numbers. In 1299 the garrisons were well provided for, since there was no army to feed, but without a large-scale military presence it was difficult to disperse victuals safely.

Carlisle, like Berwick, was staffed by officials other than Abingdon specifically to maintain the supply line. The two other full-timers were Richard Mistone, based at Carlisle priory to supply flour made from wheat brought from the stores in Carlisle, and Robert Fikeis who had charge of the wine. Nevertheless, despite the construction of a new store in and around the Carlisle castle bailey, the accounts suggest that, once the shipments had come in, Abingdon and his staff had to use all the available space in the area, including granaries belonging to local citizens.

A great deal of part-time employment was also created when the provisions arrived from Ireland from May 1299 onwards; at least sixty-one men were paid to ensure that they ended up safely stored either in and around Carlisle or at Lochmaben.[93] The possibility of increased employment opportunities, even if only on a part-time basis, is an aspect of this war, as with all wars, that should not be overlooked. While the expense of trying to conquer Scotland generally made the conflict unpopular, there were still opportunities.

This picture does somewhat contradict the desperate state of affairs described by Sir Robert Clifford in July; however, the arrival of ships on the coast off Carlisle was by no means the same as the arrival of victuals at Lochmaben. That required more time, luck (with the weather), and good management (in avoiding the Scots). The men-at-arms at Lochmaben, via its constable (Sir Robert Cantilupe was replaced by Sir Robert Felton during this year), were eventually well-supplied. Payment for the healthy amounts of grain, meat, wine and fish sent to them was presumably deducted from the constable's *certa* (the agreed fee) without the need for any money to change hands. The same happened with Bruce of Annandale's[94] men (Sir Humphrey Gardinis, Sir Hugh Mauleverer, Sir Hugh Heriz, Sir Thomas Torthorald and their fifteen esquires), who continued to defend Lochmaben for their master, even, if necessary, against his own son. Others, including Clifford himself, Sir Richard Siward and the energetic John Halton, bishop of Carlisle, were granted gifts of victuals, presumably as a reward for their services on the Scottish border.

On the other hand, the footsoldiers hired to defend the new pele seem to have paid cash for their food, which made it imperative not only to keep the stores healthy, but also to make sure money was available to pay their wages. Time and again the social mores of the age seem to have ensured that the expendable unmounted soldier was left to his own devices for his survival or at best ended up at the end of a very long queue in which horses came higher; that such treatment might prove counterproductive in terms of overall military strategy does not seem to have been considered. Perhaps there were many more where they came from, unlike men-at-arms.

The financial situation presided over by Abingdon was also comparatively healthy in this year. In total his receipts amounted to £1,287, coming from the sale of victuals, a grant from the wardrobe, and issues from Cumberland, Westmorland and Carlisle; his expenditure was only £1,122, which left him in credit by (but owing to the exchequer) £165.[95] However, on 23 September, Abingdon was promoted to be a baron of the exchequer at York; though he continued officially as receiver, Master James Dalilegh began to take on more responsibility at Carlisle.[96]

Immediately after Edward's marriage to Margaret of France in September 1299, summonses were issued for a winter campaign in Scotland, a clear sign of the king's impatience to cross the border. The muster was to be wholly in the east, with the intention of relieving Stirling castle. Sixteen thousand footsoldiers were ordered to assemble at Newcastle by 24 November; those men-at-arms receiving personal summonses were to be at York by the same date.[97] While winter campaigns were not particularly common, for all number of reasons, the climate was perhaps not as cold, wet and miserable as it would soon become.

All the same, and rather unsurprisingly, Edward found it difficult to transmit his enthusiasm for spending the winter in Scotland to his army and the muster date was postponed to 13 December at Berwick. The new summonses contained the revealing addition that any reasonable form of financial bribery should be used to persuade footsoldiers to serve.[98] At the same time, it was considered worthwhile only to ask the northern counties of Northumberland, Yorkshire, Westmorland, Cumberland, Derbyshire, Durham, Shropshire and Staffordshire to send men. Shropshire and Staffordshire still refused to send any at all, though as the two counties furthest from the border, this is perhaps not surprising.[99] High-ranking government officials, including Sir John Droxford, the keeper of the wardrobe, and the treasurer and justiciar of Ireland, met at York to coordinate arrangements for the provision of further supplies.[100]

Edward finally arrived back in Scotland on 13 December. However, despite all the hard work, a mere two thousand five hundred footsoldiers turned up and the only cavalry seems to have been a force of less than forty men serving for a grand total of nine days under Sir John de St John. A number of esquires did come to Berwick from Yorkshire, sent by knights and other freeholders at the king's request for the keeping of the Scottish march. They remained there under the command of Sir William Latimer, still captain of the eastern garrisons, from 20 November to 24 December 1299.[101] Any thoughts of an expedition were now completely out of the question.

The failure to marshal an army, caused partly by continuing attempts by the English nobility to try to limit the king's demands, and partly by the obvious unpopularity of a winter campaign, must have been a bitter pill for Edward to swallow. Much work clearly needed to be done but, as in September 1298, he was not able to do it without an army. Most worrying was the failure to chase away the Scots intent on taking Stirling castle. The king re-crossed the border on 1 January 1300, doubtless a most unhappy man.[102]

Despite the abandonment of the military expedition, a number of key royal officials, including Sir John Droxford, the keeper of the wardrobe, Sir Walter Beauchamp, steward of the household, Sir John Benstede, the wardrobe comptroller, and Sir Ralph Manton, the cofferer, remained behind at Berwick. Their brief was to 'organise fully the garrisons on the Scottish march and Edinburgh castle' and to arrange for ships to carry victuals hastily to Edinburgh, from where they would also be distributed to the garrisons at Roxburgh and Jedburgh.[103] From 8 to 20 January 1300 they travelled between the various castles, hearing the accounts of their commanders and assessing the state of the victuals in their stores. This gives us some indication, as shown in Tables 1 and 4, of the numbers maintained at Edinburgh, Jedburgh, Roxburgh and Berwick.

As with 1298, a large force, comprising sixty-five men-at-arms, one thousand four hundred and seventeen archers, twenty-one mercenaries, six serjeants-at-arms and one hundred and five crossbowmen, defended Berwick town. Their role was still presumably to reinforce the other south-eastern garrisons when necessary and to fend off attack from the Scots.[104] Unusually, Dirleton castle, apparently held privately by Sir Robert Maudley since its capture in 1298, was also given provisions from the royal store, probably as compensation for the three months spent by Maudley and his men in the garrison of Berwick town over the summer of 1299.[105]

Having finished their tour of inspection, Droxford and company returned south. Sir Alexander Convers and Sir William Rue, who were responsible for supplying the garrisons of Edinburgh, Dirleton and Stirling, went with them to York to present this year's accounts at the exchequer. War or no war, proper procedure had to be followed. Nevertheless, this veneer of normality undoubtedly obscures the continuing vulnerability of the English position even where they were comparatively well provisioned and defended.

Convers, well aware of his responsibility to keep the Stirling garrison fed and watered, duly hired John FitzWalter, master of the *Godale* of Beverlay, and his crew of six, to take victuals from Newcastle to Berwick, and from there up the River Forth. But they still had to look out for the Scots lurking round Stirling. On 13 November 1299 a letter was sent by the guardians and the community of the realm to King Edward from the Torwood, between Stirling and Falkirk. In it, they offered a truce, to be concluded through the mediation of King Philip of France, an offer which the English king was not yet inclined to take up, not least because at that point he was still planning his campaign.[106]

In December 1299, Ralph Kirby, a clerk at Stirling castle, came to York with three valets 'to reassure him [Edward] of the state of the garrison'. The fact that the king was actually still at Berwick (though about to return south) suggests that those at Stirling were effectively cut off from the rest of English-held

Scotland. The valets, but not the clerk, remained at York through-out January before returning to the castle. Kirby had meanwhile gone to Berwick to catch up with the victuals carried there in the *Godale*. Intriguingly, these supplies included large quantities of fish, luxuries such as cheeses and spices, and military hardware, but no wheat, oats and malt; this may mean that the garrison was well-stocked with these basic supplies, or that they were able to procure them from elsewhere, or even that someone somewhere was extremely incompetent.[107]

Kirby was back in York in January 1300, this time to inform the king of the surrender of the castle. It seems strange that it should have surrendered so soon after being resupplied, suggesting that the garrison was not, in fact, starved into submission. However, Kirby and the *Godale* could easily have arrived too late or been unable to get through. In any event, the constable, John Sampson, handed the castle over to Gilbert Malherbe, the Scottish sheriff of Stirling, in return for safe passage for himself and his men, who reached Berwick by 18 January. They numbered sixty-three, the majority of whom seem to have been men-at-arms.[108] 1299 had indeed been a most unsatisfactory year with no campaign, threats to almost all the English-held garrisons and, to crown it all, the loss of Stirling, that most strategic of castles and gateway to the north.

Since 1297, Edward's administration in Scotland had faced a variety of problems, revolving primarily around the logistics of conducting a successful campaign, and, perhaps more impor-tantly, sustaining permanent forces in those areas brought back under English control. When Edward appointed his sheriffs and garrison commanders in 1296, he had envisaged the role of the Scottish castle as the backbone of his administrative system, fulfilling the needs of both the crown and the local community in areas such as justice and defence, as well as symbolising his own authority. That system had collapsed, through a combination of English highhandedness and Scottish recalcitrance, and even the victory at Falkirk failed to restore it.

The English garrisons in south-east Scotland and parts of the south-west, with the exception of Berwick, sat gingerly on the edge of the communities which they were supposed to administer, usually isolated from the food supplies of their hinterland and eminently vulnerable to attack. It has been claimed that 'control of the Firth of Forth lay with the possessor of Edinburgh; control of the Clyde lay at Dumbarton; control of the neck of Scotland itself lay at Stirling. With control of all three and with reasonable vigilance, Edward could hold Scotland'.[109] By these criteria, he clearly did not hold Scotland between 1297 and 1304.

The Scots were aware of the weaknesses of these military outposts, even in the comparatively well-held south-east, and sought on every possible occasion to sever the umbilical cord which tied them to each other, England and supplies. That strategy, combined with a continuing reluctance to engage with Edward's armies in battle, might negate the effects of even a hugely impressive and successful military campaign through raiding and harrying supply lines in the winter months. Nor did the Scots forget the usefulness of terror tactics and, even if they did not actually cross the border in the second half of 1298 and throughout 1299 (this is not proven either way), the communities of the northern counties lived in constant fear of invasion.

This was the basic situation under which the English and the Scots operated between 1298 and 1304. It was not entirely a stalemate – Edward was utterly determined to win this war and it cannot be denied that he made steady, if uninspired, progress in extending English control well into the south-west in the following years. It should not be forgotten either that intense diplomatic initiatives were engaged upon by both sides and that these had a profound effect on the progress of the war in the field. Nevertheless, the confidence exhibited by the Scots, in such sharp contrast to the timidity of 1296–7, should remind us that they certainly did not believe English victory was inevitable. Equally, it must be recognised that, while Edward could not conceive of any outcome other than success, he found it extremely difficult to persuade the English nation to throw vast quantities of time, money and resources at 'the Scottish problem', even if everyone believed it was natural for the Scots to be overcome by the English. This was not a situation likely to improve as the war dragged on.

CHAPTER FOUR

STALEMATE

The start of the new century did not, initially at least, appear to promise better things for Edward's reconquest of Scotland. Indeed, the Scots, buoyed up by their success at Stirling, probably went on to tackle Bothwell, a huge and outwardly impregnable fortress on the River Clyde. Its English constable, Stephen Brampton, later complained bitterly to the king that he and his men endured fourteen months of siege, after which they languished for three years in a Scottish prison.[1] If the sieges of Stirling and Bothwell happened consecutively, then the latter probably fell in the spring of 1301, around the time that Edward was planning that year's campaign. They could, of course, have taken place concurrently but this seems less likely given the resources needed to maintain a Scottish army for that length of time without its size becoming the butt of jokes on the battlements. Even so, the ability of the Scots to reduce such strongholds is quite remarkable, though their success probably says more about the inability of Edward's regime to save them.

There were some good omens for the English, however. On 5 January 1300 the issue of the wardenship of the western march was finally resolved with the appointment of Sir John de St John to that office. As with Clifford, the area over which his jurisdiction extended was much greater than that originally conferred on Sir Henry Percy in 1296. St John was now captain and royal lieutenant 'over all the men-at-arms and all affairs of arms, both of cavalry and infantry' in the sheriffdoms of Cumberland, Westmorland and Lancashire, in Annandale, and the whole

Scottish march as far as the western boundary of the sheriffdom of Roxburgh, the beginning of Sir Robert FitzRoger's jurisdiction. On the other hand, we shouldn't forget that the Scots had their own warden of the western march, Sir Adam Gordon, whose core lands were in the south-east.[2]

St John was also given certain confidential instructions. On 25 September 1300, having presumably fulfilled them, he was paid £433 12s. for 'secret expenses made by him by order of the king and council ... on 5 January [1300]'.[3] These were presumably expended on activities intended to establish English control more effectively throughout the western march. The element of secrecy, and therefore of surprise, was essential to the prosecution of this war, as any other.

Sir John de St John was a most important acquisition as royal lieutenant. Although a soldier, like Surrey and Clifford, he was also a proven administrator, having served as Edward's governor of the duchy of Aquitaine (Gascony) at a time when relations with Philip of France reached rock bottom. On the outbreak of war between England and France in 1294 over the status of the duchy, St John led the advance guard, along with the king's nephew, John of Brittany. Despite the failure of forces to arrive from England, thanks to the outbreak of rebellion in Wales, they were remarkably successful in containing the French until a counter-offensive forced them back. In 1297, however, St John and many of his battalion were captured and Edward's lack of credit worthiness meant that the £5,000 ransom was not raised until 1298; he made it home just in time to join the king for the Falkirk campaign.[4] Sir John was not merely competent; his rule in the duchy had been popular.[5] A man of this calibre was sorely needed in Scotland.

St John could also call on the services of Sir Robert Clifford, still denied access to Caerlaverock, which had been granted to him after Falkirk; he agreed to serve in the new warden's company from 2 January to 24 June 1300 for the handsome sum (if it was actually paid) of 500 marks. Clifford and his men were also allowed to stay in the houses that he had had built in the new pele of Lochmaben 'without dispute from anyone'. However, he was not allowed to go off on his own business unless St John agreed and then only if enough of his men-at-arms were left behind. On the other hand, if he couldn't maintain his own retinue fully, he could leave freely or else reduce the numbers, with a corresponding deduction in payment.[6] The safety of the garrison was absolutely paramount but, on the other hand, there was no point in forcing service out of those who had no wish to be there or who were having to bankrupt themselves to serve. Ultimately, as Clifford well knew, it was the warden's job to maintain an effective fighting force, despite the difficulties in providing both wages and food supplies.

There was to be no honeymoon period for the new warden. At the same time as news of St John's appointment reached them, the men under his jurisdiction were ordered 'to hold themselves in readiness to be at Carlisle, properly appointed,[7] within eight days of their summons'.[8] Though we have no direct evidence for their subsequent activities, the king did make offerings in the chapel of Westminster on 14 February 1300 'because of good' – but unfortunately unspecified – 'rumours in Scotland'.[9] The next day, St John was ordered to maintain at royal wages twenty or thirty men-at-arms (presumably in addition to Clifford's thirty) and as many hobelars as he thought necessary. The use of hobelars (soldiers on small ponies), still an unusual occurrence outside Ireland, was wisely seen by the king as crucial in getting to grips with the difficult hilly terrain of Galloway in particular.[10]

By 1 March St John was engaged in a military offensive against the enemy operating within his jurisdiction. As ever, Abingdon was also placed on red alert at Carlisle, not least because if any castles were captured or surrendered voluntarily and it was thought advisable to place an English garrison in them, the receiver was to cover the costs of provisioning them with men, victuals and equipment.[11] The eight-days' summonses were presumably issued at this time, although the power given to St John and Abingdon on 1 March to punish those who failed to turn up may well be evidence of an understandable war-weariness among those being called upon to fight almost constantly in Scotland as well as to withstand Scottish attacks in their own areas.[12]

Within two weeks one success can certainly be inferred. On 11 March 1300 offerings were made in the chapel of Berwick castle 'because of good rumours heard from Scotland' (a curious turn of phrase that might suggest Berwick was no longer considered part of Scotland); a few weeks later, on 24 March, Sir John Dolive was granted the royal castle of Dumfries, suggesting that it had been successfully restored to English control. This was much better news indeed! At the same time, Sir John de St John was permitted to retain John le Skirmisher and his crew with their galley to victual the new acquisition. However, silence fell upon St John's activities until 22 April when Sir Thomas Borhunte, one of the warden's knights, arrived at Westminster 'hastily from parts of Scotland'. Fortunately, another messenger arrived on 30 April 'to reassure him [the king] of the state of the march', implying perhaps that a Scottish counter-offensive had been repulsed.[13]

Meanwhile, the struggle to maintain the supply line continued unabated. On 2 May 1300, Edward wrote to his treasurer, Walter Langton, at York, informing him that he had heard from St John that the victuals at Carlisle were almost all gone. Langton was therefore to arrange immediately for the purveyance being gathered for that year's campaign in Ireland to be sent there as quickly as possible. The Scots were still engaged in a war of attrition against the English garrisons, attacking their lines of supply to make the most of victualling difficulties.[14] St John and his men were not out of the woods yet, however busy they might have been.

*   *   *

Sir Robert FitzRoger's position as captain and lieutenant of Northumberland and of the garrisons of Berwick and Wark was confirmed on 1 March 1300, but only for another two months. Yet again all was not well on the victualling front; it was stated in no uncertain terms that '. . . it is necessary to have come to Berwick a great store of victuals and other things needed for the support of the men who are staying there and elsewhere in our service for the keeping and defence of the said marches'.[15]

When FitzRoger's current contract ran out on 30 April, the king ordered that he was to be persuaded to remain until 23 December. Whatever the inducement, it wasn't enough; he stayed only until 23 June and no replacement was appointed until around 29 September, when Sir William Latimer was once more described as keeper of Berwick town and warden of the march. Sir Walter Teye was appointed to the former office during the interim but probably had been, and continued to be, in charge of the Berwick town garrison even while the warden technically held that office. Certainly he and FitzRoger had been jointly responsible for the payment of troops in the Berwick garrisons in December 1299.[16] The overlapping command structure apparent throughout the English administration probably reflects the need for a number of officials to share these considerable responsibilities, especially since the senior official (warden or receiver) might often be needed elsewhere.

Expeditions against the Scots were not confined to the western march; the Scottish contingent left in the south-east under Sir Ingram d'Umfraville and Sir Robert Keith was still a force to be reckoned with. In April 1300 a skirmish took place at Hawick and five horses belonging to various members of the south-eastern garrisons were killed, though unfortunately we have no idea of the damage inflicted on the Scots.[17]

Despite such activities, this Scottish force was probably intended merely to contain the English garrisons there and maintain access to and from Selkirk Forest; the real theatre of war, for both sides, was now firmly the south-west, and Galloway in particular. Sir John Kingston, at Edinburgh, provided yet more bad news of Scottish activities, this time to Sir Ralph Manton, the royal cofferer, who was becoming increasingly involved in Scottish affairs. The worst came first: on 10 May 1300 a Scottish parliament was held at Rutherglen. The ability of the Scottish government to hold such an event and do so that far south was concrete proof that Edward's was not the only administration in Scotland; it was arguably not even the more successful.[18]

Fortunately, there was good news, from the English point of view, on the faction-fighting front. A serious quarrel had broken out yet again, this time between the obligatory John Comyn and his senior guardian, the bishop of St Andrews. Lamberton was supported by the Steward and the earl of Atholl, traditionally Bruce allies; Carrick himself was nowhere to be seen. The upshot of it all, and perhaps the source of the quarrel, was that Sir Ingram d'Umfraville, a Balliol-Comyn man, was chosen as guardian. There can be little doubt that Bruce had been pushed out, a testament to the strength of the Comyns, who now resumed their firm grip over Scottish government.

It might be supposed that the eclipsing of Carrick caused problems in terms of commitment to the war effort, even if no-one actually changed sides – yet. Unfortunately for the Bruces, subsequent events suggest that the dominance of one group minimised the need for consensus politics and allowed policy/strategies to be executed more quickly. To add to the misery, allies like Atholl and the Steward continued to play a role in Scottish government after Carrick's withdrawal/expulsion from power, suggesting that the Bruce star was considered even by them to be on the wane. Carrick surely came to the uncomfortable conclusion that he was now by no means essential to Scottish politics and government or the war effort.

Of more interest to the English, however, was the news that John Comyn, earl of Buchan could not attend 'because he was away in Galloway to treat with the Galwegians'. The Rutherglen parliament was therefore adjourned until 17 December, to be held in the same place, 'on which day the earl of Buchan and all the great Scotsmen will be there with their power'.[19] The Galwegians had a longstanding antipathy towards the centralising tendencies of the kings of Scots, though it should be remembered that Balliol had been lord of the region.

Edward had long recognised the uses to which a sense of Galwegian separatism might be put, releasing Thomas of Galloway, illegitimate son of the last Celtic lord of Galloway (John Balliol's mother was Thomas's half-sister), and issuing a charter of liberties for the region in 1296. Thomas, who had been in prison in the Balliol stronghold of Barnard Castle, was thus being used to underline King John's loss of the lordship of Galloway, as well as of the kingdom itself.[20] Most of the region's important families, such as the MacCans and the Macdoualls, tended to side with Edward after 1296, though it is ironic that he should be regarded as their best hope for regional autonomy. Nevertheless, this is not the same as saying that the English controlled this inaccessible part of the country.

The fight for Galloway was therefore just as important to the Scots as it was to Edward. The nearby Bruce lands of Annandale, together with the rest of Dumfriesshire, were coming under increasingly effective English control. The capture of Caerlaverock, which had surely been planned as far back as August 1299 with the construction of siege engines at Carlisle, would make that control secure. On the other hand, if Caerlaverock remained in Scottish hands, Dumfries and Lochmaben would continue to operate largely as outposts of English-occupied Scotland and the conquest of Galloway would still elude Edward.

Almost immediately upon his return from his frustrating sojourn in Berwick, Edward set the wheels in motion for the next campaign. He meant to focus on three main areas of difficulty for the English in southern Scotland: Caerlaverock, Galloway and

Selkirk Forest. Demands for purveyance from all over the country went out on 17 January 1300, to arrive at Berwick by 24 June. The large-scale state acquisition of victuals had always been unpopular but, after four years of war, resistance was becoming more stubborn, in part because funds were dwindling rapidly.

On 2 May 1300 Edward wrote to the treasurer at York, informing him that the 1000 quarters of wheat, 1000 quarters of oats and 500 quarters of malt ordered from the counties of Cambridge and Huntingdon had not been collected because the sheriff of these counties 'has scarcely anything in his hands with which he could make this purveyance' (i.e. he had no money to pay for it). Again, these counties were far removed from the war zone and had every incentive to avoid contributing if they could, but we cannot discount the possibility that there was a large grain of truth in the assertion. Equally Yorkshire, which does not seem to have been asked to provide anything this year (presumably because of the extent of the county's commitment in previous years), still managed to find 505 quarters of wheat and small amounts of other goods to send north. As Table 5 indicates, the shortfall between what the king demanded and what arrived was significant, though perhaps there was always a degree of over-demand precisely because of the likelihood of a shortfall.

The collection of these victuals was imperative, however, because, as the king knew from experience, a 'lack of victuals on this journey that we wish to embark on in Scotland would place us in the hands of our enemies or force us to return hastily'. Cambridge and Huntingdon were not let off the hook, though the purveyance was to be made, yet again and rather euphemistically, 'to the least grievance of the people'. In the end the county did provide something, though generally only half of what was demanded.[21] Purveyance was also made of the equipment needed to transport these goods to their final destination further into Scotland from the stores at either Berwick or Carlisle.[22]

Table 5: *Purveyance 1300 – demand and supply*

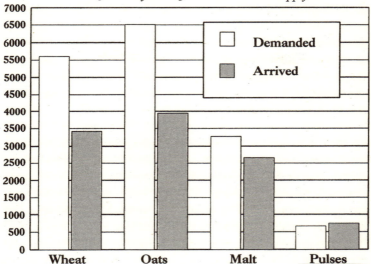

The writs for feudal service had been sent out at the end of December 1299.[23] The total numbers of men-at-arms actually serving the following summer reached the respectable total of around seventeen hundred men-at-arms but a mere thirteen per cent derived from this traditional feudal source. Of these, only the earl of Gloucester, Sir Hugh Despenser and Sir John Hastings actually fulfilled their service in person: '. . . the majority of great men appear simply to have detached some members of their retinue to do it on their behalf, even when they were themselves present on campaign'. The feudal military organisation introduced to Britain by the Normans was no longer the mainstay of the late thirteenth/early fourteenth English war machine.

A total of sixteen thousand footsoldiers from Nottingham, Derby and 'the four most northerly counties' were summoned to the muster at Carlisle, but only about nine thousand were actually recruited by the commissioners of array. The Welsh were excused 'because of all the great work which they have done in our service in the past'.[24] The evidence for their contribution in 1298 alone suggests this was nothing less than the truth. A small contingent of around three hundred and sixty Irish soldiers were also present at the siege of Caerlaverock 'and joined the king in his aimless marching through Galloway'. Edward had also requested the services of three hundred Irish hobelars, whose suitability for the Scottish terrain he had noted in 1299, but he got only a rather pathetic fourteen.[25]

As with purveyance, Edward was facing serious problems in keeping numbers of soldiers up to scratch. The men of the northern counties, who had been on the front line since 1297, were extremely unwilling to serve 'for they were afraid to leave their homes lest they should be devastated by retaliating raiders'. The men of Durham and Yorkshire 'constantly mutinied and deserted'. Only the counties of Lancashire, Derbyshire and Nottinghamshire, and, to a limited extent, Chester and Shropshire, 'seem to have been properly organised and good fighters, and willing to keep the field for more than a few days'.[26]

Finally, the regularisation of the role of the fleet, prompted by its dismal performance in 1298, should now have improved matters in terms of getting supplies (nearer) to where they were needed. Edward I, as usual, played a major role in giving greater coherence to the basic institution he had inherited from his father. A total of fifty-seven boats of varying sizes was now to be provided annually by the Cinque Ports for a period of fifteen days at their own costs.[27] In 1300 royal accounts show that thirty Cinque Port ships and fifty-nine ships from forty-eight other ports were sent to Scotland. This is also the first year in which mention is made of an admiral – Gervase Alard of Winchelsea. There were also four captains of the fleet, William Pate and Justin Alard of Winchelsea, William Charles of Sandwich and John Hall of Dover.[28] Even if the Cinque Ports did not provide a majority of vessels, they maintained control of naval operations.

Various nobles also owned ships and galleys which they put at the king's disposal – a safe-conduct was granted in July 1300, for example, to Malcolm le fiz l'Engleys (MacQuillan) to allow him to harass the Scots on the western seaboard in his own galleys. MacQuillan, who seems to have had interests on both sides of the Irish sea, had been granted Kintyre by Edward in 1296; he thus had every reason to try to make English control of the north-west a reality.[29] However, in general too few individuals displayed an interest in sea-power to play a significant role in Edward's fleet.

The Irish ports of Waterford, Youghall, Ross, Drogheda, Dublin and Cork also had a quota of one ship each to provide as their *servitium debitum*, while Cork owed two. The ships of Drogheda, across the Irish Sea not too far south-west of Carlisle, naturally figure most prominently in the transportation of purveyance.

This service was likely to become a great burden for some of the smaller ports for the simple reason that, while quotas were variable in size, demand was almost annual. All ships were to be furnished and kept for fifteen days at the towns' expense. If a crew comprised a master, a constable and nineteen men (the minimum for a Cinque Port boat), then the wages alone came to £4 6s. 3d. for each ship, a considerable sum (over £3,000 today). Quotas of soldiers imposed a similar strain on the shires, but the boroughs must have felt a particular burden since there were fewer of them to provide for the navy. On the other hand, there was money to be made transporting goods at all times of the year.

As with his armies, the king could not force the ships' crews to remain in his service any longer than the fifteen days they owed him if they did not wish to do so. Even if the mariners did agree to stay on, they would now be at the king's wages; it was becoming increasingly difficult to pay them, as well as the rest of the army, for the amount of time required to make an impression on the areas of Scotland still beyond his control.

Three years into the war, then, Edward was not having it all his own way either in his martial exploits or on the domestic front.

Having survived a full-blown crisis in England thanks to the patriotic backlash provoked by the defeat at Stirling Bridge, the English king still had to bargain for support for the Scottish war. This was particularly true in 1300, when a parliament held in March managed to extract a number of 'royal concessions, known as the *Articuli super Cartas*, which were clearly part of the price that Edward paid for the grant of a twentieth in this parliament.' But though they might grumble, the élites were behind their king now; they were merely concerned that there should be no abuse of the law and that local affairs should be run as effectively as possible.[30]

Edward arrived at Carlisle on 27 June 1300, reaching Caerlaverock thirty-five miles away on 9 July.[31] He and his army were joined there by a considerable force of up to ninety-three men-at-arms, five hobelars, three crossbowmen and nearly fourteen hundred archers drawn from the garrisons of Berwick town, Roxburgh, Jedburgh and Lochmaben.[32] The south-eastern garrisons lost a total of eight hundred and fifty men from their defence. Although the main area of contention was currently the south-west, there was still a threat to the south-east from Scots operating from Selkirk Forest; the removal of so many men was something of a gamble if it left these garrisons vulnerable.

According to the contemporary poem, *Le Siège de Karlaverock*, a total of 'three thousand brave men-at-arms' massed before the castle,[33] though this figure probably owes something to poetic licence. The army was divided into four squadrons under the earl of Lincoln, the earl of Surrey, the king, and the prince of Wales, now sixteen years old.[34] Within them were a number of prominent members of Edward's administration in Scotland, past, present and future, notably Sir Henry Percy, Sir Robert Clifford (in whose honour the poem may have been written, given the gushing and lengthy entry devoted to him), Earl Patrick of Dunbar, Sir Richard Siward, Sir Simon Fraser, Sir John de St John, Sir William Latimer and Sir Alexander Balliol.[35]

The siege commenced after the arrival of the navy – 'fortunately', according to the poet – with engines and provisions, again proving that little could be done without this vital support. But despite the stirring account of the brave exploits of the army in the poem, it was the skill of the engineers, who bombarded the castle with a constant stream of missiles, that brought about its submission. The Scots apparently held out for a day and a night and until the following day at terce (9 am), when mounting casualties and the fact that the roof had fallen in persuaded them to give up. Around sixty men survived the siege, to be rewarded, again according to the poet, with a new robe each, though royal records certainly don't reveal this.[36] Edward was more in the habit of imprisoning, or worse, any 'rebel' Scots who fell into his hands, while the poet's job was quite clearly to put a chivalric gloss on what was really a rather short and inglorious siege.

The Scottish army was obviously in no position to challenge Edward's army, but it could still harass it. Between 6 and 9 August, the English were attacked at the mouth of the river Fleet some forty miles west of Caerlaverock, presumably while foraging for food; a number of horses, including one belonging to a certain Piers Gaveston, were killed.[37] The Scots came off worst, however: Sir Robert Keith, Sir Thomas Soules, Robert Baird, William Charteris and Laurence Ramsay were all captured and the king rejoiced that some of his 'worst enemies' were now in an English jail.[38] Presumably Keith and at least some of the force under his command in Selkirk Forest had moved west as the English advanced into Scotland.

The rest of the Scottish army now moved even further west and faced the English from the other side of the Cree. The three Scottish cavalry brigades were, according to Rishanger, commanded by the earl of Buchan, Comyn of Badenoch, and d'Umfraville. In an action reminiscent of Falkirk, they fled when the English, divided into three brigades under the earl of Hereford, the king, and his son crossed the river. However, the lack of hobelars to pursue them over such rough terrain prevented the English from inflicting greater damage on the Scots.[39]

Edward's original intention was to continue west and then north, since Sir Ralph Manton was sent to Carlisle to enlist more footsoldiers and find extra victuals 'for the passing of the king to Ayr'. But he was once more to be disappointed as the army returned to England, though the king did cross the border again in mid-October to oversee the construction of a pele at Dumfries, like the one already built at Lochmaben.[40] The lack of resources – both men and supplies – compounded with the lateness of the season were the most likely causes of this change of plan, which included the agreement of a truce. Thus, despite the appearance of an English army in Scotland, and the impotence of the Scots before it, Galloway was still not brought firmly under Edward's control. The situation there is made crystal clear in a grant of 11 September 1300, by which the royal lieutenant in the south-west, Sir John de St John, was given

> ... lands, farms and rents in England to the value of 1,000 marks a year, for life or until he can be put in seisin and enjoy the issues and profits of land to that amount in the land of Galloway heretofore granted to him, and which he cannot enjoy at present by reason of the war in that land'.[41]

The failure of the royal army to progress into Galloway put the onus for an expedition on to St John's shoulders to 'bring to a satisfactory conclusion his [the king's] business in these parts'. Sir Alexander Convers, a royal clerk more usually attached to the south-eastern garrisons, went with the lieutenant between 18 October and 4 November to pay wages, though there is no evidence to indicate how many men took part.[42] The purpose of this enterprise was 'to receive the men of those parts to the king's peace', though surely this was based more on the hope, rather than the firm expectation, that the Galwegians would submit.

The Scots were also, very wisely, putting pressure on the less well-protected garrisons in the south-east. At the end of August, William Camera (probably one of the Berwick town garrison) lost a horse while in Selkirk Forest with Sir Simon Fraser, suggesting that the Scots were still lurking. However, the network of Edwardian officials in the area was further bolstered by a grant of Hermitage castle to Sir Simon Lindsay, already captain in Eskdale and keeper of Liddel castle, on 20 September. The issues of the surrounding area were to be used to 'provide supplies for himself and his men in our service in parts of Scotland'. The castles of Liddel and Hermitage, forfeited by the Soules family, had been granted to Sir John Wake, who recently died. Despite the ostensibly private nature of the grant, Lindsay's public service ensured that he was given supplies for the castle from the royal store at Berwick as a gift.[43] These valleys giving access to and from the border were crucial to England's defence, as well as that of the garrisons of south-eastern Scotland, and the king was happy to blur the lines between private and royal just as he had in the Bruce lordship of Annandale on the western border.

In October two royal clerks were sent to the south-east from the king at Dumfries with instructions for the officials there. Since Sir John de St John was otherwise occupied in Galloway, they were ordered 'to make some good expeditions upon Selkirk Forest and elsewhere where they think it good and that they exert themselves to do as well as possible so that the king can have good news of them and that they are always busy with what the king has charged them to do'. Despite the disintegration of his army, Edward was determined to maintain the military pressure on the Scots for as long as possible; he clearly continued to feel uneasy about his garrisons in the south-east so long as there was a threat from the Forest.

The clerks were to return to the king to inform him '. . . how they [the constables of Roxburgh and Jedburgh] are undertaking these matters and how they are taking them to heart after they have heard the king's will'. Finally, Sir Richard Bremesgrave, at the Berwick store, was given strict instructions to inform Sir William Latimer, warden of the eastern march, 'that by all means he is to stay in these parts to attend to these matters and make expeditions on the forest according to the initial plan, as often and as effectively as possible until he gets further orders from the king'. There is more than a hint here that Latimer, like so many before him, did not relish his position even as Edward was determined that his own work should not be undone. But his words smack more than a little of desperation.[44]

An expedition under Latimer did take place between 26 and 31 October 1300, though there is no evidence that it actually engaged the enemy.[45] Other, more drastic, tactics also seem to have been used: Michael Whitton, the head forester at Selkirk, was compensated on 20 November for having 'recently burned his houses and other property in the forest of Selkirk for the king's service'. He was not alone, either – the men under him were considered equally loyal to the English king. It says much for the growing acceptance of the English presence in the south-east that the leader of the foresters, who fought so heroically on the Scottish side at Falkirk, was now with Edward. On the other hand, given that the village of Whitton is in Northumberland, it is possible there had been a resettlement of the Forest by English incomers from 1298 onwards in order to try to secure the area.[46]

Meanwhile, Bremesgrave at Berwick was also working hard to account for the movement of goods to and from his store. Even though the army was operating in the west, he received a certain amount of the purveyed supplies, most of which went to sustain the garrisons within his jurisdiction. Table 6 indicates the proportions of foodstuffs brought in, compared with the amounts then sold or given away. In the case of wheat and flour particularly, there wasn't much in it, and more beans and peas seem to have gone out than were actually in the store!

Both Master Richard Abingdon and Sir James Dalilegh, a clerk of sir John Droxford, keeper of the wardrobe, received and issued money, victuals and equipment at Carlisle throughout this regnal year. However, by August 1300, Dalilegh had largely taken over from Abingdon as keeper of the store as the latter became more heavily involved in his exchequer duties.[47] The Carlisle store obviously received most of the purveyance since it had to supply not only the garrisons of Dumfries and Lochmaben, but also the army itself. Table 7 indicates just how hand-to-mouth a task that was.

Abingdon, who was still the principal receiver at Carlisle in this regnal year, sold £3,247 1s. 1d. worth of victuals, in comparison to Dalilegh's £862 10s. 4d. worth. Bremesgrave's receipts, amounting to £1,739 2s. 9d., were naturally less because most of this year's action was in the west. The receivers thus brought in a combined total of £5,848 14s. 2d., which still put them ahead of the cost of the victuals (i.e. what was paid to those who provided it) at £4,063 2s.[48] The Crown was certainly not above profiting from its wars. But then again, it desperately needed to.

Table 6: *Berwick store, 1300*

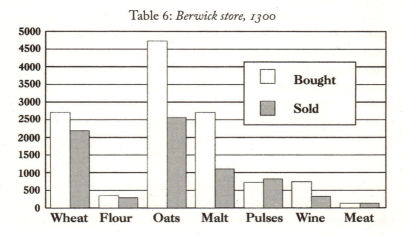

Unlike the second Welsh war, when military accounts were kept separately, it is not possible to assess the exact costs incurred by Edward, and England, during his wars in Scotland. However, it is possible for this regnal year, thanks to the survival of the *Liber Quotidianus Garderobae* (Daily Wardrobe Book). The garrisons accounted for the largest part of the year's expenditure at £13,574. Victuals came to £5,063. The army which besieged and captured Caerlaverock cost £8,561, and a further £2,000 was paid out as compensation for horses lost during the campaign. Thus, out of this year's total wardrobe expenditure of around £64,000, nearly half (£29,198) was spent on the prosecution of the war.[49] We might imagine that other years with campaigns in them were similarly heavy on Edward's purse.

Table 7: *Carlisle store, 1300*

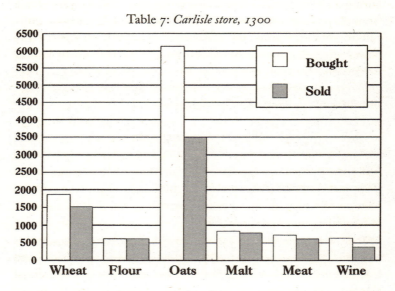

On 30 October 1300, Edward concluded a truce with the Scots, through the mediation of Philip of France, to last until 21 May 1301. This was the first oblique admission on the king's part that Scotland was far from conquered; it is also generally regarded as an acknowledgement of the failure of the campaign of 1300.[50] Edward had agreed to it in principle the previous October (1299) while at Dumfries.[51] English activities in the 1300 campaigning

season had therefore been geared towards bolstering their position before the truce came into effect.

That the truce indicates a degree of failure in Edward's prosecution of his Scottish wars is fair; nevertheless, he had made some progress during the campaign of 1300 that, looking on the bright side, could not now be recovered by the Scots when he and his army made the inevitable return journey to England in the autumn. The fall of Caerlaverock provided security for Dumfries and Lochmaben, even if Galloway itself was still scarcely under control. And while English garrisons could not make expeditions during a time of truce, they would at least not come under attack (though private initiatives on both sides would have been difficult to prevent completely). Edward was always aware of the power wielded by his enormous armies, even if this was largely psychological in nature now that the Scots refused to give battle. Given that he had failed to keep his army together to consolidate his position, the logic of the truce must surely have been to use the gains made in 1300 as the springboard to the final conquest of the south-west the following summer. In the meantime, Edward's officials in Dumfries and Annandale were now able to make their presence felt far more tellingly in the areas under their jurisdiction; it is surely no coincidence that Abingdon's account for this year included forty ox carcasses sent by the men of Moffat 'to have peace'.[52]

It now only remained for the garrisons to be paid and their accounts and stores reviewed. Lochmaben, Dumfries and Caerlaverock were visited by no less than the Treasurer of England, Walter Langton, and Sir John Droxford, the keeper of the wardrobe, between 14 and 24 November. Sir Ralph Manton was despatched to Berwick, Edinburgh and Roxburgh at the same time.[53] Since this was a period of truce, with (theoretically) no military activity, the numbers in the garrisons, as shown in Tables 1–4 did not need to be as high, which was also a bonus for Edward's finances. Nevertheless, the protection of the south-east was still dependent on a decent-sized force in Berwick town, even if the small standing army had gone. Seven hundred and thirty men served Edward in the Scottish castles held by him (excluding other castles in private hands, such as Dirleton, Liddel and Hermitage) at a total cost of £13 5s. per day (at least £9,000 now). The store at Berwick, without an army to feed, was able to maintain reasonably healthy levels of provisions in the stores within each of its satellite castles. However, the situation at Dumfries (and presumably Lochmaben) was rather less reassuring, with only twelve barrels of flour left.[54]

Since 1298, the exchequer at York had played an extremely important role in Scottish affairs, governing all financial aspects of the administration of the northern kingdom. This role replaced the fully functioning and independent administration in Berwick that had been envisaged in 1296 and is in itself a reminder of the very different circumstances of the English presence in Scotland from 1297. However, from 1300 Sir Ralph Manton, the king's cofferer, began to play an increasingly important role within the Edwardian administration north of the border, even if he occupied no properly appointed office within it and many of his activities could be regarded as an extension of his duties as a wardrobe clerk. The most important aspect of these duties was the payment of, and accounting with, the royal garrisons, a financial role which, as with Hugh Cressingham before him, did not endear him to those he had to deal with. In 1303, in the aftermath of a skirmish between Scots and English at Roslin, Manton was furiously accused of avarice by Sir Simon Fraser, who by then had switched sides but had once been one of Edward's officers:

> You have betrayed the king who made you treasurer,
> And me and many others, of whom not one is acquitted
> Of the wages which you owe by reckoning and by writing.[55]

A similar charge was made against Cressingham. It's entirely possible that both men were unscrupulous in the discharge of their duties, but they might also have been blamed as the most visible symbols of the hard-pressed regime, caught within an ever-increasing spiral of debt caused by the war. Fraser and the other Edwardian military officers no doubt viewed the conflict more traditionally, as a route to glory and riches. In reality, as the constant pleas for wage payment and the redundant role of the army at Caerlaverock illustrate rather poignantly, serving in Scotland for the higher echelons of English society was both costly and dull.

The truce with the Scots, in operation since 31 October 1300, was due to expire on 21 May 1301. On 1 March 1301 the earls of Surrey and Warwick, Sir Aymer de Valence, Sir John de St John and Sir Hugh Vere were appointed to 'treat with the envoys of Philip, King of France, touching the rectification of the disobediences, rebellions, contempts, trespasses, injuries, excesses and losses inflicted by the Scots'. This was hardly conciliatory talk.

The meeting was to be held at Canterbury at mid-Lent (around 8 March) but was later postponed until 16 April. On 26 March 1301, safe-conducts were issued to Sir Adam Gordon, Sir John Inchmartin, Master Nicholas Balmyle, the Scottish chancellor, and Master Thomas Bunkle, as the Scottish representatives.[56] However, a week later, the king ordered that, 'having determined not to renew the truce with the Scots', a force was to muster at Berwick under his own command, and another at Carlisle under his son, the Prince of Wales. It is seriously to be doubted that Edward ever intended renewing the truce, since preparations for the campaign had begun as early as February.[57]

On 8 April 1301, with still over a month and a half of the truce to run, the magnates and royal officials of Northumberland were warned to prepare for Scottish attacks on its expiry, since the king knew 'not what may result from the conference between the Scots and the French ambassadors now taking place at Canterbury'. Edward knew exactly what would result. His refusal to grant an extension of the truce and his desire for a treaty with the French alone meant that a resumption of hostilities was inevitable. On 25 April he finally announced that '... the *parlance* to have been lately held at Canterbury between his people and those of the king of France on the affairs of Scotland is broken off to his advantage and the great loss of the French ...'[58]

There was certainly some cause for optimism in the English camp, not least because of the increasing evidence for a partial re-establishment of normal government in certain areas under English control. In 1299 Sir Philip Vernay, keeper of Berwick town, Sir John Burdon, sheriff of Berwick, and Sir Robert Hastangs, sheriff of Roxburgh, were all able to hold inquests. Two of these were into lands confiscated from 'rebels' and now regranted; in both cases it was also established how much was owed as service to the Berwick exchequer. Even if there was really no exchequer in Scotland, there was clearly an expectation that some revenue might now be forthcoming.[59] In the same year, Master Richard Abingdon managed to bring in £23 13s. 4d. (at least £17,600 today) from the issues of Annandale, which was an awful lot better than nothing.[60]

Then, in 1300, the sheriff of Edinburgh, Sir John Kingston, accounted for certain 'receipts of the king's money', including the farms of North Berwick, Tyninghame, Haddington, the town of Edinburgh, Lasswade, Aberlady, Easter Pencaitland, East Niddrie and Lowood, the tolls of Edinburgh town, and the tenth of Inveresk, Lasswade, Roslin, Aberlady, Ballencreiff and Carrington. Other receipts included £16 3s. 4d. as part-payment of a fine owed to the king by the abbey of Newbattle, 30s. from five men of the sheriffdom 'coming to peace', and various other fines. The total received was £66 8s. 3d. or around £50,000 today. Kingston also received a further £25 from the 'issues of Scotland', namely the farms of Tranent and Seton, and the sale of hides and grain belonging to certain fugitives in Carrington.

He had also been able to buy victuals and equipment for his garrison from the surrounding area. The purchases were mostly of cattle and interesting items such as 'ferrets of Dirleton', while local smiths had also been used to service the mounts of his men-at-arms. With this evidence for the increasingly effective authority of the sheriff of Edinburgh, it is not surprising to find references to 'captured grain', to 'hobelars and archers who were assigned to look after enemies' beasts at Lowood', and finally to Scots coming to Edward's peace.

However, the evidence is not completely one-sided. Despite the dearth of records for the Scottish government, there are some clues as to its overall capabilities in the north-east particularly. In 1300, for example, John, earl of Buchan, was able to hold a court in Aberdeen as justiciar of Scotland. John, earl of Atholl, who would once have aligned himself with the Bruces rather than Balliol and the Comyns, was nonetheless described as sheriff of Aberdeen, 'perhaps indicating that a normal peacetime cross-section of interests still prevailed'. More significantly, John Comyn of Badenoch had, as guardian, 'been able to prosecute successfully two pro-English landowners in the area, one of whom was the earl of Strathearn'. Comyn's ability to hold courts and, most importantly, to execute the judgements of these courts, speaks volumes about the success of his regime'. He also seems to have done so independently of his co-guardians.[61] There can be no doubt that the Scots maintained firm control of the kingdom north of the Forth.

On 12 May 1301 Sir John de St John's appointment as captain and lieutenant of the western march was renewed for the third time, doubtless to Edward's great relief.[62] Nine days previously, St John had been empowered 'to receive the knights and middle men of Scotland to peace, as the king enjoined him *viva voce* [orally]', presumably while the lieutenant took part in the pretend truce negotiations at Canterbury. On various dates between 5 April and 26 May, Sir John Kingston, Sir Robert Hastangs, and Sir Hugh Audley, perhaps already keeper of Selkirk Forest, were all similarly ordered to admit the 'middle' or '*mesne*' men of Scotland to the king's peace.[63]

This was an unusual stipulation. Certainly, every English official in Scotland had the authority to receive any Scot to Edward's peace; however, this deliberate targeting of the 'middle men' may indicate a belief – or at least a hope – within the English government that certain Scots were now at least as fed up with the war as many of those south of the border. Such orders, issued immediately before the outset of a campaign, were presumably to be used as an amnesty to encourage these small landholders or burgesses, who played an important role in their own communities, to adhere to the English cause. The Scottish government would then find it much more difficult to exercise their authority in military, administrative and financial matters, even when most of Scotland's senior nobility were not at Edward's peace.

A similar mandate was granted to Sir Gervase Alard, the admiral of the fleet now operating off the coast of north-west Scotland. On 6 June 1301, he was given

> ... full powers, to last till 1 November, to receive to our peace ... Alastair of Argyll, John and Duncan, his sons, and Lachlan, son of Alan [MacRuari], who married Alastair's daughter, the daughter herself and all their domestics and each of them and also all other husbandmen and middle people of the Scottish isles who wish to come to our peace, except barons, bannerets and other rich and great lords.[64]

This is the first proper reference to the situation in the region since 1297 apart from Lachlan MacRuari's raids on the north of Scotland with Alexander Comyn of Buchan in 1299. Such activities did not necessarily have much to do with any fervent loyalty to King Edward. The likeliest explanation for the submission of the MacDougalls is the (undocumented) success of the MacDonalds in English service, prompting a change of heart among the former, who now seem to have taken the view that the only way to regain their position was through similar service. If so, it is likely that they soon changed their minds since the release of King John from papal to French custody took place only a month or so later, putting a quite different complexion on Anglo-Scottish politics. There is unfortunately no evidence for Admiral Alard's activities in the north-west over the summer of 1301, though Edward must surely have been prepared to divert the fleet only in the knowledge that the MacDougalls were definitely seeking reconciliation.

The exclusion of the 'barons, bannerets and other rich and great lords' is most striking and corresponds to the general principle now adopted by Edward's officials in targeting the 'middling sort'. These lords included James the Steward and John Comyn of Badenoch, who were certainly most unlikely to submit at this time, but Edward may have been particularly angered by what he considered the treacherous behaviour of such high-ranking Scottish nobles and was deliberately seeking to isolate them from the communities they represented.

There is no evidence for large-scale submissions in 1301 or, indeed, in any year before 1304, though that may be because the senior Scottish nobility, who tend to monopolise the written record, did not submit until then. Nevertheless, English accounts do make odd references to small anonymous groups who chose to 'have peace'. Equally, the revenues raised in 1300 and 1301 by the sheriff of Edinburgh could only have been achieved if exactly that section of society which Edward was now targeting had accepted the English regime in reasonable numbers. Nevertheless, in 1301 it was also asserted by Sir Robert Tilliol, constable of Lochmaben, that some Scots were forcing those in the surrounding area who had submitted to Edward to return to the Scottish fold.[65]

None of us should be surprised that the passage of time might have persuaded some that Edwardian government was here to stay and that it might be prudent, if not essential, to make terms with it. Though the English administration still fell dramatically short of the one set up in 1296, it is clear that the military achievements of the king and his army from 1298 onwards were accompanied by similar, small-scale improvements to the state of the permanent English administration of southern Scotland in certain areas.

There was no doubt in Edward's mind, whatever the feelings of his subjects, that yet another campaign would take place in 1301. Not only that, but he intended to raise the stakes much higher by wintering in the north in order to prevent the Scots from taking advantage of an English withdrawal without the demeaning need for a truce. Doubtless it was hoped that even the most recalcitrant would soon realise that continued resistance was futile. This had worked well in Wales,[66] but the downside was the huge resources (money and supplies) needed to persuade men to serve over the winter. England was to be asked not only to keep paying for the reconquest of Scotland, but to pay even more, though presumably the king hoped that such an extreme measure would bring an end to it.

This was a high-risk strategy indeed and Edward surely realised that the grievances behind the crisis of 1297 were not going to go away so long as there was a war to pay for. It was his job as king to sell his military objectives to his own subjects; although the war in Scotland lacked both glory and rich pickings, there was still an element of national pride involved, as the portrayal of Edward I as a king who had brought great fame to England through martial exploits in contemporary poems illustrates. On the other hand, there was surely a limit to such patriotic feeling. The longer the Scots held out, the more likely this stand-off might raise serious questions about the king's abilities and the wisdom of endlessly squandering the kingdom's resources on Scotland.

On 1 March 1301 the inevitable writs for purveyance were issued. The demands made on the northern counties were noticeably smaller than elsewhere and must again reflect not only the considerable resources which they had already contributed to the war, but also the devastation inflicted by both sides.[67] Since

Edward's forces were to be divided into two, purveyance was required at both Berwick and Carlisle. In addition, while half the Irish purveyance was to be sent as usual to Skinburness, the port for Carlisle, the other half was to go to a port on the island of Arran, held for Edward since 1298 by Sir Hugh Bisset of Antrim.[68] The aim was presumably to bring the whole of Scotland south of the Forth-Clyde line under English control.

This was still easier said than done, however. The northern English counties were not alone in suffering from a dearth of foodstuffs. On 18 April, the demands made on the county of Essex were reduced by reason of 'a scarcity of oats and malt in that county'. The merchants there also appear to have fallen victim to profiteering during the previous purchase of their goods since those ordered to supervise the collection of this year's quota informed the king that: 'As regards payment ... [they] cannot give their goods with confidence except to persons named, who have power to tax, collect and pay when the time comes'.[69]

The king arrived at Berwick on 5 July 1301 and had his army mustered by 12 July. According to the payroll for the period up to 29 September, it numbered around six thousand eight hundred footsoldiers, with a further two hundred and seventy-two drawn from the garrisons of Berwick, Roxburgh, Jedburgh, Edinburgh and Selkirk Forest. The earl of Angus also provided two hundred archers, presumably from his Northumberland lands.

The king had also negotiated for the service of the Irish nobility, who had not come to Scotland since 1296 because of continuing payment problems. Edward's terms were extremely generous, including the pardon of two-thirds of all debts owed to the exchequer. Even so, the earl of Ulster, Ireland's most powerful nobleman, refused to go. Nevertheless, an Irish force numbering two hundred and twenty-nine men-at-arms, three hundred and five hobelars and nearly fifteen hundred footsoldiers arrived on the island of Arran by 15 July, joining the Prince of Wales on the mainland at Ayr shortly thereafter. A separate force under Sir Eustace Poer and Sir Thomas Mandeville, numbering forty-five men-at-arms, eighty-six hobelars and one hundred and twenty-eight footsoldiers (most likely sent by the earl of Ulster), probably took part in the siege of the earl of Carrick's nearby castle of Turnberry.[70] Though the cavalry and footsoldiers were doubtless welcome, the hobelars were probably of most use as the prince's army moved into hilly Galloway.

The fleet continued to prove vital to the success of this year's endeavours. Despite their *servitium debitum* (owed service) of fifty-seven, the Cinque Ports were requested to send only twelve 'good, large ships'. This was perhaps a reflection of their previous good service and the fact that it was becoming so constant, though Edward may also have felt that large vessels of good quality were preferable to a greater number of smaller, inferior boats. Sir Gervase Alard remained as admiral and captain of the Cinque Ports. In addition, the non-Cinque Port ports of Bristol and Haverford were to provide three ships between them, to go with these twelve ships to Dublin by 11 June 1301.[71] They would then presumably cross the Irish Sea to Skinburness or Ayr to provide supplies and give aid to the prince of Wales.

Additional summonses were sent to forty-four English, one Welsh and six Irish towns to provide a further sixty-eight ships to join the king at Berwick by 24 June.[72] This fleet should therefore have totalled eighty-one ships, though there is no way of knowing exactly how many actually turned up.

Having mustered at Berwick in July 1301, Edward's army moved west, staying at Peebles for two weeks and arriving at Glasgow on 21 August, attacks by Scottish raiding parties causing problems along the way.[73] The more leisurely pace taken by the eastern army may be a reflection of Edward's rather hopeful desire that his son – in the west – should attain 'the chief honour of taming the pride of the Scots'.[74] The prince's army arrived at Ayr in August. On the 25th his father, at Glasgow, heard unspecified 'good rumours'.[78] There is no evidence for a siege at Ayr, nor any reference to a harassing Scottish force, though there may well

A youthful and almost affable Edward I. *Reproduced by permission of the British Library (Royal MS 2A XXII f219v)*

King John swearing homage and fealty to a rather more implacable Edward I, leaving no-one in any doubt as to who was boss. *Reproduced by permission of the British Library (Royal MS 20c vii f28)*

The inglorious face of war; mass death and destruction at Berwick in 1296. However, such scenes of carnage were probably all too familiar to the average foot-soldier.

Reproduced by permission of the British Library (MS Add. 47682, f40)

Above. An evolving constitutional position. Warrant of Edward I as overlord of Scotland, using the seal of the guardians. After the conquest of 1296, Edward had his own seal made.
Reproduced by permission of the Keeper of the Records of Scotland

Right. The paltry remains of the nerve-centre of English-occupied Scotland – Berwick Castle. The Great Hall, where judgement on the Great Cause was given, is now the railway station.
Photograph: author's own

The siege of Bothwell castle, showing just how busy the engineers were.
Reconstruction drawing by David Simon, courtesy of HES

The siege of Caerlaverock castle. While the engineers were on overtime, this siege provided very little opportunity for Edward's knights to indulge in deeds of derring do.
Reconstruction drawing by David Simon, courtesy of HES

Dumbarton castle, controlling the fords across the Clyde. Many an English officer forced to submit to Sir William Wallace spent some time here in less than comfortable conditions. *Courtesy of HES*

Dirleton castle, captured by Bishop Antony Bek before the battle of Falkirk in 1298 and garrisoned with English soldiers thereafter.

Stirling, Scotland's most strategic castle, which, unsurprisingly, changed hands more often than any other. It is also not surprising that most of the main battles of this period took place within sight of its walls. *Courtesy of HES*

Kildrummy castle, seat of the earls of Mar and a temporary Bruce stronghold in 1306 because Robert Bruce had care of his young nephew, Donald of Mar. *Reconstruction drawing courtesy of HES*

Urquhart castle, played host to one of the most northerly garrisons after 1296, but was forced to submit to Andrew Murray and the burgesses of Inverness in 1297. *Reconstruction drawing courtesy of HES*

Inverlochy castle, a Comyn stronghold near Fort William, commanded access to the Great Glen, the easiest way through these imposing mountains (including Ben Nevis on the right) to Inverness and the east. *Crown copyright: HES*

have been one or both. Strategically, winning Ayr was a considerable triumph for the English, even if it had taken three years to achieve; direct control had finally been extended right through to the west coast, allowing shipments from Ireland to come directly to Scotland. The Gascon, Sir Montasini de Novelliano,[76] became constable of the castle and Sir Edmund Hastings the sheriff. Both had already served in other Scottish garrisons.[77] Overall keepership of the castle and the sheriffdom was granted to Patrick, earl of Dunbar and March. Though essentially an eastern landowner, Earl Patrick also owned Cumnock castle, twenty miles east of Ayr, and so had interests in the area.[78]

The chief stronghold of the earldom of Carrick, Turnberry, lies some thirteen miles south along the coast from Ayr. This time there was certainly a siege, since the first reference to any English presence there was on 2 September but the king, still receiving 'good rumours' at Glasgow, did not hear of its reduction until he was at Bothwell on 5 September at the earliest.[79] Its fall, even if only temporary, must have come as a considerable blow to the earl of Carrick, the younger Robert Bruce.

Around the same time, John Comyn's castle of Dalswinton, situated around six miles north-west of Dumfries, was given to Sir John Botetourt, who had perhaps been responsible for its capture. However, the wage payment for the four men-at-arms sent to garrison it was cancelled, suggesting that the English did not manage to keep it for very long. Certainly Sir Robert Tilliol, the constable of Lochmaben, wrote on 10 September that the Scots, who were attacking him, 'went to lodge near Dalswinton'. The English were making considerable progress in the reconquest of the south-west but even the 1301 campaign by no means ensured complete security.

The king had now himself settled down to a siege. The barony of Bothwell, including its state-of-the-art castle, and other lands in Scotland to the value of £1,000 had been granted, in anticipation, to Sir Aymer de Valence on 10 August 1301; Edward's progress to Lanarkshire was thus deliberately planned to turn this generous grant into something of real value. The Scottish owner of Bothwell was three-year-old Andrew Murray – posthumous son of Wallace's co-commander at Stirling Bridge – who was growing up in the safety of the north-east. The defenders put up an admirable resistance but had surrendered by 22 September.[80]

Sadly, nothing is known of the fate of the garrisons of any of the Scottish castles captured by the two English armies in 1301. However, the account of the sheriff of Cumberland notes payments to 'two knights and thirty-two serjeants, Scottish prisoners in Carlisle castle, and a constable and eight warders to guard them' made in regnal year twenty-nine (20 November 1300–19 November 1301).[81] It is certainly possible that these are the unfortunates who surrendered to the English in this year's campaign. The lack of references to footsoldiers means we cannot rule out the possibility that they were summarily hanged.

Despite all this English success, the Scots did their best to counteract it. There had been further changes in the Scottish administration since the previous year, with Sir John Soules replacing the bishop of St Andrews and Sir Ingram d'Umfraville as guardian, apparently at the behest of King John, who was probably forcibly transferred from papal to French custody at some point over the late summer of 1301. It is unclear whether Sir John Comyn continued to govern, but the balance of probability is that he did.[82] Soules, whose lands lay largely in the southeast, had been part of the Scottish embassy to Europe in 1297–8, returning to Scotland around the same time as King John was released into papal custody. He could be considered a more pro-Balliol figure in not being so closely tied to the Comyns like Umfraville. The bottom line remained, however, that Scottish resistance would have been almost pointless without the active support of the Comyns and their allies.

Having said that, Sir John Comyn does not seem to have been with the Scottish army in the south-west, but his cousin, the earl of Buchan, led a force, together with Soules, positioned at Loudoun in Ayrshire. Another force under Sir Simon Fraser, Sir

Alexander Abernethy and Sir Herbert Morham (whom we last met in prison in Edinburgh) lay at Stonehouse near Strathaven, thirteen miles to the north-east. Sir Robert Tilliol at Lochmaben sent information on their activities to the king, still at Glasgow. The Scots, controlling the road from Glasgow to Ayr, were clearly hoping to prevent the two English armies from joining up.

So, Sir Simon Fraser had finally joined the Scottish side. He left in dramatic fashion, stealing Sir William Durham's horse and armour from Wark castle in order to make his escape. The last reference to him in official English documents is as late as 27 June 1301, when £40 was issued to his valet at York as payment for two horses bought from him by the Treasurer.[83] The fact that he was to be found leading a Scottish contingent only three months later does admit the possibility that he had been acting as a double-agent; his swift departure from Wark might also suggest that he had just been found out.

There may have been other reasons, however. The fact that Sir Hugh Audley, though not described as keeper of Selkirk Forest until August, was active in the south-east in the spring of 1301 may mean that Fraser had been, or was about to be, removed from office or, at least as likely, no longer wished to serve as keeper himself. This, together with Guisborough's description of the accusations of wage defaulting levelled by Sir Simon at Sir Ralph Manton, suggests that the benefits of English service were no longer obvious to the Scot, who at least had a choice about whom to serve.[84]

The arrival of Sir Simon Fraser and Sir Herbert Morham in the Scottish camp in mid-1301 is a good indication that the Scottish position was still regarded positively: there is little point in changing on to the losing side. This assessment was probably based less on Scottish military activity, which was now about avoiding battles and using guerrilla tactics targeting English garrisons and armies, but rather on increasingly fruitful diplomatic missions. However, the Scottish army still had work to do to prevent English gains from becoming overwhelming.

When the king left Glasgow for Bothwell on 5 September, the two Scottish contingents at Loudoun and Strathaven probably came together. Certainly, a large Scottish force under Soules and Umfraville arrived outside the walls of Lochmaben on 7 September 1301. It numbered, according to Tilliol, 'forty bannerets, twelve score men-at-arms [and] seven thousand footmen or more.' Allowing for inevitable exaggeration, this must have been the main Scottish army.

After attacking the pele for several hours, the Scots withdrew to Annan where they 'burned and pillaged the country round about'. They returned to Lochmaben the next day but seem to have come off worst since Sir David Brechin and Sir John Vaux were injured 'and many others were killed and wounded'. There were a couple of English casualties, but the pele again stood firm. Later that day the Scots withdrew to Dalswinton, apparently en route for Nithsdale and Galloway 'and they are causing to return to them those who came to peace and are collecting a greater force to come to our marches'. The fundamental strength and weakness of the Scottish military position is exposed by these activities. On the one hand, they could not reduce an English-held castle when it was protected from a long siege by a nearby English army; on the other hand, their harrying tactics did make life extremely difficult for the garrisons, and terrified the local inhabitants. The western march was still clearly in a state of flux, with the loyalties of the native population changing at the approach of an English or a Scottish army. Patriotism was a luxury that many – perhaps most – could ill afford.

Tilliol also inadvertently laid bare the fundamental strength and weakness of the English position when he informed the king '. . . that you have rejoiced us much with the rescue which you have promised us . . .' and 'that your honour shall never be injured by us as long as our victuals last'.[85] There is no denying the might of the English military machine; but the Achilles' heel of the supply line, in this fifth year of war, was still capable of placing the reconquest in jeopardy.

Lochmaben's rescue was presumably not to be brought about by the king himself, since he was about to leave for Bothwell. The prince did move south from Turnberry around this time, en route to Loch Ryan, which was nevertheless over ninety miles from Lochmaben.[86] Sir John de St John was at Knockdolian, near Ballantrae, on 14 September. Since this was between Turnberry and Loch Ryan, it seems likely that he and at least some of his thirty men-at-arms[87] were with the prince's army. The withdrawal of St John's men from Dumfries and Lochmaben seems to have placed those garrisons in a vulnerable position, which the Scots were not slow to exploit. However, a contingent under the command of the earl of Lincoln was detached from young Edward's army at Loch Ryan, arriving at Lochmaben by 21 September.[88] This forced the Scottish army to move on.

The south-eastern garrisons were being kept informed of Scottish activities in the west and were aware of the possibility of an enemy attack on the east since it was a relatively easy matter for the Scots to slip down one of the valleys that cut through the Southern Uplands, linking the two. Around 13 September, Sir Robert Hastangs at Roxburgh wrote to the king, having just received Edward's letter informing him of the measures to be taken by English officers in the south-east to repel the Scots. All the remaining soldiers in each sheriffdom were put on a twenty-four-hour alert under the utmost secrecy in order to maintain the initiative against the enemy.[89] Nevertheless, the king was becoming edgy about the security of the area, believing that he was not being kept properly informed. Sir Hugh Audley, warden of Selkirk Forest, was ordered to write quickly 'containing all we know for certain'.

Edward seems to have had some reason to be critical of his officers' abilities to work together effectively. On 17 September a meeting had been arranged which Hastangs, his brother Richard at Jedburgh, Sir Alexander Balliol, probably already keeper of Selkirk castle, Sir Hugh Audley, and Sir William Durham, the new sheriff of Peebles, were all supposed to attend with their men in order to work out a strategy against the Scots. Unfortunately, only the Hastangs brothers and Audley turned up, 'and very few of the country folk, except our foresters, who came loyally and are ready to perform all your commands'. As a result, nothing was organised, and the king was requested to order the other officers to 'come quickly since we have things to do'.

The need to send messages to and from Bothwell cannot have done much for either speed or secrecy. It is highly likely that the reluctant Sir William Latimer, captain of the eastern march in 1300, was no longer in that office and the lack of a coherent command structure in the south-east was clearly causing real problems. However, Edward was well aware of this and Audley and the rest were ordered to await the orders of Sir Walter Burghdon, who had become keeper of Carstairs castle and sheriff of Lanark by 21 September 1301.[90] From his position in the middle of the country – an area only recently brought under even nominal English control – Burghdon was now well placed to organise the defence of the eastern march against a Scottish attack from the west.

There were still problems, however, particularly with the security of the sheriffdom of Peebles. Situated on the north-western edge of Selkirk Forest, Sir William Durham's appointment undoubtedly indicates a degree of English success against the Scots who had previously been able to come and go as they pleased. It is striking that this increased control took place around the same time as Sir Simon Fraser changed sides and also in the year following the capture of Sir Robert Keith, the Scottish warden of the Forest, though again it must be stressed that any double-dealing on Sir Simon's part as Edward's officer cannot be proved.

In the meantime, English spies within the Scottish army were busy gathering information for their masters in the south-east. Durham's spy, who came straight to Peebles from Nithsdale on 21 September, provided the rather inconclusive news that the

Scots were still in Galloway, hiding out in Glentrool Forest, but that it was impossible to tell where they were heading. It was also reported that the prince of Wales was on pilgrimage to Whithorn, prompting the Scots to remove relics there to Sweetheart abbey. However, the English seem to have found them and taken them back, indicating that the two forces were still in close proximity to each other.[91] Since Sweetheart lies only a few miles south of Dumfries, this also implies that English control in the south-west was certainly not unchallenged even in the environs of the garrisons of Dumfries and Lochmaben.

Sir Alexander Balliol, at Selkirk, informed the king rather peevishly that 'the writer and fellow keepers of the march are threatened by a possible Scottish raid to destroy the writer's lands and to seize and defend the forest . . .' Balliol was lord of Cavers near Hawick in Roxburghshire. Meanwhile, the spies were to keep up their good work, so that royal officers in the east might be sufficiently prepared for an attack. Another meeting 'to inspect forces' was arranged for 24 September.[92] Although those in the south-east appear rather panic-stricken and disorganised in the face of this threat, the Scottish army also seems to have run out of ideas. Five years of war was taking its toll on both sides.

Ordinarily, September would have marked the beginning of a retreat by the English army, whether that had been Edward's original intention or not. The decision to remain in Scotland over the winter of 1301/2 naturally put a strain on the administrative machinery already stretched to the limit to provide for the summer campaign. On 14 August various English sheriffs, including those of the northern counties of Northumberland, Cumberland and Westmorland, were ordered 'to induce merchants and others of those counties who wish to sell victuals and other necessaries by land and sea to the king and his army in Scotland . . .'. These orders were concluded with the thinly veiled threat that each sheriff was:

... enjoined to conduct himself so in executing this order that the king may be able to realise that the sheriff has this matter specially at heart and that he desires its speedy and happy expedition, and so that it may not be delayed through lack of victuals and other necessities to the damage of the king, the sheriff and of all the people of the realm.[93]

Although credit could be used to a certain extent during a campaign, not least to offset wages with payment for victuals, hard cash still had to be transported north. As 1301 progressed, the lack of coin began to cause more and more serious problems, coming to a head in spectacular fashion. According to a letter to the king, probably from Sir Ralph Manton, the late arrival of £200 ordered by the king before he left Berwick in mid-July provoked a mutiny on 28 August among 'the foot crossbowmen and archers in the garrison [Berwick], joined by some of the men-at-arms of Sir Ralph FitzMichael, who was with them in Gascony and is their leader and *mestre abettour* (prime mover) in all riots'.

The next day, despite threats to himself and the men-at-arms with him, Manton 'rode up the great street, which they were blocking to prevent the guard being mounted'. Though his people were 'molested ... most vilely on returning', the cofferer was able to reach the castle and place 'two men-at-arms at each post'. He then 'consulted Sir Walter Teye, the captain of the town garrison, who said that he didn't blame the mutineers, for when the earls of England were in the town [presumably with the king in July], they had only got three days' pay, and were now a month in arrears'. The implication here is that most of the hard cash had gone on keeping the aristocrats happy.

Manton and his men remained on guard at the palisade and were joined the next day (Wednesday 30 August) by Sir John Seton and four valets. Sir Walter then held a meeting in St Nicholas' church of all the men-at-arms, who were so far staying out of the mutiny. Each man was asked if he would mount guard and 'All replied that they would willingly and that they had no concern in the mutiny of the foot'. However, they did sympathise with the mutineers since they agreed to remain at their posts only until the following Friday (1 September). Fortunately, the £200 arrived that same day (Wednesday 30 August). The next morning (Thursday) it was counted out in front of the sheriff of Northumberland (who presumably brought it) and part was set aside for the garrisons of Roxburgh and Jedburgh.

The Berwick garrison was finally paid the next day (Friday). Sir Walter seems to have taken fright, however, since he ordered Manton 'to pay the whole sum to the garrison and none other', claiming that this was the meaning of the wording of the king's letter to him. Manton's response, with some justification, was that 'the king always treated Roxburgh, Jedburgh and Berwick as one'. Sir Walter then claimed ignorance until he received more specific instructions from Edward, 'he being only a lay man', and payment duly went ahead at Berwick only. Manton therefore 'suffered evil and annoyance through want of this, for in place of Sir Walter only getting £14. 14s., he has taken £36 from him, whereby he has nothing to pay his own people'.[94] The rebellious footsoldiers presumably grumbled their way back to their posts.

This extraordinary episode at Berwick, the very heart of the English administration, must have been extremely worrying for Edward, though, sadly, we know nothing of his reaction to Manton's news. There was little point in organising a successful campaign if the English garrisons were in danger of disintegration for lack of money and supplies, not least because the Scots had been able to pick off garrisons suffering similar problems in the past. Such an appalling eventuality was only narrowly avoided on this occasion. The route to progress was circuitous indeed.

Things were not looking likely to improve in the immediate future either. On 25 September an anonymous letter – probably from Sir John Droxford, keeper of the wardrobe, in York – was sent to the king describing the overall financial situation, given that two armies, as well as the garrisons, still needed large amounts of money to keep them together. A total of 2,000 marks had been sent to Berwick around 14 September (presumably to go to the king, rather than to pay the garrisons). Five hundred marks had also been sent to Carlisle to the prince, who 'greatly needed money', bringing the total received there also to 2,000 marks. The writer now hoped that 'by Michaelmas [29 September] there will be enough to pay both the king's army and his son's, if not otherwise disposed of by the king, and if as much as possible of the 'proffer' (taxation already promised) is taken beforehand'. Without this, it would 'be difficult to help ... Berwick or Lochmaben', indicating that the writer was aware of continuing problems in the former and that they were reaching similar proportions in the latter.[95]

Manton remained in the south-east to organise the garrisons before returning to the king at Dunipace, about five miles south-east of Stirling, at the beginning of October. In the meantime, arrangements were made to strengthen the English forces in Selkirk Forest in continued anticipation of a Scottish attack. A total of twenty men-at-arms and one hundred and twenty foot-soldiers from the garrisons of Berwick and Roxburgh had been sent to Sir Hugh Audley there, along with the Northumberland knight Thomas Grey[96] and his three knights, who were 'no longer at Ayr with earl Patrick'. This brought the total number of men-at-arms patrolling the Forest to fifty, excluding a further six with the sheriff of Peebles.

Manton had also spoken with the Hastangs' brothers, Sir Alexander Balliol and Audley, instructing them on behalf of the king 'to send out scouts and each warn the other and also the country'. Balliol was still in touch with his spies in the Scottish army and had reassured Sir Ralph that 'whenever the enemy issue from Galloway, he will know two days before and will warn the king by two or three messengers of what road they take, and so will the others'. The cofferer had not managed to see Sir William Durham, 'who neither came nor sent an excuse', but he was to be informed of the king's commands. It was vitally important that the Scots should not regain a foothold in south-eastern Scotland.

As already mentioned, Manton was supposed to divide '£200 of the fine made by Newcastle for the fifteenth (tax) among the garrisons of Berwick, Roxburgh, Jedburgh and the Forest, to his best judgement, for fifteen days' wages', thereby reducing the likelihood of another mutiny. However, he was not at all happy about the situation generally, telling the king that if he had not gone there himself, 'all the garrisons on this side would have been scattered for want'. The money from the exchequer arrived at Berwick on 28 September but was not as much as he had expected 'and should have had'. Supplies there were also getting dangerously low, as he had told Sir John Droxford, who was asked to collect as much as he could everywhere, 'for your [the king's] business in Scotland depends much on *vivers*'.[97] Edward could have told Droxford that himself and probably did.

The situation was not much better in the south-west, where St John was experiencing the familiar problem of trying to make ends meet, not least because his wages were so greatly in arrears. According to a letter written to Manton on 27 August 1301, he was due money from both the previous financial term (up to 29 May) and the current one (up to 1 November). Cash was urgently required because 'he had great works to do and he is heavily indebted to the poor people of all parts who dolefully beseech him for victuals and other things he has taken from them'.[98] St John surely knew perfectly well that Edward's administration would only find real acceptance in Scotland if it was not perceived as oppressive. However, the situation, if anything, deteriorated: according to a letter of 23 October from the Prince of Wales to the treasurer at York, 'the castles of Lochmaben and Dumfries [were] feebly garrisoned with troops and lacking in victuals and other provisions'.[99]

Edward was well aware of the options available to him and what would best suit his purpose. He was also not a man to leave any stone unturned in pursuit of his objectives, though he also knew when to give up, in the short term at least. He left Bothwell around 22 September 1301.[100] His original intention seems to have been to move westwards to Inverkip on the west coast, close to the mouth of the River Clyde and whose owner-in-waiting was the earl of Lincoln. The earl wrote impatiently to the king from Galloway on 21 September and 2 October, 'understanding that as soon as he has taken Bothwell castle, the king will attempt that of Inverkip'. Lincoln claimed it as part of a grant of the lands of Strathgryfe, forfeited from James the Steward. The initial plan had probably been for the prince's army to link up with his father's at Inverkip in a pincer movement; this strategy had been abandoned for quite some time, not least because the prince's army was now busy making pilgrimages deep in Galloway.[101]

Unbeknown to Lincoln, and doubtless to his severe disappointment, the king had also changed his plans and gone north to Dunipace by 27 September.[102] The intention now was presumably to attack Stirling castle, as Manton's activities around 30 September suggest. The cofferer was busy gathering together various engines, engineers and carpenters at Berwick to be sent west. He had also ordered the sheriff of Northumberland to send north twelve carpenters and twelve masons, though 'he has not yet one'. On 4 October Sir John Kingston sent various bits and pieces of siege equipment to the king from Edinburgh.[103] Other preparations included the building of a road and a bridge near Dunipace and repairs 'on a bridge beyond a certain river [probably the river Carron] ... for the passage of the king's carts there'.[104]

Edward remained at Dunipace throughout most of October. On 29 September, several members of the army, perhaps on a foraging trip, encountered a group of Scots at Airth, east of Stirling, and a fight ensued in which two horses on the English side were killed.[105] By this time the English army had spent four months in Scotland and was supposed to remain there for several more. But finances were dire. On 11 October Edward informed the exchequer of his 'surprise', like Manton's, at how little money had been sent. Therefore, the king complained, he could not pay his men, most of whom had already left, and he could not 'prevent the daily desertions' of the rest.[106] Edward put the blame for this situation squarely on his officials at York, ordering them to ensure that their inefficiency did not force him to withdraw. That was the wonderful thing about being king; if a certain course of action did not work out, the fault lay with those implementing it, not with the policy itself.

Much of Edward's ire stemmed from the fact that the lay and clerical taxes – the fifteenth and the tenth – and the usual issues for the Michaelmas term should all have been collected by now. Two days later, on 13 October, the king wrote again to poor Droxford. Referring to Manton's letter about 'the state of the king's supplies', Edward now required 'hasty purveyance' to be made, especially since the prince's army was now making its way to Dunipace, and the queen and her household had also joined the court for the winter.

Droxford, no doubt aware of how hard a taskmaster Edward could be, had already left York for London before he received this barrage of complaint. However, the barons of the exchequer opened the second letter and quickly informed the king that 5,600 quarters of corn and other supplies were being collected, to arrive at Berwick by Christmas and to be paid for from the Michaelmas issues and the proceeds of the fifteenth. There was an element of disingenuousness to this nevertheless, since the writs ordering the purveyance had only just been sent out. Further purveyance was ordered from Ireland, three-quarters of which was to be sent to Skinburness by 2 February 1302, for the use of the garrisons of Dumfries and Lochmaben; Ayr was to receive the rest.[107]

However, this did not alter the fact that those in charge of purveyance and the collection of royal revenues required the latter to pay for the former. Thus, most of the money raised did not even reach the border, despite the fact that cash was desperately needed for the wages of those serving in the garrisons and the army. Desertion had always been a disease, but it was now in danger of becoming an epidemic.

On 16 October, a mere three days after the last letter, Edward fired off an even more desperate and irate missive to the exchequer. The lack of money meant that none of his promises of payment had been kept and desertions continued. But for this, the king wrote in frustration, he would have 'completed the bridge across the Forth', presumably at Stirling. If he had managed to do so 'this season', he further lamented, he would have 'made such exploit against the enemy' that the reconquest of Scotland would have quickly reached 'a satisfactory and honourable conclusion'.[108] It is tempting to ask which fantasy land Edward was now inhabiting, since he was clearly asking for the impossible; England's considerable resources – not to mention the patience of his subjects – were being stretched to the limit. Nevertheless, he had already achieved much more than most would have believed possible through the judicious use of carrot and stick, so why should he not push his luck – and his subjects and his own officials – even further?

The king now ordered that all money sent north should come only to him, except for what was meant for the garrisons of Dumfries and Lochmaben and others guarding the western march – where the Scots were still active – as well as the new garrison at Ayr. £1,000, which had to be borrowed in York, was sent north immediately. Droxford was still in London, desperately searching for more funds; those in York assured the king that they were constantly urging the sheriffs to hasten the raising of their revenues. They also admitted that £9,789 16s. 5d. already assigned from the fifteenth – including £4,000 owed as wages for the Welsh soldiers with the prince – was not now to be paid 'since this seems the only way to save the royal expedition'.[109] The English footsoldiers were thus not, in fact, bottom of the list; the Welsh and the Irish footsoldiers held that dubious honour.

Such desperate measures were perhaps inevitable in the circumstances; however, they had some disturbing implications. On 18 December 1301, letters of credence[110] were issued to those in charge of purveyance in the English counties. They were ordered to explain to those who had 'granted to the king last year certain corn for his maintenance in Scotland' that they would not now be paid from the proceeds of the fifteenth, as they had been promised, but would have to wait until the following Midsummer. Alternatively, if they preferred immediate payment, 'they are desired to advise and ordain how the king may be best served with the corn that he needs now for his maintenance henceforth'. In other words, money for past service would only be forthcoming in return for further supplies. Payment for these would then be made from the fifteenth at Midsummer 1302 – allegedly. The king did categorically promise that he 'will pay for the corn that he has ordained to take or that he shall take in the respective counties readily to everyone without making prise of corn by any of his ministers [i.e. that a market price would be paid]'.[111] But many would have heard that before.

The reference to prise – a royal right to take supplies at a fixed low rate, originally intended to feed the household, not the army – was perhaps a veiled threat; nevertheless, Edward had to tread very carefully or face the distinct possibility that provisioning would become even more difficult than it clearly already was. Robbing Peter to pay Paul was only possible for a short time before Peter put his foot down.

There was nothing more to be salvaged from this year's campaign. On 22 October 1301 the king informed the exchequer that he was retreating to Linlithgow for the winter, since so many of his troops, 'both horse and foot', had deserted and he was 'in danger of losing' what he had already won. Yet again he ordered that as much money as possible should be sent north. He declared that he would not accept the 'excuse' that 'it is dangerous to transport large quantities of [coin]',[112] though this may well have been a genuine concern.

Edward was not alone in his need for cash; the south-western garrisons under Sir John de St John were still in a desperate state. On 13 October it was arranged that £25 from Lancashire and £25 from Westmorland and Cumberland would be paid to him as part of a debt of 200 marks. A further £100 from Lancashire was assigned to him on 20 October. A month later, the king ordered that the proceeds of the fifteenth in Cumberland and Westmorland were to be sent to Dalilegh, the receiver at Carlisle.[113] Although there is unfortunately no evidence of how much was actually handed over, it is no wonder that other payments from the fifteenth were being cancelled in a desperate attempt to target hard-pressed resources where they were needed most.

But these measures were still not enough. On 31 December Edward wrote to the exchequer, explaining that 'since we have heard that Sir John de St John and the good people who are staying in his company in the garrisons of the castles of Lochmaben and Dumfries, as you know well, have been and still are in great danger and hardships for lack of money', sufficient amounts were to be sent to St John as soon as possible.[114] The situation was swiftly spiralling out of control and there was little that Edward, or any of his officials, could do.

To add to these undoubtedly pressing difficulties, some rather depressing news was emerging from the continent about Anglo-Scottish affairs. A letter dated 1 October 1301, perhaps again from the cofferer, Ralph Manton, informed the king of the removal of King John from papal custody, to which he had been committed in 1299, to his family estates at Ballieul in Picardy.[115] The winter of 1301–2 witnessed the zenith of French support for the Balliol cause, although there was one other to whom this was of at least as much concern as King Edward.

The stalemate evident since 1298, when it became clear that Scotland was not going to fall back into Edward's lap even after a military defeat, was not broken yet; nevertheless, so long as

England was prepared to devote so much of its resources to this piecemeal reconquest for the foreseeable future, there was every hope that Scotland would one day yield, not least for the lack of an alternative. On the other hand, there was surely a limit to the patience of the English, not to mention Irish and Welsh, who were being asked to expend considerable resources year after year on an enterprise that so far had provided very little return on the investment. This situation was exacerbated by the fact that so much time, energy and expense was also required to keep the threat of a diplomatic coup by the Scots at the courts of the pope and the king of France at bay. Delaying tactics were certainly used to good effect, but they did not necessarily resolve anything. Edward's best hope was to upgrade his activities to a continuous military pressure on his enemies within Scotland, as well as maintaining an effective diplomatic presence on the continent. However, as the failure to winter in Scotland in 1301–2 makes clear, it remained to be seen whether there were sufficient resources, or public will, to sustain such pressure. Progress had been made, but the final outcome remained profoundly uncertain.

CHAPTER FIVE

TURNING THE SCREW

On 26 January 1302, the Treaty of Asnières, granting another truce to the Scots until 1 November 1302, was ratified by the king at Linlithgow.[1] The English army began its weary journey south shortly after. Letters of credence on behalf of Edward's ambassadors to the king of France, which gave them full powers to grant a truce to the Scots, had been issued as early as 24 August 1301 when the king and his army were still at Glasgow.[2] Edward may, of course, have just been taking precautions; a truce could again prove useful in preventing the Scots from undoing the year's good work if all did not go according to plan. It's curious that he was prepared – on the face of it – to expend huge resources on wintering in Scotland in the anticipation that military activity would be suspended throughout the next campaigning season thanks to the truce. Perhaps he did not enter negotiations honestly. Perhaps he really did hope that this would be the campaign to end all campaigns. Or perhaps – and most likely – he knew perfectly well that the superhuman effort required to stay on in the north meant there would be almost nothing left to fund another campaign in 1302.

When he ordered his ambassadors to the continent, Edward already had reason to be concerned. Soules and the main Scottish army had never gone east, but had taken the opportunity, as the prince marched north to join his father at Dunipace near Stirling, to move through Carrick and the districts of Kyle and Cunningham. John Marshall, the earl of Lincoln's baillie in his barony of Renfrew – only recently acquired in practice as opposed to theory – reported that the guardian was advancing towards him with a large army. On 3 October, the recently captured castle of Turnberry was besieged 'with four hundred men-at-arms and *petail* [footsoldiers] enough to damage it as much as they could'.[3] On 25 October 1301, as the English army decamped for Linlithgow, a servant was 'sent to Glasgow to learn of rumours there of the Scots'.[4]

It is significant that Soules' army was attempting to win back the lands of both the earl of Carrick and his friend and neighbour James the Steward, whose lands of Renfrew Lincoln now held. Indeed, it's surely very likely that, despite his exclusion from power, young Robert Bruce rode out with Soules to try to expel the English from his lands.[5] The constable at Ayr, Sir Montasini de Novelliano, and the sheriff, Sir Edmund Hastings, were expecting the Scottish army there by the end of October and urgently required reinforcements 'for the Scots are in such force that they and the other loyalists there cannot withstand them'. They had heard nothing as yet from Earl Patrick, who had overall custody of the area, 'at which they wonder much'. The earl was, in fact, still at Dunbar, according to Sir Ralph Manton, intending to join the king at Dunipace. He almost certainly had a quick change of plan, since he claimed in February 1302 that the Scots had begun to besiege the garrison at Ayr 'after his own arrival at the castle'. It was only the start of another truce that had brought this siege to an end towards the end of January.[6]

To add insult to potential injury, a Scottish contingent – perhaps under Sir Simon Fraser – was still active in and around Selkirk Forest. On 29 October 1301 a member of the Berwick town garrison was captured at Melrose, despite the presence of fifty men-at-arms and one hundred and twenty footsoldiers under Sir Hugh Audley in the Forest itself.[7] Far more alarming, however, was the capture of Sir Robert Hastangs near his own castle at Roxburgh in December. Fortunately for Hastangs, his brother Nicholas agreed to stand in as a hostage for his ransom and he was back at his post by February 1302.[8] Yet again the Scots were proving that, no matter how impotent they might appear when facing an English army directly, they could still inflict some fairly telling blows through guerrilla tactics. Now it was Edward's turn to look on helplessly.

Despite the profound difficulties experienced by the English administration in trying to keep Edward's two armies together, they still needed to ensure that the garrisons were safe and secure. On 8 October 1301 a daily rate of pay, beginning on that date, was calculated for both the royal armies and the fortresses in English hands. It was agreed on 17 November that Sir John de St John should maintain a small standing army of one hundred and twenty men-at-arms 'constantly arrayed to make forays on the Scots in Galloway until next Easter [22 April 1302].' This strongly suggests that, at that point, Edward did not expect a truce to halt military activities.

The garrisons of Lochmaben and Dumfries were each to contain ten men-at-arms and one hundred footsoldiers, and a clerk was to be sent 'without delay to see to their weekly pay, and also to the proper munition of these castles with dead stock, corn and wine and other *vivers*, as he hears they are insufficiently provided'. However admirable these arrangements might appear on paper, they were likely to prove extremely difficult to implement. Sure enough, on 31 December, the king had to send further orders for money to be sent to St John, 'who is in great want of it for these garrisons'.[9]

The amount paid out in wages for English-held castles, apart from Lochmaben and Dumfries which were accounted for separately, totalled £12 7s. 2d. per day, or £4,510 1s. 7d. per annum. Although this compares well with the daily figure of £13 5s. in 1300, it is by no means the full complement. There are no figures for Ayr, suggesting that it was cut off from the rest of the English administration by enemy activity. And Berwick, as had become standard, played host to a small standing army of twenty-five men-at-arms, sixty crossbowmen and two hundred and seventy archers. This is just as well, since the figures given for Roxburgh and Jedburgh are noticeably smaller than usual, presumably because there were now more English garrisons for which men had to be provided and paid.

A garrison at Linlithgow under Sir William Felton, as keeper of the castle, was set up in this regnal year (20 November 1300–19 November 1301). Felton had recently been the constable of Beaumaris, one of Edward's new Welsh fortresses.[10] Eighty-five men-at-arms and one hundred footsoldiers were ordered to reside at Linlithgow, though ten of the men-at-arms formed the retinue of the new sheriff, Sir Archibald Livingston. Carstairs and Kirkintilloch also feature in English accounts for the first time in 1301, most likely acquired as the king's army passed them en route to Glasgow, in the case of Carstairs, and then to Dunipace, in the case of Kirkintilloch.

The fact that the constable of Carstairs, Sir Walter Burghdon, was also sheriff of Lanark indicates that the castle, belonging to the bishop of Glasgow, had been appropriated by the Crown to act as the centre of a sheriffdom. Perhaps there was nowhere in Lanark itself worth putting a garrison into, perhaps as a result of Wallace's early activities, though the motte is still visible today, or perhaps, given the terrible death of its first English sheriff, the town had been demoted. However, the Scots maintained their own sheriff, Sir Walter Logan, in the area, and it is likely that Burghdon did not have it all his own way even after 1301.[11]

Kirkintilloch, another Comyn of Badenoch castle, was probably garrisoned shortly after Linlithgow, since Sir William Fraunceys, the constable, chose twenty archers from the latter garrison to go there. They were joined by a total of twenty-seven men-at-arms and nineteen crossbowmen.[12] The English garrison community in Scotland was expanding annually, a sign of success, but equally an administrative nightmare. Even some of the private castles needed looking after; Dirleton in Lothian, for example, was again found to be so badly supplied that it was allowed to buy victuals from the Berwick store.[13] Though it is possible that non-payment of dues by the local populace was a major cause of this lack, it is equally likely that the area was suffering from a surfeit of military activity to the detriment of grain production.

Two more royal stores also emerge in 1301. The one at Ayr came under the overall control of James Dalilegh, the receiver at Carlisle who, despite enemy pressure, was able to issue flour, oats and wine from there in September. A royal clerk, John Jarum, had been appointed its keeper, under Dalilegh, by December.[14] The establishment of a garrison at Linlithgow – not to mention the king's residence there – brought about the first mention of a store at Blackness on the River Forth. Without this store, provisions could probably only have been brought up safely as far as Leith.[15]

The only evidence in this year for 'normal' administrative activity was once more in the sheriffdom of Edinburgh, where Sir John Kingston, the sheriff, was again able to collect the issues normally owed to the Scottish crown. Though we cannot rule out the generation of similar paperwork from other sheriffdoms which has not survived, it might also be the case that Edinburgh was the most secure sheriffdom in English hands; the garrison was certainly not involved in the preparations for a potential enemy attack. The variety of issues was very similar to those collected in the preceding year, indicating that the sheriff and his officers were still able to enforce their authority across the area under their jurisdiction.[16]

The Scottish administration was also busy in this year, to judge from the scraps we have left to work from. In July 1301, Sir John Soules issued letters patent confirming Sir Alexander Scrymgeour in certain rights belonging to the constableship of Dundee, presumably still firmly in Scottish hands, proving that the Scottish chancery, revived under Wallace, was still operational even if there is no evidence for the use of a royal seal. More important, however, was the appointment by 31 January 1301 of Master Nicholas Balmyle as chancellor. Since any revenues which found their way into the coffers of the Scottish administration were doubtless needed for the prosecution of the war, 'the rich abbey of Arbroath was made responsible for paying Master Nicholas's fee . . .'[17]

On balance, Edward and his mighty military machine made considerable progress in the process of reconquest in 1301 while the Scots, in military terms, had been forced into a largely reactive position, though there were moments when guerrilla tactics might regain the initiative. Nevertheless, the English military machine was reaching the limits of its capacity, for which the king's impotent fury at the frustration of his plans is evidence in itself.

Since we have practically no evidence for the Scottish side of this coin, the guardians may have experienced similar difficulties. However, the ability of the Scottish army to maintain itself in the field throughout much of the year suggests there was still widespread support for the restoration of King John and we should not forget that, even by the end of 1301, most of Scotland remained beyond even the nominal control of Edward's administration. Thus, although on one level the Scots looked increasingly likely to succumb to the intense pressure inflicted by these impressive English armies year after year, the whole picture suggests that the issue was far less clear-cut as English garrisons remained vulnerable to starvation and attack as Edward's coffers grew emptier and emptier. To this must be added another dimension which has hitherto played little part in this story, though it has been grumbling away in the background: continental diplomacy.

The truce of Asnières not only demanded the suspension of hostilities between Scotland and England until 1 November 1302, thereby ruling out a summer campaign; it also, far more controversially, stipulated that the French should hold certain lands in Scotland for its duration. These were:

... the lands, possessions, rents ... which the king of England or someone on his behalf has taken or acquired which the king of France says were occupied from John Balliol or from the Scots since the messengers of the king of France came to the king of England, or which will be taken before the ratification of this present treaty made by the king of England, that these shall be in the hand of the said king of France until the Feast of All Saints to come [1 November 1302].

All this territory was to be handed over by 16 February 1302, to be administered by King Philip as he saw fit. Provision was also made to preserve the rights of the *menu people*, the lesser folk who held land by heritage, perhaps the peculiarly Scottish 'kindly tenants', who maintained such rights because of the continued occupation of their land by themselves and their ancestors.[18]

Since English ambassadors had been appointed on 24 August, presumably shortly after 'the messengers of the King of France came to the King of England',[19] the terms of the truce probably encompassed most of the castles captured during the summer campaign, such as Bothwell, possibly Kirkintilloch, Turnberry and Dalswinton. Ayr and Carstairs might just have avoided inclusion. Thus, according to this extraordinary agreement, a large chunk of the south-west was to be handed over to the French. Taken at face value, this would have been a remarkable humiliation for King Edward, not to mention a dreadful waste of the summer campaign if the revenues from captured lands were to find their way into the coffers of King Philip rather than his own.

So why agree to such humiliating, even dangerous, terms? The answer surely lies in the fact that warfare in this period, just like any other, was inextricably bound up with politics. It was thus profoundly affected by shifts in international opinion, most particularly, in this case, centring on the pope, Boniface VIII, as well as the powerful French king. The Scots at the papal court

– Master William Frere, archdeacon of Lothian, Master William of Eaglesham and Master Baldred Bisset – had been extremely busy in May 1301, pressing forward the Scottish counter-arguments to the case presented for Edward's claim to the overlordship of Scotland in the previous year. They claimed to be able to directly refute more than one of the English arguments: the Scots had never acknowledged Edward's suzerainty 'by a decree of their entire nation', as the latter asserted, nor did the English king have 'full possession of Scotland ... but only of certain places in the dioceses of St Andrews and Glasgow'. The Scots at Rome hoped that the pope 'will pronounce judgement on this affair between them and you [King Edward] and that he [the pope] will immediately forbid you to engage in any kind of warlike acts against them'. The Scottish request for a papal pronouncement on the status of Scotland's kingship – an issue that most rulers felt was none of the pope's business – surely made dealing with a fellow king, even one as wily as Philip, a more acceptable alternative to Edward.

French pressure on both the pope and the English was also vital to the Scots. Of crucial importance to the events taking place in Scotland itself was the release of John Balliol from papal custody at some point over the summer or early autumn of 1301; he then returned to his ancestral estates in Picardy in France. The imminent return of King John to his kingdom was expected not just by the Scots, but by Edward as well, provoking the extraordinary admission that '... [it is feared] that the kingdom of Scotland may be removed out of the king's hands (which God forbid!) and handed over to Sir John Balliol or to his son ...'[20]

It was against this background that the negotiations between the French and the English were conducted at Asnières. Edward was undoubtedly very concerned about his diplomatic position. He faced the possibility that the pope would explicitly prohibit him from continuing the war – a ban that would have been difficult for even the diplomatic skills of his chancellor Walter Langton to circumvent, since the ultimate sanction of excommunication would certainly have followed. At the same time, the possibility of King John's return can have done little to boost English morale in Scotland, while the Scots must have believed that victory would soon be theirs.

So, although the financial and supply difficulties encountered by the English army meant that the king and his men endured a miserable winter in Scotland, this cannot have been what caused Edward to conclude the truce since he had apparently already agreed to it in principle in August 1301. The period up to February 1302 was therefore used to consolidate the English hold in Scotland, primarily through building programmes for most of the new castles in Edward's hands in preparation for future campaigns. The purveyance ordered in October 1301 was needed to feed English garrisons and the army until it came home at the beginning of the truce.[21]

But that still leaves a few questions. Most particularly, if Edward knew of the likely conditions of the truce, why did he want to reduce Stirling castle over the winter of 1301–2, which would, if captured, have then been handed over to the French? Perhaps he was gambling on the likelihood that the agreement would never actually be implemented, given that France hadn't lifted a finger to help Scotland when he invaded in 1296. Alternatively, with the arrival of news of John Balliol's release into King Philip's custody, the *raison-d'être* for the truce – so far as Edward was concerned – may have been to prevent a French invasion in 1302. At the same time, the English army's presence in Scotland would preclude a surprise winter attack on King John's behalf before the agreement was struck.

Balliol's release, implying as it did the active support of King Philip, if not Pope Boniface (we don't really know if this was a formal release or a less formal kidnapping) marked the zenith of Scottish achievements in the diplomatic arena.[22] The English king was now firmly on the defensive, even if Scottish military activities were also curtailed. However, this diplomatic success had another important consequence: the return of the earl of

Carrick to King Edward's peace. Now nearly twenty-eight years old, it had been one thing for the earl to act as guardian in King John's name with the latter very much out of the picture; it was quite another to remain on the Scottish side if Balliol really might return to reclaim his throne.

While not denying patriotism as one possible motivation, the main reason behind Carrick's attempt to work with the Comyns in maintaining Scottish government and its military machine was surely his obsession with the throne and the elevation and maintenance of his position within the Scottish political community as a step towards it. That claim was, of course, currently vested in Carrick's father, Bruce 6, who remained resolutely on Edward's side, but this does not decrease the volumes spoken by Carrick's action in 1302. A free Scotland and a Bruce king were surely synonymous in his mind even if a free Scotland and a Balliol king were rooted in the minds of most Scots and certainly those running the patriotic administration.

The capture of Turnberry in September 1301 may also have influenced Carrick's decision to change sides. The English were now making headway in his own earldom, as well as controlling his father's lordship of Annandale.[23] Although the silence about his activities throughout 1301 suggests that he was already effectively a neutral figure, the lack of information on Scottish military operations should make us wary of presuming that he failed to try to protect his own lands. We should also remember that Carrick had been here before, the family losing first their earldom in 1293 and then the rest of their Scottish lands with the death of the Competitor in March 1295.

According to one chronicler, Bruce gave himself up to Sir John de St John, presumably at his own family's castle at Lochmaben. St John was certainly not with Edward and the rest of the court at Linlithgow, though he was imminently expected there to help to organise the planned building of a pele, according to a royal letter of 21 February 1302. A petition from Bruce, probably from 1305, implies that he indeed met with Sir John.

He was then granted certain conditions, including a grant of Sir Ingram d'Umfraville's lands in Carrick (possibly as a payback for d'Umfraville's replacement of the earl as guardian) 'in the presence of many good people'. Carrick was perhaps then sent on to perform homage to the English king personally.[24]

After Edward's departure for England from Linlithgow on 1 February, Bruce remained there as part of a Scottish council along with Sir John Segrave, Sir John Botetourt, Sir Robert Clifford, Sir William Latimer, Sir John de St John, Sir Thomas Furnivall, Sir Hugh Audley, and Sir Nicholas Malemeyns. These nine were all issued with victuals by Ralph Benton, the keeper of the store at Linlithgow, on 4 March.[25]

The exact meaning of Carrick's submission terms has been argued over in detail and there is still dispute as to whether *le droit* in the document that formalised his return to Edward's peace refers to Bruce's claim to the throne, or merely to his Scottish estates. But it is surely fair to say that the degree of speculation over a document which, by its very nature, should have been unambiguous, suggests that one or both parties wished to leave part of it vague.[26] It is also significant, that the word 'le' is used with 'droit', rather than 'mon', until one remembers that the Bruce claim to the throne did not rest with the earl of Carrick, but with his father; he could not, therefore, refer to it as his own.

It is perhaps useful to speculate what Carrick's submission terms might have been if he had submitted a year earlier, or a year later, when the imminent return of King John was not uppermost in everyone's minds. It is likely that he would have been confirmed in his lands and property on similar terms to those granted to Sir John Comyn, on behalf of the Scots in general, in February 1304. The difference in 1302 between the earl of Carrick and every other Scottish noble of a similar rank and background was his family's claim to the throne, a claim which Edward was perhaps prepared to recognise, albeit covertly, only at a time when the return of King John with the backing of a French army was a realistic possibility. If that possibility became reality, Edward could have attempted to divide the Scottish nobility by proclaiming Bruce of Annandale as king, reversing the judgement of his court in 1292 and his own decision, in 1296, to abolish the Scottish kingship in 1296. There is perhaps only one element in this difficult period about which we can be certain: if Edward gave the Bruce claim to the throne any kind of credence, it was only because of the difficult circumstances in which the English king found himself in 1301–2. This was plan B, but plan A had not failed yet.

On 12 and 14 February 1302 the king – en route back to England – and his council at Roxburgh made various ordinances for the keeping of the garrisons during the truce (see Tables 1–4). The standing army in Berwick town was now relatively small at ten men-at-arms, forty crossbowmen and one hundred and forty archers under Sir Edmund Hastings. However, Sir Alexander Balliol in Selkirk Forest had access to six hundred footsoldiers at four days' warning and one thousand at eight days' warning, should any infringements of the truce take place in that area. It is not clear where these footsoldiers were to come from, although, given the numbers and the time needed to raise them, at least some were probably to be sent from south of the border. No agreement survives with St John for the keeping of the western march and the garrisons of Dumfries and Lochmaben. However, he was still paid £150 for his service with sixty men-at-arms for the Easter term up to 10 June 1302.[27]

As in 1300, no payment was to be made for the loss of horses during the period of the truce. It was also ordained that some of the footsoldiers in the garrisons of Roxburgh, Berwick town, Jedburgh and Berwick castle should be carpenters and masons to make repairs to the walls and houses, in the case of the castles, and to begin the construction of a pele (essentially a palisade) and other defences, in the case of Berwick town. Berwick castle was apparently in something of a state. On 17 March 1302 Edward ordered John Droxford, on the advice of Ralph Manton, 'who has seen what is lacking in the said castle, to bring about such repairs as you see should be done'.[28] On 12 and 14 February 1302 detailed ordinances were also made for the building works to be constructed at Linlithgow and Selkirk.

The defects of the royal manor at Linlithgow – set on a broad plain twenty miles west of Edinburgh in what was probably prime hunting country – had come to the king's attention upon his arrival there in October 1301, prompting him to enlist the services of eighty-one diggers and ninety-one carpenters from 12 November. Cementers, scythers and coverers were also involved in making the 'king's chambers' up until 28 November. The town's defences were to be strengthened with various kinds of crossbows, quarrels and belts sent up from England.

Edward had had plenty of time over the winter to work out his plans for the pele he wanted built around the existing manor house. Sir John Kingston, the sheriff of Edinburgh and Sir Archibald Livingstone, the sheriff of Linlithgow, were appointed 'overseers and ordainers' of the building of a 'forcelette'. A clerk, Henry Brandeston, was appointed to pay the wages of those involved in the building work and each sheriff was to provide a clerk to act as comptroller. The master carpenters were to be Master Thomas Houghton, who had previously resided at Edinburgh, and Master Adam Glasham, who had worked on Edward's first pele in Scotland at Lochmaben. The sheriff of York was to send as many carpenters, masons and diggers as were deemed necessary, and the sheriffs of Edinburgh, Linlithgow, Stirling[29] and Lanark were all to provide carts and wagons.

Lastly, as a measure of the importance, and indeed the scale, of the works envisaged at Linlithgow, the king sent for the man who had been the architect of the great Edwardian castles in Wales, the Savoyard, Master James de St George. Both Master James and Master Thomas Houghton had been involved in the works at Beaumaris in Wales, where Felton – the new keeper of Linlithgow – had also served.[30] These construction projects were clearly intended to raise the status of the existing structure to that of a fortified stronghold, effectively a castle.[31]

Master James arrived in Scotland by the end of April 1302 and on 23 May an indenture giving exact details of the works to be undertaken was issued. A ditch was to encircle the fortification, as deep and wide as possible so that water from the nearby loch could flow through it. A stone gate and two stone towers had been originally planned, but the king now changed his mind – presumably because of financial constraints – and 'would have the gates and towers of timber and the peel itself to be built of untrimmed logs'. The tower of the adjacent church of St Michael and the church itself were also to be reinforced. Finally, another 'good defensible ditch' was to be made behind the castle from one end of the pele to the other, beyond a ridge near the loch, to protect the new construction from an attack by water. Another palisade was to be constructed on top of the ridge.[32]

Progress was swift. By 14 September 1302, it was reported that there was 'nothing to do here, except fourteen perches [75 yards] of "pele" and six brattices [wooden parapets]'.[33] But despite the success of the building programme, the enterprise was still plagued with the usual money problems and payments to those working at Linlithgow were soon badly in arrears. In 1303, when the king was planning works at Dunfermline, the Linlithgow men categorically refused to be sent there, because they were still owed so much.[34]

Selkirk castle also required attention because of the basic nature of its structure. The first reference to it occurs as early as 1120, in the foundation charter of Selkirk Abbey. The royal burgh, situated on the junction of the rivers Ettrick and Yarrow on a natural escarpment, grew up around the castle, which was a favourite residence of the early kings of Scots – William the Lion issued at least twenty-seven charters while staying there.[35] However, an earthwork located in the grounds of a Georgian mansion house on the outskirts of the town is all that remains of both the early castle and the Edwardian pele constructed in 1302.

The tower dominating both was placed on the summit of this mound, which has a diameter of 40 feet.[36]

The detailed plans envisaged for Selkirk were very similar to those for Linlithgow though the use of stone suggests that it was meant to be a more impressive edifice, perhaps because of its importance to the security of the Forest. It would also join the important network of south-eastern garrisons comprising Berwick, Roxburgh, Jedburgh and Edinburgh. Sir Alexander Balliol and Sir Robert Hastangs were to oversee the work and provide workmen and transport, while the clerk, William Rue, was to be responsible for paying wages and 'attendant expenses'. Balliol and Hastangs were also each to provide a comptroller to double-check the finances. Master Reginald the engineer, who was usually at Berwick, and Master Stephen of Northampton were appointed as master carpenters. The sheriff of Northumberland was to send enough carpenters, diggers and masons for the work and sufficient carriage for transporting the 'necessary materials'.[37] By September 1302 it was not quite completed:

> The tower of the fortress is finished, except the roof, from a lack of 'plunk' [planking]; a postern is made out of the same to the west, faced with stone; a drawbridge and portcullis, with a good brattice above; the stone work of said bridge is half finished. And fourteen perches [75 yards] of 'pele' have been completed from one part of the tower to the other. There are forty-three perches [237 yards] of 'pele' yet to make. The stonework of the main gate of the fortress is raised above ground to the drawbridge.

These figures suggest that the new structure covered a couple of acres in area, at a total cost of £1,372 13s. 10d.[38] The reason for the delay may be connected, at least in part, with continuing Scottish attacks; on 6 June 1302, Sir Robert Hastangs, as 'keeper of our works at Selkirk', was paid 100 marks to make an expedition 'without delay'. Five months later, on 8 November, £200 was issued by the exchequer at York, together with twelve crossbows and the equipment to go with them, to be taken safely to Roxburgh in dangerous conditions to Sir Robert Hastangs for the works at Selkirk.[39] Although the Forest was not as much of a problem for the English garrisons as it had once been, it could still provide cover for Edward's enemies.

1302 began well for the Scots. A Scottish parliament met at Scone on 23 February and was informed of Bishop Lamberton's success in including Scotland in the Anglo-French truce of Asnières.[40] The defection of the earl of Carrick had presumably also come to the attention of his erstwhile colleagues by this time. Although this meant that his earldom's 'army' could probably no longer be called out on behalf of King John,[41] we should not presume that his defection was hugely significant. Bruce was both a particular case and already something of a political has-been, rather than the thin end of the wedge.

If anything, there is more evidence during this year for the devastating effects of Scottish military activity, particularly cross-border raiding. On 14 August 1302, the sheriff of Northumberland was ordered to choose a coroner in place of one Nicholas Middleton 'whom the king has caused to be amoved from the office as it is testified before the king that Nicholas's lands have been much destroyed and wasted by the Scots . . .' Ten days later Edward also informed the chancellor, Walter Langton, that the people of Northumberland were excused from their duties of castleguard [the obligation of a tenant to defend his lord's castle for a fixed period of time] at Newcastle because their lands had been '. . . destroyed by the Scots enemies'. In October, the sheriff of Cumberland, Sir William Mulcastre, sought respite for just over half of the £222 9s. 11d. he owed to the exchequer, claiming that he had not been able to levy this money 'as the county was so wasted and destroyed by the Scottish war'.[42]

The Scots should not, of course, have inflicted this damage in 1302, because of the truce, and probably reflects what they'd been doing in any year between 1298 and 1301, suggesting a long-standing, and surely systematic, policy of attacking, terrorising and destroying the lands and people of the north of England. Though King Robert Bruce adopted this policy and, as he so often did, made it his own, it had become a particularly unpleasant feature of this bitter war from as early as 1297.[43] The inhabitants of Northumberland and Cumberland, particularly, were caught between the rock of Edward's continuing demands to sustain the English war effort, and the hard place of being on the front line when the Scots crossed the border.

The timing of the indentures for Linlithgow and Selkirk (12 and 14 February 1302) are extremely significant when it is remembered that the date set for handing over castles captured during the previous campaign to the French was 16 February. The building works, together with arrangements for their garrisons, make it clear that Edward had little or no intention of handing them over. There is no way of telling, of course, whether he had ever meant to fulfil that part of the truce. Given the number of castles recaptured late in 1301, his inclination would surely have been to default if he could possibly get away with it. Presumably as the winter progressed and there was no sign of a French expedition on behalf of King John before the ratification of the truce, Edward began to feel confident enough to ignore the 16 February deadline and retain the castles taken in the previous year.

This policy was vindicated on 11 July 1302 when the Flemings defeated the French army at Courtrai (modern Kortrijk), destroying all hopes that Philip IV would take direct action in Scotland on behalf of King John.[44] Although the English king could not have predicted such a defeat, he may have been ready to call King Philip's bluff, based on the shrewd suspicion that the French rarely wished to expend much cost and effort – as opposed to making diplomatic threats – on the Scottish cause. To make matters considerably worse for the Scots, papal pressure on the English king had also eased by the end of 1302 as a result of the worsening quarrel between Boniface VIII and King Philip, re-establishing King Edward as an attractive papal ally. Indeed, the pope now turned directly on the Scottish church, supporting Edward's claims; the Scottish bishops were encouraged to submit and the bishop of Glasgow was explicitly ordered to cease his rebellious activities.[45] It would be naïve to suggest that the support of these important European powers for Scotland had ever been based on altruism rather than pragmatism but the bottom line was that both now had need of England, or at least could do without English enmity. The Scots were equally motivated by political expediency and doubtless had little sympathy for the burghers of Flanders and their blow for freedom against the French at Courtrai. In practical terms, the battle for Scotland was now once more entirely dependent on the war of attrition being played out on the ground rather than in the courts of Europe, a battle that neither side seemed to be winning.

In the meantime, the truce of Asnières was perhaps indirectly responsible for the finalisation of the town-planning exercise for Berwick which had been initiated to so little effect in 1296. Even though the new English burgesses there were responsible for reviving Edward's interest in the town, the truce provided him with some time to reconsider matters which had moved to the bottom of the pile during the years of war.

On 4 July 1302 the king ordered an inquest to be held 'to inquire by what services a burgage and four 'places' are held by Nicholas Carlisle, the king's serjeant in Berwick, and whether forty acres lying between said town and its fosses [ditches] ... might be granted, without damage, to Nicholas to hold of the king'. The policy of giving garrison members a stake in the communities to which they now belonged, as at Carlisle, was clearly in operation in Berwick.

The inquest was held on 30 July before Sir Walter Amersham, Edward's Scottish chancellor, Sir Edmund Hastings, warden of Berwick town, and Sir John Burdon, the sheriff, by a jury of sixteen. These sixteen asserted that Nicholas Carlisle held the burgage 'which was Ralph Phelipe's' and three places belonging to the bishop of Moray, William the Scriptor and Henry Stirling. These four had presumably forfeited their lands in 1296. As for the forty acres, it was asserted that they were held:

> ... in the late King Alexander's time by various burgesses of Berwick freely without any *reddendum* [payment], as is pertinent of their burgages, and when the said burgh was founded [pre-1124] they were given to the burgesses to build, if any wished to do so, and there are streets in said ground arranged for this.

Now, however, these lands were held by 'various burgesses of the king of England for a yearly payment of 2s.'

These 'various burgesses', numbering thirty, are named and include the main English officials in Scotland, including Amersham, the chancellor, Sir John Weston, the receiver, and Master Robert Heron, the comptroller and keeper of the customs at Berwick. Five were English burgesses resident in Berwick, who also sat on the jury of inquest (so no conflict of interest there then!). The remaining twenty-two included Reginald the engineer, currently at Selkirk, and two ship owners, John Spark of Newcastle and John Packer of Sandwich, who had served the king faithfully over the years in bringing up supplies to the north. Edward had at least been successful in making Berwick a base for those who formed the backbone of the English administration of Scotland.

Though four of the jurors appear to have been burgesses of Berwick before 1296 – as the tone of their findings also suggests – none of those holding land in the forty acres can be described without doubt as long-standing Scottish inhabitants of the burgh. Though technically the term 'burgesses of the King of England' now applied equally to any 'British' burgess, it is highly likely that these thirty had been among those sent north in 1297. But, no matter how recently they, or the other jurors, had come to the town, they did not mince their words on the subject of their rights, stating categorically that:

> ... this ground cannot, without the greatest injury to the king and the confusion and destruction of the aforesaid town be held wholly [*integre*] by Nicholas or any other; for he might build as good or a better town there than the present and the burgesses have no other place within or without their town where they can have a handful of grass or pasture, or any other easement, except these forty acres, whereon all the burgesses, both small and great, have common pasture in open time by use and wont, and they [the 40 acres] are divided in small divisions as in the time of King Alexander among the burgesses.[46]

This was not the only petition addressed to Edward by the burgesses of Berwick in this year. Of far more importance was their quest for a charter of liberties, because 'they are new men come into the town and had and have great need of the king's aid and have several times asked him, for his own benefit and the profit of his town of Berwick, as well as of the burgesses inhabitant'. Edward had, in fact, promised them certain franchises when he was at Roxburgh en route for England in February 1302, which had encouraged a further influx of 'merchants and sufficient persons' to the burgh.[47]

As a result of this petition, Edward granted Berwick a charter of privileges on 4 August 1302. These consisted of the right to be a free burgh, with burgesses and a merchant guild and 'Hanse' (guild entry fee), the right to elect a mayor and four bailiffs yearly, as well as a coroner. The burgesses were also permitted to have a prison inside, and a gallows outside the burgh, as well as a twice-weekly market on Monday and Friday, and a fair each year from 3 May to 24 June.

This charter of privileges restored to Berwick the rights and privileges which it had long enjoyed – there had been a provost, burgesses and common seal attached to the burgh since at least 1212,[48] and a mayor and commune since 1235. But many of these privileges had presumably fallen into abeyance during the difficult circumstances of the conquest of 1296. A letter was sent to the keeper of Berwick town, Sir Edmund Hastings, on the same date, informing him of these concessions and ordering him to present the new mayor to the chancellor of Scotland, as Edward's representative, to make his fealty. Hastings was then ordered 'not to intermeddle further in the custody of the town'.[49]

Having been awarded the status of a free borough, Berwick was now included among the other English trading centres for administrative purposes. Thus, on 13 August 1302, John Spark and William Brown, two of the 40s. acre burgesses, were appointed as 'collectors and receivers in ports of the new customs of 2s. a barrel, which the merchant vintners of the duchy [of Aquitaine] have granted to the king, in addition to the old customs'.[50] Berwick was now to all intents and purposes in England.

It could be argued that the granting of this charter of liberties at the prompting of the burgesses indicates a considerable degree of confidence in the English grip on this furthermost south-eastern corner of Scotland. There is likely to be much truth in that, though doubtless if the military situation degenerated once more, it would have been necessary to restore the burgh to military control.

Berwick's good fortune was not the only indication that the previous year's military gains were being translated into advances in administrative control. Thomas Fishburn, a former keeper of the Rolls of Scotland, chose this year to petition the king again regarding the restoration of '20 marks of yearly rent in Ednam in the sheriffdom of Roxburgh'. He had been regranted it in 1296 but Surrey had been unable to enforce the king's writ. Whether or not Fishburn's perception of increased English authority was accurate is, unfortunately, impossible to say. Given that Sir John de St John, who was given the writ to execute, died a few weeks later, it is likely that poor Thomas remained bereft of his twenty marks; on the other hand, the fact that there is no evidence that he petitioned the king later – when most such outstanding demands were made – suggests he was successful in 1302. The important point is that he considered it worthwhile making the petition in the first place.[51]

There were the first stirrings of advances in administration further west too. On 15 August 1302, in the indenture setting out the arrangements made with Sir Walter Burghdon for the keeping of the sheriffdom of Lanark, it was stated that 'Sir James Dalilegh, the escheator there, is to inquire and certify ... what sum Sir Walter has received in his bailiwick and deduct the same'.[52] Dalilegh, more usually the receiver at Carlisle, had probably been appointed escheator – a particularly Scottish office – in 1301, when the English grip on the south-west was extended into Lanarkshire and Ayrshire. However, the mere fact that he was supposed to account for the issues of lands in English hands does not mean there was necessarily much revenue to account for. Edward's edicts were often issued more in the hope than the realistic expectation that Scotland might start to pay for itself.

It has certainly been suggested that the orderly set of accounts produced by Dalilegh in his office as escheator for regnal years 31 and 32 (20 November 1302 to 29 November 1304) shows that 'whenever the English won any Scottish territory they were able to use an established revenue-collecting and accounting system'. Be that as it may, this set of accounts – the first of its kind since Edward laid claim to ruling Scotland directly – began only in the Martinmas term (c. 11 November) for 1303, when the conquest of Scotland was once more within the English king's grasp. Even then, it was noted more than once that lands even in Lanarkshire could not be accounted for in the previous Pentecost term because they were 'in the hands of the Scots'. On balance, there is only clear-cut evidence at Berwick and in the sheriffdom of Edinburgh (as well perhaps as Roxburghshire and Berwickshire, which were expected to make a contribution to the upkeep of their garrisons from 1302) for the ability of Edward's officials to make a coherent account of the potential revenues of their bailiwicks before late 1303, though small amounts were undoubtedly collected. On the other hand, it was probably true that 'the Scots . . . must have been able to keep this system in operation', though to what degree is, of course, impossible to ascertain for lack of evidence. But the guardians had to pay for the war effort somehow, even if some parts of southern Scotland surely evaded paying anything to either government.[53]

And in a significant departure from attitudes in 1296, it seems that Edward's officials were now aware of the need to administer their offices effectively and impartially. However, there were undoubtedly conflicting attitudes among royal officials, highlighting the fact that this was still a war situation. In September 1302, Edward received two letters, from Sir Robert Hastangs, sheriff of Roxburgh, and Sir Hugh Audley, the keeper of Selkirk Forest. The pair had recently been involved in the pursuit of thieves in the sheriffdom of Roxburgh.

According to Audley, whose letter reached the king first, an arrangement had been made between himself, the sheriff of Roxburgh, the latter's brother, Sir Richard Hastangs, and Sir Alexander Balliol, 'that they should attack at three points the moor of Alkirk [near Selkirk] in which some robbers infesting the county of Roxburgh had taken refuge'. Audley and his foresters came across them first 'in a house' and captured them all when they fled, returning to the house to collect the stolen cattle. Hastangs, as sheriff, then demanded that Audley hand them all over. 'As he [Audley] wished to avoid strife, he gave up the beasts but kept the prisoners till he knew the king's will. The foresters pray the king for the goods of the resetter [the fence for stolen goods], as others have what they can gain on the enemy'.

Hastangs' version of these events was basically the same, with the additional information that the twelve thieves captured by Sir Hugh 'in one of their greatest retreats' had already been indicted before him as sheriff of Roxburgh. Though Audley did indeed give up 'a part of the bestial', the thieves had been sent 'to the prison of Berwick or Bamburgh, he [Hastangs] does not know which'. The problem, as Hastangs himself put it, was that Sir Hugh 'claims them and their ransom as prisoners of war, under the king's grant of what he can gain upon the enemy'. The sheriff, on the other hand, asserted that 'they are common and notorious thieves and have made such riot in the county that the people told him that they expected him to clear them out'. Hastangs wanted them returned to prison at Roxburgh 'or he will find no man in the county willing to obey him after his authority has been defied'.[54]

This was a classic catch twenty-two situation. Audley and his men, in Selkirk Forest, were, or at least had been, in the middle of a war zone and regarded the potential profit to be made from this conflict as a condition of their service. Indeed, the extent to which individual officers were forced to use their own money in the king's employ meant that some form of return from the enemy was the least they could expect.

Hastangs had a quite different perspective on this issue. He had been sheriff of Roxburgh now for five years and the local population were presumably used to the idea that if any justice was to be done, he was the man to do it. Criminal activity did not stop just because there was a war on; indeed, the collapse of normal government tended to make theft in particular more lucrative and easier to get away with. And, of course, Wallace and subsequent Scottish leaders had given cattle-reiving the kudos of a patriotic endeavour. For the inhabitants of Roxburgh, the issue was equally simple; their goods had been stolen and their acceptance of Hastangs' administration and, through him, that of Edward himself, depended on the sheriff's ability to bring the perpetrators to justice. If only we knew the king's judgement on the subject.

The most substantial example of an increasingly confident English administration was the court held at Linlithgow between 8 October and 5 November 1302 in the presence of Master James de St George as lieutenant of the keeper of the town, Sir Archibald Livingston, and Sir William Felton, constable of the castle. It is not entirely clear whether this was a burgh court, or a shrieval one, since Livingston was both keeper of the town and sheriff.

A variety of crimes and misdemeanours were brought before it and a few Scots sought to take advantage of this opportunity to pursue claims, though English also sued Scots. The most interesting case concerned an action brought by Christina of Edinburgh against Master Adam Glasham, one of the master carpenters. He was accused of 'unjustly keeping from her a plumb-line, to her damage'. Adam claimed the lead was his. Interestingly, Christina's pledges were both members of the garrison, Master Thomas Houghton, the other master carpenter, and Adam Tyndale. Glasham was found guilty and he and his pledges ordered to be fined.

But Glasham then allegedly compounded his crime by beating up Christina. When he was brought back to court, he then made a plea of essoin (excuse) against her, but she challenged the validity of this plea because 'according to the law of Scotland, after the law had given bail, essoin should not be allowed'. The hearing was adjourned, presumably to allow the English officers to find out if Christina was correct about the legal position. However, Glasham managed to avoid subsequent court hearings by pleading illness and there are no records of any further proceedings.[55]

Despite earlier accusations against Edward's regime, the English officials running this court do appear to have made an effort to be even-handed, as witnessed by the fact that a local woman, supported in her testimony by two members of the garrison, was successfully able to prosecute another garrison member. Not only that, but the reference to essoin makes it clear that it was expected that those making judgement would adhere to the laws and customs of the northern kingdom, rather than English practice.

This cannot have been easy for the Edwardian government, given that most officials were presumably unversed in Scots law and would require the services of native experts. Nevertheless, the fact that they were prepared to tolerate Scottish sensibilities on this issue – in contrast to 1296/7 – indicates the degree to which this reconquest relied on a two-way relationship between 'victors' and 'vanquished'. Christina's original involvement with the garrison, together with the activities of Eva of Stirling, indicate that that relationship went on at all levels, though the fact that both of these examples involve women might lead to some interesting conclusions about gender, patriotism and pragmatism if it were not for the fact that two is really too few from which to draw any conclusions.

Basic economics – the need, above all, to make a living and provide for dependants – meant that those for whom the English presence was now an apparently permanent reality would find it difficult to avoid interaction and co-operation, which in turn might promote greater acceptance. Though it could be argued that such evidence just happens to have survived for this year rather than others, it is far more likely that it does represent an increased ability, in certain restricted areas, to run a normal administration. The gains of the previous few years surely derived less from the establishment of nominal English control throughout more of Scotland than in the removal of the Scottish government's ability to challenge Edward's rule in areas which had long been dominated, but not completely convinced, by the English presence. The king knew what he was doing in singling out the 'middling folk'.

Edward's demands on his own subjects, though certainly lightened by the truce and the absence of a campaign, by no means disappeared altogether, not least because of the backlog of debt from previous years. For example, the Welsh troops who had served with Prince Edward in 1301 were supposed to receive the £4000 owed to them as wages from the fifteenth to be raised in the counties of Hereford, Gloucester, Worcester, Devon, Warwick, Leicester, Shropshire and Stafford in 1302. Unfortunately, this was still not enough and, on 13 June 1302, the exchequer was ordered to assign even more counties to make the payment 'so that the king can have them [the Welsh] at other times more readily for his business'.[56] By this point in the war, expediency, rather than one's place in the payment queue, played the most crucial role in dictating where hard-pressed royal issues were spent.

The garrisons also obviously needed to be paid. On 2 May 1302 Sir Walter Amersham, described again as chancellor, and Master John Weston, the paymaster, were ordered to lay out £536 13s. 4d. on the second instalment of wages for the Easter term (9 May – 1 June), indicating that the men-at-arms were certainly being paid in advance. This was divided among Sir John de St John and his retinue, and the garrisons of Berwick town, Berwick castle, Roxburgh, Jedburgh, Carstairs, Edinburgh and Bothwell. £200 was also to be sent to Linlithgow and Selkirk for the works there. The total expenditure came to £547 1s. and the shortfall was to be met, in the case of the garrisons of Berwick, Roxburgh and Jedburgh, from the issues of these areas.[57]

Payment was also to be made to Sir John FitzMarmaduke, keeper of the earl of Lincoln's lands of Strathgryfe. On 15 February, he was issued with a full month's wages while he was still with the king at Roxburgh. At the end of that month, and for each month following, the money was to be sent to Edinburgh, from there to Carstairs and on to Bothwell on the River Clyde, less than ten miles south-east of Glasgow, where Sir John would pick it up, a distance of over one hundred miles of fairly rugged terrain. Such an excessively complicated procedure suggests that the king did not feel happy about money being transported inland from the store at Ayr, and so it had to come from Berwick. Indeed, FitzMarmaduke's job was explicitly 'to save this land [Strathgryfe] and the surrounding area'. He could not yet run it effectively.[58]

Even though the truce ruled out a campaign, purveyance was also still required for the garrisons. One-third of the supplies collected in England was to be sent to Berwick, while the rest was to be delivered to Edinburgh. The advances made in the last year are reflected in these arrangements – the new garrisons at Linlithgow, including the workmen building the pele, Carstairs, Bothwell and even the earl of Lincoln's men in Strathgryfe were probably all supplied from the east. Edinburgh, which was nearer to them than Berwick, thus became more important as a store. The western garrisons of Dumfries, Lochmaben and Ayr were to be provisioned from Ireland.[59]

By 1302 Edward had decided that those to whom he had granted lands in Scotland could now, and definitely should, provide castleguard – men-at-arms for duty in the garrisons there.[60] Fifty-one individuals, including the earls of Lincoln and Warwick and Sir Walter Beauchamp, Edward's steward, as well as those, like Sir John de St John, Sir Robert Clifford, Sir Henry Percy, Sir John Kingston, Sir Robert Hastangs and Sir John Burdon, who had served, or were still serving in Scotland, were to provide the services of one hundred and fifteen men-at-arms. Obviously, this would prove a considerable saving to the crown.

However, it is clear from the memoranda concerning these troops that the arrangement was by no means working properly: thirty-two were recorded as 'not yet come' and so '... it is not surprising that no more was heard of this particular system', even if the majority do seem to have been provided. The important point to be drawn from the failure of men such as St John and Beauchamp, whose loyalty to the crown is beyond question, to fulfil their quotas is that they were not yet truly in possession of the lands for which they were to provide this service. Either that, or they were still owed so much that they had little incentive to give the king anything more.[61]

The fleet was another element of the military machine that needed to provide its service despite the lack of a campaign, again simply because the garrisons needed supplies all year, every year.

Edward was prepared to be lenient towards the Cinque Ports in particular, simply out of need;[62] however, the one offence he was more than ready to punish was the non-fulfilment of promised quotas.

The unprecedented regularity with which service was now demanded ensured that by 1302 many ports were refusing to send their ships. On 10 August 1302, two royal clerks were appointed to punish the townsfolk of no less than thirteen ports, including Portsmouth, Southampton and Plymouth, who had been ordered to supply a total of fourteen 'well-armed' ships for an expedition in that year. They had apparently taken 'no measures to do so, to the harm of that expedition' though it is not clear if this refers to a military endeavour planned for after the end of the truce.

At the end of the same month, an inquiry was ordered into the conduct of the men and mariners of one of the ships from Bristol, the *Michael*, 'who came in the company of the other ships towards Scotland on the king's service, and, after receiving the king's wages at Dublin, withdrew without leave'.[63] Such audacious behaviour was quite unacceptable. This point was made to the recalcitrant sailors, who now found themselves in prison, and on 13 November the constable of Bristol castle was ordered to release them because they had promised to serve the king 'faithfully' on his next expedition.[64] As was increasingly the case, Edward's need was greater than his wrath.

As the end of the truce (1 November 1302) approached, further arrangements were reached with the various garrison commanders and their men to guarantee their services from 1 September until Christmas.[65] As mentioned above, sixty of the four hundred and eighty-five men-at-arms were provided by those holding lands in Scotland. Each castle's store of provisions and military equipment was also checked, and any insufficiencies remedied. The numbers stated for each garrison in the surviving indentures (see Tables 1–4) indicate that there was little or no increase from the truce level, despite the expected resumption of hostilities.

However, Sir John de St John's retinue was increased from sixty to seventy-one men-at-arms with a brief 'to make mounted expeditions and to stay in the garrisons of the castles of Dumfries and Lochmaben'. Sir William Latimer and Sir John Segrave, based at Roxburgh and Berwick respectively, were appointed specifically 'to make horsed expeditions in various parts of Scotland as necessary', with a total of ninety-one men-at-arms between them. This was in addition to the usual force of seventeen men-at-arms, forty crossbowmen and one hundred and forty archers who remained stationed within Berwick town. The keepers of the castles of Linlithgow, Edinburgh, Jedburgh, Roxburgh and Berwick town were all to be allowed full wages while engaged on *chevauchées* (mounted expeditions) outside their own areas of jurisdiction, to be deducted from their *certa*.[66]

As the end of the truce approached, much had changed since its outset, though that was probably not all that obvious within Scotland itself. Yet there was still nothing inevitable about victory for King Edward. Despite the extremely disappointing diplomatic setbacks, the Scots could pride themselves on having contained the English south of the Forth/Clyde line for the past five years; despite, or rather, because of, Edward's military gains, the supply line was if anything in a worse state than ever. However, the stakes for both sides were increasing. By the end of 1302 the Scots had no immediate hopes of the return of their king, in whose name this war was being waged; Edward, on the other hand, though now free of diplomatic obstacles, was finding it more and more difficult to raise the required resources needed to finish the Scots off once and for all. Despite the truce, which had worked out surprisingly well for the English, the financial burden was still immense.

But such problems cannot have been restricted to Edward's exchequer; presumably the Scottish government was also finding it difficult to sustain an apparently endless war. The status quo was perhaps still an option, but 1302 provides sufficient evidence to suggest that, while Edward's subjects had complained longer, many Scots had now reached the point where they would protest loudest. And that meant that Edward's regime was finding increasing acceptance among the people of lowland Scotland, so long as the reward was firm and effective – but not too heavy-handed – government.

CHAPTER SIX

CHECKMATE

Safe-conducts to six Scots were issued on 15 August 1302 to allow them to meet two envoys of Philip of France in England, presumably seeking an extension of the truce. But Edward had other ideas, arranging for the reassertion of military pressure even before a full-scale campaign could be organised. On 11 September, Sir John Segrave and Sir Edmund Hastings at Berwick, Sir Alexander Balliol at Selkirk, Sir William Latimer at Roxburgh, Sir Walter Huntercombe (captain of Northumberland), and Sir Robert Clifford (keeper of the bishopric of Durham) were informed that, despite recent orders summoning them to a parliament in London in October, they should not 'in any way depart from Scotland or its marches'.[1] Edward was extremely concerned to ensure the security of his garrisons; nothing was to endanger future military success on the road to reconquest. On 24 September he wrote to Langton, the English treasurer, ordering him to be:

... attentive in such manner that our affairs should prosper, that the wages be well and promptly paid to our people who stay in these parts; and that you have well overlooked the castles of Scotland, the fortresses and other places which concern us there and that they be well provisioned, so that there will be no want and that the new castles which we are having made there have all that they need for the completion of their works. For if they are well provisioned everywhere, this will be a great security to the whole of our business there. And if our business goes well there, we hope that it will go well everywhere.[2]

On 14 September 1302, Edward received the news of the death of Sir John de St John, to whom he was 'much bound'. Indeed, this loyal servant was owed so much from the crown that writs had to be sent to the escheators and royal officials ordering them to 'take nothing' from his estate until the king had spoken to them. All the same, it took another two months for St John's executors to be given free administration of his affairs and for his debts at the exchequer to be discharged. His office as warden in Scotland was awarded to his son, another Sir John, until further orders, though local lord Sir Richard Siward took over in the meantime, 'that the district be not left unprovided'.³

By late September Edward had, in fact, decided that Sir John Botetourt should become warden in St John's place. The situation in the south-west was again worrying – as it tended to become the minute English armies disappeared back over the border – with starvation proving the biggest challenge to the security of the garrisons there. At the end of October 1302, the king received a message from Siward, delivered by 'his dear friend', Sir Ralph Manton. The latter had recently visited Lochmaben, but since his departure things had taken a turn for the worse. Siward supposedly had 'not above ten men-at-arms there [at Lochmaben] or at Dumfries . . . As to sustenance, he [Siward] has received nothing since he [Manton] left them except £10 then paid to him'. This was worrying news, especially considering that the late warden's retinue supposedly numbered seventy-one men-at-arms, split between the two garrisons.⁴ Sir Richard could report, however, that 'the country is quiet' and that 'the earl of Carrick went to parliament on Sunday 21 October', suggesting that the younger Bruce was now living at least some of the time on his father's lordship of Annandale, perhaps at Lochmaben itself, though he could also have 'popped in' coming south from his own castle of Turnberry.

As the autumn progressed, Edward continued to make arrangements for his garrisons with a view to the renewal of full-scale military activity as soon as possible. To that end, and before the expiry of the truce made any English movement outside their secure zones more dangerous, the king wished to find out exactly the state of the country west of Stirling. Speed was clearly uppermost in his mind. On 29 September, he wrote to Sir John Segrave at Berwick, ordering:

> that the expedition lately arranged between you and Ralph Manton, our cofferer, should be done with all haste and in the best manner that you can, so that you go by Stirling and ... the ... by Kirkintilloch, as near as you can by our enemies in the lands which are in our hands, so that it can be done in safety ... and the foray being thus done (inform us by your letters), send a special man to tell us the manner in which it was done, together with the condition and news from parts of Scotland with all possible haste.[5]

The enemy seems to have been largely concentrated north of Glasgow and Stirling. Segrave and Manton could certainly have gone west in comparative safety along the southern banks of the Forth, via Linlithgow, towards Kirkintilloch, avoiding Stirling. But the king was still preoccupied with 'the gateway to the north'. Without control of Stirling castle, the English were hemmed in below the Forth, while the Scots could move about freely at least as far south as Lennox north of Glasgow and Menteith, west of Stirling.

On 7 November 1302 the first summonses went out for a campaign planned to begin on 26 May 1303. The muster point was Berwick. A request for service was also issued to 'the magnates and commonalty of the land of Ireland', under the considerable inducement of a reduction or cancellation of any debts to the king.[6]

Orders for purveyance were sent out to seven English counties, who were to send supplies to Berwick before the soldiers were due to arrive. The king ordered that 'all purchases are to be paid for', presumably, and as usual, as the only means of persuading those to whom he was already in debt to part with their goods. However, ordering payment was one thing; doing it was quite another. Royal officials were to turn the screws with strict orders to ensure that 'no debts are to remain owing to the king, either of the issues [of the areas under their jurisdiction] or of the moneys which are leviable and for which [they are] answerable at the exchequer, or of the aid granted to the king for marrying his eldest daughter'.[7] Such strict accounting was doubtless essential to the successful collection of supplies. But the pressure on royal officials to exact every last penny owed to the crown cannot have done much to endear them to the tax-paying population.

Summonses also went out for the fleet. The Cinque Ports were ordered to provide twenty-five ships out of their quota, but these were to be crewed with the same number of men as if they were the full fifty-seven. They were to arrive at Ayr by 16 May 1303, along with a further twenty-five ships from the abbot of Battle, the prior of Christchurch and forty-one towns on the coasts of Sussex, Hampshire, Somerset, Dorset, Devon and Cornwall. These were all counties whose service in the Scottish war was usually conspicuous by its absence, except when it came to the fleet. A royal clerk, Walter Bacun, was also sent to the counties of Essex, Norfolk, Suffolk, Cambridge, Huntingdon, Lincoln, York and Northumberland to find a further fifty ships to go to Berwick by 26 May.[8]

December 1302 was a very good month for Edward and marked the vindication of his diplomatic campaigns over the last few years. On 2 December the treaty of Amiens, between France and England and *excluding* Scotland, was ordered to be proclaimed by all English sheriffs. Walter Amersham, as chancellor of Scotland, was also commanded 'to issue orders to all the sheriffs of that land to cause the like proclamation to be made'.[9] Though this statement is disingenuous, given that Scotland beyond the Forth was still not his, the fact that Edward bothered to issue such an order suggests that a form of English administration, presumably centred on Berwick, was beginning to take shape again, at least in southern Scotland.

In the meantime, the garrisons were preparing to repel any new Scottish offensive as the truce expired. On 4 January 1303, Sir John Segrave and Sir John Botetourt were appointed captain of Northumberland and captain of Cumberland, Westmorland, Lancaster and Annandale to the western boundary of the sheriff-dom of Roxburgh respectively. Both were ordered to assemble the men-at-arms of these counties within eight days of their appointment, as had been agreed with their inhabitants on 27 December 1302.[10] An expedition under Botetourt's command was organised soon after. Though it had initially been planned for December 1302, most of the men-at-arms were paid from 5 to 28 January 1303, apart from Sir Robert Clifford and his retinue who received wages from 13 December. The numbers involved were quite substantial, reaching a peak of one hundred and nineteen men-at-arms and over two thousand footsoldiers and twelve hobelars around the middle of January. Half of the footsoldiers came from the counties of Cumberland and Westmorland.[11]

The garrison of Dumfries was also strengthened between 1 and 27 January 1303. A further twenty archers took up residence there at the end of that month and were paid right up until the end of April 'against the coming of the Scottish army'. In addition, 'bretasches, barriers and a certain palisade' were constructed 'outwith the gate of the pele of Dumfries by order of Sir John Botetourt, Sir Robert Clifford, Sir John de St John junior, against the coming of the Scottish army between 6 December 1302 and 7 January 1303'. Repairs were also carried out on both the castle and pele at Lochmaben around the same time.[12] The south-west was clearly expecting a major Scottish attack. Given that Sir John Soules – along with other Scottish notables – had left for a major embassy to the continent to try to shore up their severely weakened diplomatic position, the army was now presumably led by Sir John Comyn of Badenoch as sole guardian.

In fact, the Scots seem to have gone east, rather than west, in a move that was clearly unanticipated and perhaps suggests that the English in the south-east had relaxed rather too much. On 7 January Sir William Latimer at Roxburgh informed the king rather melodramatically that 'we are daily in peril of our lives'. On 13 January Sir Ralph Manton was in the northern English counties, having been 'sent there to advise touching the protection of those parts and of divers lands in Scotland in the king's hands'. A week later he was ordered back to Scotland to arrange the payment of wages to men-at-arms en route north. On 20 January the archbishop of York received notice to supply men, horses and arms; twenty-five magnates, mostly northerners with long experience in border warfare, were summoned:

> . . . to go in person to John Segrave . . . with horses and arms and all his power . . . until the king's Scottish enemies have been repelled, who, as the king learns from John for certain, have invaded the land in those parts that are in the king's hands and it is feared that they may invade England.[13]

It is not possible to ascertain how much of a threat the Scottish army actually posed; nevertheless, its successes in early 1303 indicate perhaps an element of grim determination on the part of the Scottish political community, as well as a rather worrying display of panic and disarray in the English camp. Despite the precautions of 20 January, Segrave and his company at Berwick were unable to prevent Edward's newly constructed fortress at Selkirk from falling into enemy hands. The castle must have been captured in January 1303, since orders to arrest its keeper, Sir Alexander Balliol, and bring him to the king were issued on 3 February. Balliol was freed by 14 March, having promised to 'serve the king well and safely in time of peace and war with all his power', though his son Thomas remained as a hostage. All the same, it took until March 1305 for the king to forgive Sir

Alexander 'for the loss of the pele at Selkirk' and restore his lands to him.[14]

Edward had certainly been furious. He may also have been unduly suspicious of his officers in and around Selkirk Forest, though there is absolutely no evidence that Sir Alexander Balliol ever sought to emulate Sir Simon Fraser's career pattern. The harsh measures taken against Balliol perhaps reflect less on his own conduct than on Edward's determination to bring about the final conquest of Scotland sooner rather than later, and his growing frustration at events, and people, thwarting that ambition, however unintentionally.

Having achieved success at Selkirk, the Scots then turned their attention to Edward's other new project in the south-east, the pele at Linlithgow. The castle was besieged in February 1303, but this time its defences proved strong enough to resist. The Scots, led by the guardian and Sir Simon Fraser, had given up by 24 February, moving first to Biggar, which sits on an important east–west route. But then, having presumably received word of Sir John Segrave and his company's approach from Berwick, they rode quickly east for twenty-five miles over rough terrain under cover of darkness to surprise the English at Roslin, seven miles south of Edinburgh.[15] Comyn had hand-picked those who rode with him, supposedly those who 'preferred to die rather than be shamefully subjected to the English nation.' These were now hardened men-at-arms with some seven years of military experience under their belts. They were, in other words, worlds away from those who fought so ineffectively at Dunbar in 1296, including the guardian himself.

Sir John Segrave, appointed keeper of Berwick castle on 5 August 1302,[16] resided there with fifty-three men-at-arms to make expeditions throughout the south-east; Sir William Latimer had thirty-eight men-at-arms with him at Roxburgh for the same purpose. According to Guisborough, Segrave, 'being near to Edinburgh at the beginning of Lent [20 February 1303]' and not knowing 'about the Scottish ambush', divided his men 'into three troops and were distanced from each other by about two leagues [about 11 kilometres or 7 miles]'. On 24 February he was informed by 'a boy' that the Scottish army was nearby and decided not to retreat, despite being separated from the other two troops. His own brigade supposedly numbered three hundred men, suggesting that it had been reinforced, probably by the men-at-arms ordered north on 20 January.[17] The Scottish chronicler Andrew Wyntoun says that the 'Treasurer' – meaning Manton – brought an army of 20,000 horsemen north before the battle, a figure that we can quite happily disregard. The Scottish army, by contrast, supposedly numbered an equally unlikely seven thousand. Wyntoun describes the battle itself with much glee:

> And with them the Scotsmen
> Then fiercely fought, and laid on then
> Where many hard blows were seen,
> Many there lay dead on the green:
> The Scotsmen embarrassed them so,
> That many were forced on to their backs there:
> They took many prisoners
> And divided among them wilfully
> The armour and other gear
> Of war that they won from them there.

Five of Segrave's valets lost horses at Roslin and Sir John was himself taken prisoner, having been badly injured. The Scots then skirmished with the two other English companies. Although this was not the great battle lauded by later Scottish chroniclers, there's no doubt that it provided a marvellous opportunity to laud John Comyn as a valiant and successful military leader, not something he was long allowed to be remembered for. Scottish morale was further boosted by the fact that among the dead was Sir Ralph Manton, Edward's cofferer or chief money man in Scotland, whose career seems to have followed that of Sir Hugh Cressingham to a most unfortunate degree. At the same time, the experience left the English dispirited and unenthusiastic, a situation further compounded by a lack of money.

Perhaps, in taking on the job of taxman and paymaster, no-one could have expected to win the love of the Scottish population or even of other colleagues. On the other hand, it perhaps takes a 'special' kind of person to carry out such a job in the first place. Manton, like Cressingham before him, was doubtless sorely missed by the king, for whom his energy had accomplished much. However, the cofferer was supposedly killed by Sir Simon Fraser, who blamed Manton for failing to pay him properly when he was Edward's keeper of Selkirk Forest. In other words, this time it was an English official who viewed the financial shortcomings of his masters as oppression, a failure that almost certainly prompted Fraser to change sides. It's easy to understand why Edward was so keen to finish off the conquest of Scotland sooner rather than later.

But in early 1303, the initiative had passed to the Scots; the English could merely react to the increasing pressure unleashed by the end of the truce until the king brought his army north. Eight of those assigned to help Segrave on 20 January 1303 were summoned to attend a meeting at York with the treasurer, barons of the exchequer, certain members of the king's council and others on 15 March. They were to discuss 'the state of the magnates and others in the army against our enemies', a rather oblique way of describing the confusion caused by Roslin.[18]

At the end of March, Sir John Segrave, released from prison (no doubt on payment of a significant ransom) and back at his post despite his injuries, wrote in exasperation to the exchequer, complaining that the attack on the Scots on the march 'cannot be accomplished unless the sheriff [of Northumberland] does as he has been charged to do'. This was presumably to raise money, or perhaps men, since Segrave also referred to the respite of debts until Easter promised to those of the county who served with him. £1000 or 1000 marks was ordered to be taken to Roxburgh on 26 March to pay for this expedition, to come out of the fifteenth granted to the king in October 1302. Further supplies of money from the relaxing of service to Scotland to ecclesiastics (i.e. payment not to go) were to be at the exchequer by 2 June.[19] The only good news so far was the confirmation of the Truce of Amiens between England and France on 22 March 1303 and its extension until 26 May.[20]

In the meantime, preparations for the forthcoming campaign should have been well underway, but as usual not everything was going to plan. Edward was soon expressing concern about the state of purveyance in particular. On 26 March various royal clerks were sent to the counties where it was supposed to be happening, to inquire 'touching the diligence' of those entrusted with it.[21]

He was also facing severe difficulties in assembling a fleet. In March, the sheriffs of Essex, Norfolk, Suffolk, Cambridge, Huntingdon, Lincoln, York and Northumberland were ordered to help the king's clerk, Walter Bacun, who was trying to select the fifty ships expected from these counties:

> ... as it appears that some of such towns have refused to send their ships, others have refused to find security to send them, and others, though willing to grant a certain number, have refused to send them furnished at their own expenses without the aid of the men of the adjacent towns.

Sir Robert Clifford, as keeper of the bishopric of Durham, was also ordered to ensure that the four ships chosen by Bacun from towns within his jurisdiction were sent to Berwick by inducing 'the men, by all means that he shall see fit, to do this and distraining them [seizing property to the value of what was owed], if need be', since they were 'wholly contemning the king's order on this behalf'. Equally, the men of Yorkshire, 'although they granted that they should send a certain number of ships to the king, are not able to send them to Berwick, thus found at their own cost, without the aid of the men of the towns of the adjoining parts'.

On 16 April another clerk, William Walmsford, was sent to help Bacun, 'because the latter has been negligent in the matter', suggesting that the ships were still not forthcoming.

The eastern counties were by no means alone in their unwillingness to provide their quotas. In Bristol, already noted for the brazen behaviour of its mariners, 'certain men of the town and the parts adjoining capable of this service [two ships] refuse to go with the ships to Scotland well-found with men at their own cost'. Again, full measures, including distraint, were ordered against them. Three Cornish towns – Loo, Polperro and Ash – also claimed that they could not provide their quota of one ship, with its men and equipment, without help from four neighbouring towns. The admiral, Gervase Alard, wrote to the king, explaining that since these last four towns were not used to contributing to the fleet, the king should send a writ ordering them to do so.[22] In the end, ships were sent, but most towns joined together with others to provide the quotas, in comparison to 1301 when very few did. This ultimately made for a smaller fleet, but it was better than nothing.

The blame cannot be attributed completely to the king's demands – corruption and opportunism played their part. On 10 March 1303 an inquiry was ordered on behalf of two citizens of Southampton, Walter Frest and Alice, widow of Ralph Bishop. Their ship, 'with its whole gear and fittings', had been selected to go to Scotland and was duly handed over to one Robert Wynton, who promptly sold it to a Winchelsea merchant 'and refused to restore it or pay for it, to the damage of the said Walter and Alice, and the harm of the Scottish expedition'.[23]

Royal clerks had faced widespread problems in persuading most ports to fulfil their quotas by 1302, never mind 1303, though the Cinque Ports were reasonably reliable. The repeated threats to the non-Cinque ports underline yet again the fleet's importance to the prosecution of the war. Unsurprisingly, the regularity with which it was called out caused exactly the same problems as with the army, though the extent to which these ports were unused to performing this service seems to have made things worse.

Preparations for the campaign had been stepped up by April 1303, probably because of the set-backs earlier in the year. The muster-point was now Roxburgh, rather than Berwick. On 9 April writs were sent out to various clerks to choose footsoldiers in each county. Writs of summons were also sent out to Ireland, seeking five hundred men-at-arms, one thousand hobelars, and ten thousand footsoldiers. Altogether this Irish army totalled only three thousand four hundred when it sailed to Scotland. This time, the earl of Ulster sailed too, having demanded, and received, the pardon of all his debts at the Irish exchequer, amounting to the spectacular sum of over £16,000 [over £14 million today].[24]

Preparations for the royal arrival began long before Edward himself reached Roxburgh on 16 May. Most royal clerks were fully occupied throughout that month, ensuring that adequate supplies reached Scotland in time, making use of sixteen ships and their crews.[25] Bolts for crossbows and spears for the footsoldiers were also brought up to Berwick, presumably to be distributed among those arriving at Roxburgh. Purveyance in Northumberland provided the spears in this case, as well as horseshoes and nails.

Large amounts of hard cash were also brought up in lump sums. These sums were generally paid into the wardrobe, to be used for the immediate expenses of the expanded royal household. There were also many instances of arrears of wages paid out in May to members of various garrisons who joined the army in that month.[26] There was nothing like the royal presence to facilitate the payment of wages, though that was not necessarily true for colleagues remaining back at the castle.

Ten thousand three hundred footsoldiers were supposed to arrive at Roxburgh by 12 May; at its peak in early June, the numbers reached only seven thousand five hundred. By June there were also some four hundred and fifty men-at-arms at wages in the king's household and one hundred and eighty with the prince of Wales.[27]

Writs were also issued for the first time for levies to be raised from within Scotland itself. The earl of Carrick was ordered 'to come with all the men-at-arms he can', in addition to one thousand footsoldiers from Carrick and Galloway (presumably from ex-Comyn or Balliol lands in the latter region). Sir Richard Siward was told to bring 'three hundred chosen foot of Nithsdale'; the earl of Angus was 'to be asked to send his men-at-arms and at least three hundred foot'; and the earl of March was also to bring 'as many men-at-arms as he can'. There is no evidence to show exactly how many of these Scottish contingents actually served, or the numbers raised, though Carrick, and probably Siward, was with Sir John Botetourt over the summer.[28]

Edward and his army proceeded along the southern banks of the Forth to Linlithgow at the beginning of June. Unfortunately, the river was still unfordable at Stirling, not because of the Scottish garrison there, but because the bridge destroyed in 1297 was not yet rebuilt. However, Edward had thought of that and a specially constructed pontoon bridge saved the day, allowing the king to reach Clackmannan on the northern bank of the river on 10 June.[29] With Scottish-held Stirling castle at their backs, it was no doubt hoped that English soldiers would think twice about deserting, since they might have to negotiate the enemy on their own. The army then continued up to Perth, where it remained for over a month for what seems to have been a second muster.[30]

Not surprisingly, fresh supplies were also needed and twenty-one ships sailed up the River Tay to Perth. The names of the merchants selling these goods – men like Thomas Pody of Ravensere and William of Alnmouth – indicate they were English rather than Scottish. Edward was highly unlikely to be able to purchase supplies once he began to advance into enemy territory even if he found the burgesses of Perth more amenable – one hundred and sixty lagens of red wine were bought from various men of the burgh for the king and the prince of Wales, for example.[31] Scotland north of the Forth may have been unaccustomed to the English but not everyone was aghast at the prospect of such a large market.

The Scottish government was already well aware of Edward's intention to move north of the Forth; there was really only one military option available to them and they had taken it even before the English army reached Perth. According to the king's letter of 14 June 1303 to the bishop of Durham, the Scottish army had 'entered Annandale and Liddesdale and elsewhere within the marches in the county of Cumberland with a great multitude of armed men'.[32]

Sir Thomas Multon of Egremond and Sir John Hoddleston were duly appointed to assemble the footsoldiers and men-at-arms of Cumberland and Westmorland and the other areas over which Sir John Botetourt had command while the latter was away with the king; on the other side of the country, Sir Walter Huntercombe was to take over in Northumberland during Sir John Segrave's absence. Sir Aymer de Valence, now the king's lieutenant in the south of Scotland, was still at Berwick, where he was ordered to hold a council with these three to plan action for the defence of the march.[33]

While the Scots were undoubtedly a grave concern, the usual supply problems were also rearing their ugly heads for those left to defend southern Scotland. Dalilegh, the receiver at Carlisle, was the first to complain that he was finding it difficult to make ends meet, given that the king's priority was to feed his army via the eastern stores. However, six ships from Ireland did arrive at Skinburness between 18 April and 28 June, though the totals of 390 quarters of wheat, 427 quarters of oats and 12 casks of wine were unlikely to last long.

By the time the Scots were beginning their offensive in the south-west, Dalilegh had already written to Droxford at the exchequer requesting more funds. Given that both Droxford and Langton, the treasurer, were with the king, an official at York

wrote back on 17 June to explain that all the cash in the exchequer had been sent to Perth. Since Dalilegh had already been sent
money after Botetourt's departure for the army on 1 May, the
writer questioned his need for more. Nevertheless, to safeguard
the garrisons at Dumfries and Lochmaben, the collectors of the
fifteenth in Cumberland were ordered to send the receiver
anything they had in hand.[34]

The situation on the march was certainly deteriorating rapidly.
A letter from the bishop of Carlisle, Multon and Hoddleston
(who were now in charge in Cumberland and Westmoreland) on
23 June informed the exchequer that the Scots, under Sir Simon
Fraser and Sir Edmund Comyn of Kilbride, had crossed the
border five days earlier with a large force and destroyed lands
around Carlisle. Another contingent of Scots, this time under Sir
John Moubray and Sir William Wallace (recently returned from
his own diplomatic mission to the continent), had marched
through Galloway 'and have attracted to them most of the
Galwegians'. They then 'harassed' the countryside around
Caerlaverock and Dumfries on 23 June and 'are coming to
destroy Annandale and to join Sir Simon Fraser and his company'.

Given the potential of this combined force to wreak havoc on
the north of England, the bishop and the two knights sought
advice and assistance urgently from royal officials in York 'because
almost all the men-at-arms and footmen are with the king'.
Those whom they had managed to assemble at Carlisle naturally
required provisions. The exchequer responded immediately,
ordering Sir James Dalilegh to provide 'sufficient victuals' for
those defending the march.[35] Again, this was easy enough to
order, but difficult to execute if there was no money and no
supplies.

Despite the exchequer's attempt to rise to the situation, it soon
became clear that this was just not enough. On 16 July Multon
and Hoddleston wrote again to York, explaining that the defence
of the western march was being undertaken at their own expense
and that they were unable to recruit men into their service to

cross the border unless the king's wages were paid. They urgently requested money for equipment so that at least some retaliatory measures could be taken against the Scots; payment to them and their men was also needed as soon as possible because of their own indebtedness. They mentioned that Dalilegh had been trying to provide for them, but he had informed them that there was hardly enough in the store to provide for the garrisons in the area, let alone extra troops.

A similar story was told by Sir John le Moigne, keeper of Galloway and Nithsdale in Botetourt's absence. The Scots were also making life extremely difficult for the garrisons at Dumfries and Lochmaben by preventing supplies from reaching them from Carlisle; those remaining there required urgent relief 'before it is too late'. Le Moigne asserted that 'in the two garrisons there are neither enough knights nor esquires nor crossbowmen to mount guard nor to go to the king, if you do not command that their wages and arrears be paid by the bearer of this letter'.[36]

This implies that the garrisons were on the point of disintegrating, less as a result of direct enemy action than by the failure to make wage payments. Though this may have been affected by Scottish activity in the region, the finger of blame could most fairly be pointed at the fact that almost all available resources were being poured into the campaign north of the Forth. The men in the south-western garrisons had absolutely no incentive to remain at their posts in such circumstances; even the men-at-arms, whom we might expect to stay for reasons of honour, were on the point of mutiny. This was not a popular war. The overall picture, allowing for exaggeration on the part of royal officials desperate to provoke a reaction from the central administration, is one of extreme difficulty. The loss of these castles, through desertion or surrender, would have gone a long way to counterbalance any success which Edward might achieve in the north-east.

On the other hand, the Scottish government was now under threat in its own heartland and there was surely a degree of desperation in Scottish activities over the summer of 1303 as the east coast ports north of the Forth – a lifeline to Europe for supplies and diplomacy – came under threat. This sense of fighting against ever-increasing odds is also hinted at in the letters written to Comyn by the Scottish magnates who were over in Paris trying, and failing, to regain King Philip's active support (he was very good at making the right noises, which meant very little in practice); though the Scottish diplomats all urged the guardian and his team to continue the fight, they clearly recognised that all they were doing now was struggling on.[37] To add to the heartbreak, it must have been almost impossible to answer exactly what they were fighting for. 'Scotland' as a political concept separate from its king was not easily understood in the middle ages, even if it surely existed at an emotional level. If King John was not coming home in the foreseeable future – and in 17 November 1302 he had in fact signed over his rights to Scotland to his 'very dear lord and good friend,' King Philip[38] – it became more and more difficult to justify prolonging the fight in his name. To this thorny question of political theory must also be added the profound economic and social problems caused by prolonged warfare.

However, this does not detract from the effectiveness of the Scottish strategy. For the royal officials at Berwick, Carlisle and York, failure because of the overwhelming scale of the problem was not enough to save them from blame. On 14 August, Dalilegh was requested to pay Sir John Botetourt for the service which he and his retinue of thirty-two men-at-arms were performing in Scotland. The payment was to be made from the (unspecified) lands which the king had given Botetourt in ward. By November, however, Edward was 'expressing his surprise' that this order had not been executed, the knock-on effect of which was to prevent Sir John from making an expedition because he couldn't pay his men.[39] Given Dalilegh's own extreme lack of money, it is not at all surprising that he was loath to spare any sum, however justified, if it was not required for the direct assistance of the southwestern garrisons.

To add to English woes, there wasn't even enough money and supplies to keep the main army in good fettle. On 15 June 1303, the treasurer's lieutenant at York, Sir Philip Willoughby, wrote to Richard Bremesgrave at Berwick, ordering him to send all money received from the exchequer to the king as quickly as possible, by land or sea, so long as it was safe to do so. Scottish ships were presumably attempting to disrupt the army's supply line, though the fact that twenty-one English boats got through to Perth implies that they were not particularly successful. Even if it were not possible to deliver the money, the king was to be informed as to how much Richard had received, and when, 'so that said Philip will not be blamed for negligence if the king is lacking'. It takes little imagination to envisage the kind of letters Willoughby had been receiving from Edward. £1000 was duly received at Berwick in the next week, £300 of which was paid into the wardrobe at Perth on 24 June, though doubtless this was still far from satisfactory in the king's eyes.[40]

Victuals were not in a much better state. On 20 June Sir Nicholas Fermbaud, the constable of Bristol castle, was ordered to arrest ships and their crews so that grain purveyed in Somerset and Dorset could be taken safely and quickly to Berwick since it was urgently required to feed the army and royal household. Ships did arrive at Perth with more victuals. Nevertheless, on 30 June William Burgh, a royal clerk, was sent from Perth to York to hasten the dispatch of money needed by the royal cooks.[41]

Edward's immediate plan on leaving Perth seems to have been to capture Brechin castle. Preparations for the siege had been made throughout the previous month: on 15 July Sir Ebulo Mountz, now constable of Edinburgh castle, was ordered to send siege engines from both Edinburgh and Jedburgh to Montrose by sea as soon as possible.[42] Presumably others were told to do the same.

The army left Perth on 17 July and effectively entered enemy territory. Two days later, prayers were said at Coupar (Angus) abbey for William Redinsle, a valet of Sir Hugh Bardolf, 'killed by the Scots'. There was then a ten-day gap when Edward seems to have returned to Perth. Perhaps he was ill or, more likely, he may have been informed of Scottish military activity in the south-west and returned to Perth to consider his own strategy before ploughing on up the coast and into the mountain fastnesses of the far north.[43] Whichever, he was soon back en route; on 29 July, 'the goods of Scottish enemies found in Coupar abbey after a search by Sir Walter Teye and Sir Matthew Montemartin' were sold.[44] The English army then continued round the coast to Arbroath, and from there to Montrose, where the siege engines and more victuals were picked up from waiting ships. They then cut inland to Brechin.

As Edward and his men advanced further into Scotland, it was even more imperative (if that were possible) to arrange for the despatch of further supplies of money and victuals. On 28 July orders were sent to each English county to forward the proceeds from the fifteenth to the exchequer. On 7 August further demands for purveyance were made in six counties.[45] It is no wonder there was little or nothing left for poor Dalilegh at Carlisle. To add to the burden, the prince of Wales seems to have maintained an army separate from his father; for two weeks in July he and his men were busy in Strathearn, where they also made direct contact with the enemy.[46]

The siege of Brechin lasted around five days, until 9 August when Sir Thomas Maule, the Scottish constable, was killed and the rest of the garrison capitulated.[47] The king and his army remained there another week, presumably organising the installation of a garrison and the provision of victuals, before moving on up to Aberdeen by 24 August. Though five ships did meet them there with supplies, there was still a desperate need for more. On 28 August, the very day of, but presumably just before, the ships' arrival, Edward wrote to Philip Willoughby complaining that even though his previous letters had commanded all available cash to be sent up immediately to pay those at royal wages, it had been very slow in arriving and 'we owe treble the sum that you have sent'.

The king went on to state what was really on his mind: 'If we cannot make these payments, we cannot hold this part in peace and they [his men] will go back to their own parts, as they are already doing from day to day, because of the lack'. To make matters worse, the Berwick store had not yet fully received the goods acquired by purveyance. Willoughby was again held responsible for this and was to 'hasten the said purveyance to us so that we can leave where we are'.

Edward also mentioned the Irish, who, he said 'do not wish to serve without pay nor to suffer greatly like our other people of England have done'. These were presumably the great Irish magnates, such as the earl of Ulster, who had only been persuaded to take part in the campaign thanks to an impressive piece of financial bribery. The Irish footsoldiers, on the other hand, were left to fend for themselves and most generally returned home 'the minute their hundred days' service was complete, except for the poor souls who ended up at Linlithgow' [see below]. Ulster did, in fact, remain in Scotland over the winter, but returned home owed nearly £6,000; '. . . other leaders were owed sums in proportion to the retinues they brought with them'.[48]

The king was clearly faced once more with the prospect of his army disintegrating slowly before his eyes and the campaign grinding to a halt long before his plans had been fulfilled. But the frustration this time must have been excruciating; he knew perfectly well that it was essential nothing got in the way of what really had to be the final push. Fortunately, the arrival of the five ships at Aberdeen on 28 August seems to have done the trick and the army moved on the same day, arriving at Kinloss abbey on the Moray coast on 12 September. Given that both the king and his son were intent on 'taking much plunder, burning and destroying everything,' this victory march may also have finally given the ordinary footsoldiers in the English army something worth staying for.

Having gone as far as his progress of 1296, Edward turned back south via the difficult route over the Grampian mountains. Despite further resistance, the castles of Urquhart and Cromarty were apparently restored to English control (possibly by the prince of Wales's army); Inverness presumably also surrendered while John Comyn's castle of Lochindorb seems to have been successfully besieged. The king reached Dundee on 16 October, but not before making a special detour to spend a night or two in the Scottish guardian's seat at Boat of Garten (Gartenrothe). Ever aware of the importance of symbolism, the king even ordered in a team of mowers to cut Comyn's corn, which no doubt was baked into something tasty by the royal cooks.[49]

Despite the evidence to suggest that the south-western garrisons had been on the verge of calamity throughout the summer, the situation does not seem to have deteriorated any further. This stability can presumably be attributed, in part at least, to the organisation of an expedition under Sir Aymer de Valence, the royal lieutenant in the south, around the middle of July 1303. A detachment of men-at-arms, which included Sir John Botetourt and the earl of Carrick, had been sent south from the army to join him on the king's orders, indicating the seriousness with which Edward did indeed take the threat. The expedition had reached as far west as Lincoln's beloved Inverkip on the west coast by 24 August, remaining there until 4 September.[50] The lieutenant then moved back east again, reaching Glasgow five days later.

By the end of September 1303, while at Linlithgow, Valence became party to a most interesting development. On 26 September he was able to write to the English chancellor that he had been 'treating with the great lords of Scotland to bring them to the king's will and hopes to be successful by God's help; but cannot say for certain'.[51] Unfortunately for this putative peace process, however, Valence's army was also experiencing very visible difficulties. Thus, two days later he was forced to send word to Richard Bremesgrave and Alexander Convers at Berwick that:

The Irish troops, who are at their wages for nine or more weeks, have heard it said that money has come to Berwick, and are staying in the country around Linlithgow where they can have nothing to live on except ready money, unless they rob the people who have sworn allegiance to the king; and they see clearly that no man cares for them or their lives, so they have packed their baggage to go home. And Sir John de Menteith and Sir Alexander Menzies, who had come to treat in good form for peace, broke off their business by reason of the scarcity that they saw among the said people.[52]

In other words, English success over the summer of 1303 prompted some Scottish nobles to consider the possibility of submission, but they were then so shocked by the state of some of those attached to Valence's army that they must have become convinced Edward would not be able to stay in Scotland over the winter, just as he had failed in 1301/2. It was worth continuing the struggle after all. Poor Margaret, countess of Lennox, was then forced to send to King Edward for help against Comyn and his followers, who came south, crossing the Forth 'as far as Drymen' shortly thereafter.[53] Menzies and Menteith could, by virtue of their behaviour after 1306, be regarded as pro-Bruce, or, at least, not pro-Comyn. The pair may not be particularly representative of the Scottish leadership, but their decision to carry on the fight against Edward as a result of what they saw at Linlithgow surely indicates that the Scots did not consider all to be lost as late as autumn 1303.[54]

Unfortunately, this optimism was misplaced; Edward soon made it clear that he could, and would, winter in Scotland. This would prevent the Scots from making a coherent attempt to undo what had been achieved in the summer, including reclaiming access to the east coast ports as well as castles and manors, lands and revenues belonging to members of the Scottish government. To underline the point that Scotland was now more or less his, Edward's army marched south from Dundee to Cambuskenneth; Stirling castle, perched on the rock high above and the last to hold out for King John, was last on the hit list. On 24 October the king wrote that 'we do not wish to leave there [Cambuskenneth] until we have made headway in the best way we can'. The pontoon bridge, which had been stored at Berwick, was to be sent up to Blackness, along with six engines and further supplies of victuals, and then shipped to the king.[55] However, this was not the time of year to engage in a major siege and Edward was forced to wait until 1304 to recapture Stirling castle.

The army which spent the winter in Scotland seems to have remained a reasonable size, a phenomenal achievement in terms of resourcing. Out of a total of three hundred and sixty-three men-at-arms paid royal wages throughout the campaign, two hundred and eighteen received payment at Dunfermline. The Prince of Wales with his household left the king there on 25 November to form a separate court at Perth. This unusual arrangement was undoubtedly prompted by the knowledge that Comyn and his council were known to be in Atholl, some thirty miles further north. Edward still wanted to see his son take the ostensible credit for bringing the war to an end, even if there had been no grand military finale. He did not have long to wait; by the end of December messengers were travelling between the prince and his father with letters concerning the demands made by the Scottish government for the submission of the Scottish people.[56]

However, they had not submitted yet and Edward was still keen to maintain military pressure over the winter, perhaps to concentrate the guardian's mind, but also to influence those who were not yet intending to accept whatever terms Comyn could prise out of King Edward. In January 1304, Sir John Segrave, Sir Robert Clifford and Sir William Latimer were placed in charge of a company chosen to make *chevauchées* [mounted expeditions]. Detailed instructions were issued to ensure absolute secrecy; only those whose names appeared on an indenture were to go with them and a number of searches were to be made to ensure that no 'strangers' slipped in unnoticed.[57] This expedition was apparently heading south from Dunfermline (perhaps via the Queen's Ferry or else by the circuitous route towards Stirling to cross the Forth at the various fords), suggesting that their target was a 'rebel' force unconnected with the guardian and operating in southern Scotland, probably under Sir Simon Fraser and Sir William Wallace.

This was not the only expeditionary force retained over the winter. On 9 January 1304, immediately before negotiations began with Comyn, Sir John Botetourt wrote to Sir James Dalilegh, informing the receiver of the number of men he was retaining because 'he intends to make a foray on the enemy'. This force numbered one hundred and twenty-four men-at-arms, including Sir Robert Clifford and the earl of Carrick, nineteen hobelars and two thousand seven hundred and thirty-six foot-soldiers from the counties of Cumberland, Westmorland and Lancaster. Botetourt and his men then joined the main company under Segrave. They had good reason to continue the military offensive; on 25 February 1304, while peace negotiations were well underway, two messengers were attacked en route to the king with letters from Carrick.[58]

On 3 March 1304 the king wrote to Segrave and the other nobles, applauding 'their diligence in his affairs' and begging 'them to complete the business which they have begun so well and to bring matters to a close before they leave the parts on that side [of the Forth]'. Not all were so industrious, however; the earl of March was the object of the king's 'surprise that he let the enemy go'. The earl was to keep a close watch on the Scottish garrison of Stirling 'and cut them off if they sally'.[59]

Just over a year after Roslin, Segrave finally extracted his revenge, 'discomfiting' Sir Simon Fraser and Sir William Wallace at Happrew, on Fraser's own lands near Peebles. The greatest barrier to success prior to that date seems to have been the usual problem of locating the Scots. This was overcome by the use of a local informant, one John of Musselburgh, who was paid 10s. on 15 March 1304 for 'leading Sir John Segrave, Sir Robert Clifford and other magnates in their company, assigned to a certain horsed expedition over Sir Simon Fraser, William Wallace and other Scottish enemies of the king then being in parts of Lothian'.[60] Unfortunately for Edward, the two were neither captured nor killed.

Fraser and Wallace were now operating without the sanction of the Scottish government and the Scottish political community generally, even though both could be described as members of it and had been leaders of the Scottish army the previous summer. Their activities certainly make it clear that the decision to submit was by no means unanimous, though, in Wallace's case, the fact that, as we will see, he alone was to submit to King Edward's will with no guarantees for his life and safety surely gave the former guardian little choice but to keep his distance. He and Fraser were not the only ones still refusing to see the writing on the wall, however. A letter from the abbot of Coupar Angus which arrived at Perth on 9 January 1304 reported that 'a great part of the enemy who had gone towards Strathearn have now returned to Angus and ... they would willingly break down the bridge [across the Tay] if they could'.

The Scottish guardian, who sent his clerk to ask for a parley around the same time, was keen to distance himself from such activities. He now recognised that the Balliol star was waning, though in truth it had been in almost terminal decline for the past year and a half. The Comyns and most members of the Scottish political community would now have been concerned to secure their own positions, especially since the earl of Carrick was already two years ahead of them.

Their choices were now extremely limited. Active support for King John among many local communities had been haemorrhaging away for a number of years in areas used to the English presence; this might have been tolerable when it was limited to parts of southern Scotland but Edward's breakthrough into northern Scotland in 1303 must surely have released an overwhelming sense of exhaustion. There was of course every reason to suppose that the English might be expelled from these areas, as they had been in 1297/8, but at what cost?

The Scottish political community had governed a large part of the kingdom and maintained a credible war machine for six years against formidable opposition. During that time neither they, nor Edward, had been able to fully perform a medieval government's peacetime functions, especially the administration of justice, because their writs were only effective in certain parts of the country. Of course, the English king was not getting any younger – at sixty-four he was unlikely to be able to maintain his current level of activity for much longer, not least because he would soon show signs of serious illness. Though this might seem like an argument for continuing, there were perhaps more pressing reasons – such as the scale of damage inflicted by this war – to persuade most that it was time to end the conflict.

It is perfectly credible to argue – as many must have done as the political community worked out its decision to submit – that Scotland's interests were best served by peace, certainly in the short term. The batteries could be recharged, ready – perhaps – for better odds under Edward's less-capable son. All of this must remain speculation, of course. However, we must not presume that either altruism or self-interest can be wholly ascribed to those living at such a distance from our own times and whose motivations we can never know.

Men like Fraser and Wallace clearly disagreed with the arguments put forward, for whatever reasons; however, carrying on the fight was not *by definition* the right thing to do. For those whose lives were already hard enough, peace and order were of paramount importance. Edward had disrupted that normality when he invaded Scotland and expected its people to accept the burdens commensurate with absorption into a comparatively centralised state like England. Now many of those who had bitterly resented such impositions found that interminable warfare unleashed even more intolerable burdens. Patriotism may be a deep emotion, but it is mostly underpinned by a pragmatism that does not necessarily – for good reason – endure against all odds.

On 11 January 1304 a letter was sent from Perth to an official or noble of note at Dunfermline (possibly either John Benstede or Sir Henry Percy, both of whom subsequently became negotiators). This letter told the addressee to go to the royal castle of Kinclaven with Sir Aymer de Valence, who was also at Dunfermline, 'to hear what [Sir John Comyn] wishes to say and if he wishes to treat'. Comyn's clerk, who had been sent to Perth to arrange this meeting, was to 'return [to Perth] on Sunday [19 January] [on which day] Comyn will come to Kinclaven'. The earl of Ulster and Sir Hugh Despenser, who were both with the prince in Perth, were also to accompany them with at least two hundred men-at-arms, just in case.[61]

'Sir John Comyn and those who are of his party, both beyond the sea as here', did indeed want to make a preliminary offer of submission. The basis of their offer was, understandably, a guarantee of safety of life and limb, freedom from imprisonment and the confirmation of all lands and property for themselves and their heirs in England, Scotland and Ireland. They then asked to be pardoned for acts committed during the war for all time, including liability for all issues raised previously from royal and other lands.

Thirdly, they requested that all the 'laws, usages, customs and franchises' should be kept 'in all points as they were in the time of king Alexander'; any amendment should be made with the advice of the king and the advice and assent of the *bones gentz* of the land. After so many years of war, they by no means envisaged a return to either the letter or the spirit of 1296. The fourth clause contained specific requests from Sir John Comyn and Sir John Moubray relating to land which they had been granted by King John. The fifth clause requested that there should be no hostage-taking or other forms of surety except homage and fealty. Those Scots still in France could arrange for the extraction of their oaths independently. Finally, a document sealed with the seals of the king, his lieges and his baronage was to be given as sufficient security.

Although Prince Edward was technically responsible for these negotiations, his father was still very much in charge. By 2 February 1304 the king had drawn up his own set of conditions for those who wished to return to his peace. These terms were generous enough; he certainly agreed to the main condition, that there should be no loss of life or limb, and no imprisonment or disinheritance. However, he insisted that the Scots submit completely to his future ordinances on ransoms, amends for previous misdeeds and, most importantly, the settlement of the land of Scotland. There were also some who could not be forgiven so easily and were excepted from the general conditions 'since they are of another category than the others'. The king was also of the opinion that Comyn and Moubray had better do some crawling if they wanted any special favours.

The Scots with the guardian were now assembled at Strathord, a forest near Dunkeld, coming ever closer. On 5 February a team of negotiators – probably the earl of Ulster, Sir Henry Percy, Sir Aymer de Valence and Master John Benstede – were sent from the prince at Perth to the royal castle at Kinclaven, around ten miles from Strathord, to firm up a more definitive peace formula. A memorandum of these negotiations and a full copy of further draft terms were sent to the king the following day. The Scots basically accepted Edward's terms, with additional requests relating to the rights of heirs, the maintenance of strongholds in the hands of the current holders until the next parliament, and the release of all prisoners except Sir Herbert Morham and his father (though it's not obvious why those two were excluded).

Comyn understood what was expected of him – after all, he had led the 'rebel' Scottish government for most, if not all, of the period between 1298 and 1304 and required absolution not just for what he had done himself, but for what he had caused others to do as guardian. Having taken the trouble to place all his lands in the king's hands, he was duly rewarded for his humility by having them returned to him. Edward would not hold the previous six years against him (apart from demanding a punishment of one year's exile), so long as it was now quite clear who ruled Scotland.

The list of reprobates from whom the king wished to extract some form of punishment grew as the negotiations continued. These included Robert Wishart, bishop of Glasgow, whom Edward accused of 'great evils',[62] Sir Alexander Lindsay, who was 'to make some penance ... for the flight he made from the king who made him a knight', and Sir David Graham, who had apparently borne 'himself so falsely with regard to the discussions which he held with the members of the king's council'.

The longest period of exile was reserved for Sir Simon Fraser and Thomas de Bois (Sir Herbert Morham's esquire, who had served in the Edinburgh garrison before changing back on to the Scottish side in 1301). They were to spend three years banished not only from the British Isles and Gascony (Edward's dominions), but also from the lands of the King of France 'if they can find no greater grace in the meantime'. However, William Wallace was singled out as by far the most deserving of punishment; he was simply to submit 'to the will and grace of the king, if it seems good to him [i.e. Edward]'. Although this requirement was most onerous, implying no guarantees whatsoever, it should be noted that at one point the king also wanted Bishop Wishart to submit to his will.

The key to the severity of punishment, with the exception of Wallace, seems to have been the extent to which Edward felt himself personally betrayed. Treachery may not have been good for the state, but in the middle ages it was still seen as a crime against an individual, the king (or any other ruler). The careers of Fraser and de Bois shared one particular feature – both had at one time been a member of the English administration, changing sides around the middle of 1301.

With the finer details still under discussion, it was now felt that negotiations had gone far enough to arrange a day for Comyn and those with him to come to the king. Decisions had also to be made regarding the issue of their letters of safe-conduct for their trip to meet Edward at Dunfermline, a submission date for those such as Sir John Soules, James the Steward and the bishop of St Andrews who were still in France, and the form of guarantees which the royal messengers were to give 'to stand by the things granted'. Edward was to send back his reply by Saturday 8 February.

Sunday 16 February was chosen as the day on which the Scots would pay their homage and fealty to the king. The prince was to lead this victory parade, to which the earls of Strathearn and Menteith, who had already submitted, were also invited. However, Perth was still to be left properly defended, indicating that the peace process was still by no means universally accepted. Those in France were to come to Edward's peace by 12 April, 'each according to his condition and state' (although as late as September 1304 the English king was making representations to the king of France to encourage the departure of some of these Scots). Once Comyn and the rest had performed their homage and fealty, 'the king will have made his letters patent to keep all the things as they were discussed and granted'.[63]

These negotiations and the final terms of the Scottish nation's surrender to English rule are vitally important to an understanding of the previous years of war. It is striking that the final conditions were not, overall, vindictive or ungenerous, presumably for the simple reason that Edward was in no position to demand harsh penalties. Despite his success in wintering in Scotland, the king surely knew that he could not afford to keep his army together for much longer; the emptiness of his coffers made it abundantly clear that it was in no-one's interests to prolong the war any longer than necessary, so long as he could conclude that the Scottish political community had freely taken him to be their lawful lord.

As a result, and in marked contrast to 1296, he also found it politic to obtain the active support of the Scottish nobility as the best means of ensuring effective and acceptable government in the future, up to and including bringing some of them into it. This was no mere temporary expedient either, to judge from the fact that three of those named as Sir John Comyn's own council in 1304 became sheriffs in the new administration.[64] However, the decision to return to the landholding status quo of 1296 was not without its own difficulties and, as we will see, Edward had to spend the next eighteen months sorting out the resulting legal morass before he could finalise the settlement of Scotland.[65]

In the meantime, there was still work to be done. In March 1304 a parliament was held at St Andrews, nearly eight years after the last one held by Edward I in Scotland. This was the first important test of Anglo-Scottish solidarity, and the Scottish nobility had to be seen to be there in force. 'The parliament was clearly not Scottish, but neither was it English. Circumstances had dictated its composition. Perhaps the terminology of 'English' and 'Scottish' in this instance does not aptly describe the occasion; rather, it was the king's parliament'.[66] The assembled throng witnessed, among other things, a declaration of outlawry passed on Wallace, Fraser, and the Stirling garrison, which alone held out, *'secundum iuris processum et leges Scoticanas* [according to legal process and Scottish laws]'. Edward was now prepared to use Scottish law and custom to give legitimacy to actions which many of those present might well rather not have witnessed. A total of one hundred and twenty-nine landowners took Edward as their liege lord on either 14 or 15 March, together with the 'evil' bishop of Glasgow, Robert Wishart.[67]

The net around Stirling was now being drawn exceedingly tight. On 1 March the earls of Menteith, Lennox and Strathearn were sent to prove their new loyalty to Edward by deploying both horse and foot 'so that the enemy on the other side [of the Forth] cannot injure the people on this at the king's peace'. Around the same time Sir Alexander Abernethy was sent by the Prince of Wales to guard the fords north-west of Stirling, preventing access to and from Menteith and Strathearn. It may well have been Wallace who was the danger since Abernethy was specifically told only to receive the latter and his men if they surrendered unconditionally into the king's will. A month later the same earls (Menteith, Lennox and Strathearn) were all ordered to prevent their people from attempting to provision the garrison at Stirling, suggesting that those living in the earldoms to the north of the castle remained unconvinced by recent developments.[68]

William Biset, the new sheriff of Clackmannan, who resided at Tulliallan castle (Kincardine-on-Forth), was also experiencing trouble but it had nothing to do with recalcitrant Scots. On 17 April 1304 Edward had to write to Sir Henry Percy, having heard that the latter's 'people have come there [Tulliallan] and wish to eject him [Biset]'. Percy was ordered 'for his love to allow Biset to remain and attend to his duties'. Though it is not clear why Sir Henry was interested in the area, this would seem to indicate that those who had served Edward long and loyally were now jockeying for at least some tangible reward.

Biset had already paid for the strengthening of the walls at Tulliallan, and he was also involved in harassing the Stirling garrison cooped up about twelve miles upstream. By 17 April, he and his brother had managed to capture the garrison's boats, which were presumably used to ferry supplies. Biset was eventually rewarded with the keepership of the castle and sheriffdom of Stirling, relinquishing Clackmannan.[69]

Once parliament was over, preparations for the forthcoming siege were stepped up. On 20 March the current sheriff of Stirling, Sir Alexander Livingston, was ordered to muster 'all the forces, both horse and foot, of his bailliwick, including baronies in it, but excluding any part of the Lennox ... to come without delay before Sir Thomas Morham and Alwyn Calendar, to whom they are to be obedient'. The exclusion of the men of the Lennox is presumably a further indication of their reluctance to accept

Edward's lordship.[70] Equally, the fact that Livingston had been named as Edward's sheriff of Stirling since 1301 may also indicate that the Scots in the castle had been receiving a taste of their own medicine for some time before its recapture as they became increasingly isolated from those areas still under the control of the Scottish administration.[71]

The Linlithgow garrison was also preparing to harass the enemy, but could not acquire sufficient men-at-arms because 'the king's men were dispersed foraging and before they could be assembled the time would come for the king to move near Stirling, which he intends shortly to do'. Edward therefore ordered the constable to inform Sir John Comyn 'and other good men in those parts' of what he knew of the 'enemy's plans'. Comyn and his own garrison at Kirkintilloch, 'and any others whom they can hire are to do the best they can until the king's arrival'. In the meantime, engines and their equipment were to be sent to Stirling, a process that did not run entirely smoothly.[72]

Despite evidence for continuing enemy activity, there had clearly been a fundamental shift in Scotland's status and Edward's position as overlord. The king was now coming to Stirling as the country's accepted ruler, serenaded on his way by various women 'just as they used to do during the time of Alexander, late king of Scots'.[73] While there may well have been a note of triumphalism in this last piece of rather unnecessary administrative detail (which only royal clerks would see), it may also indicate a sense of satisfaction among some sections of the population that a king once more ruled in Scotland. Public opinion on even such a crucial issue was clearly as varied and contradictory as it is today.

Most importantly, however, Edward could now make preparations for the siege through his own officials and the Scottish lords in and around the Stirling area, instead of having to rely entirely on his own military machine coordinated from York. This surely marks the transformation, admittedly still incomplete, of the English presence in Scotland from a military regime to a peacetime administration. The parliament at St Andrews, no doubt intentionally, reinforced this transition. The measures taken against those who still refused to submit were approved there by the Scottish political community. Even though the siege of Stirling was obviously very much a military endeavour, there was a sense in which it was portrayed as a national effort in the interests of law and order.

Edward left St Andrews on 5 April 1304, arriving at Stirling seventeen days later. His first action was to refuse to grant the Scottish constable, Sir William Oliphant, permission to consult with Sir John Soules, who, as guardian, had placed the castle in his custody, presumably some time in 1301. Since Soules was currently in France (he never, in fact, returned to Scotland), the request was presumably made as a delaying tactic, and it should have come as no surprise that it was rejected.

The outcome was inevitable, not just because of the presence of much of the former Scottish government in Edward's army, but also thanks to the range and number of siege-weapons arrayed against the garrison. Having been threatened with the direst punishment for their insolence and having been forced to endure a pounding by the mighty 'War Wolf' – a brand new and extremely large trebuchet – *after* they offered to surrender, Oliphant and his men handed over the last Scottish-held stronghold on 24 July 1304. They were then led off to captivity in England. Edward doubtless thought they deserved worse, though there were many who admired their bravery. The next day William Biset took charge as sheriff and keeper of the castle. Even Sir Simon Fraser realised exactly which way the wind was blowing and submitted before the end of the siege.[74] The war was over.

Up until this juncture, Edward really does seem to have acted with uncharacteristic prudence and forbearance, albeit in order to get his own way. However, the contemptible bombardment of Stirling castle with the War Wolf does seem to mark the point at which the gloves came off. On 25 July, 'the day after the castle was handed over', Edward ordered the people of Scotland, but especially Sir John Comyn, Sir Alexander Comyn,[75] Sir David Graham and Sir Simon Fraser 'to make an effort between now and [13 January 1305] to take Sir William Wallace and hand him over to the king so that he can see how each one bears himself whereby he can have better regard towards the one who takes him, with regard to exile or ransom or amend of trespass or anything else in which they are obliged to the king'. Edward also refused to allow Sir John Soules, the Steward and Sir Ingram d'Umfraville, who had so far failed to return from France, to submit until Wallace had been captured.[76]

This was base bribery and surely any honourable man would have felt profound unease at being made to hunt down a former comrade-in-arms. Given the general tone adopted since January, it is possible that Edward would not have executed Wallace out of hand if he had indeed submitted into the king's will – Fraser certainly suffered no extra penalty for submitting late, despite being declared an outlaw at the St Andrews parliament. However, Sir William evidently could not bring himself to bend the knee and Edward probably knew this, hence the original unconditional stipulation. Certainly the fall of Stirling seems to have chased away any instinct for clemency and Wallace now without doubt symbolised the spirit of Scottish resistance in the mind of the conqueror. However shabby it might seem to demand that the Scottish nobility hand over their erstwhile colleague, Edward was doubtless determined to test their commitment to the peace, not least because they had been so ready to go back on their oaths of homage and fealty in 1296.

The reconquest of Scotland was by no means a foregone conclusion even during the summer of 1303. Militarily, the Scots were still able to prove, as they had done throughout the war, that the English supply line was extremely vulnerable and that a sustained attack might well jeopardise the maintenance of Edward's immense war machine.

However, a number of factors now worked against the Scottish government's ability to compel Edward to change his plans through pressure on his garrisons, a strategy that had proved at least partially successful before. Most of these factors were psychological and related in part to the diplomatic isolation the Scots now found themselves in, as well as the unpalatable reality that King John was unlikely to return to Scotland in the foreseeable future (indeed, ever). This meant that the authority in whose name the war was being waged was now a symbol with no substance.

It is important not to judge the thirteenth and fourteenth centuries by our own standards. We have no difficulty with the concept of a country existing independently from whoever actually runs it; in the middle ages, such a concept – though it might exist in theory, if some of the rhetoric in the Declaration of Arbroath is anything to go by – ran contrary to the ethos of personal lordship underpinning relationships between king and political community. Though the guardians had proved more than equal to the task of governing in John's name, they were no substitute for the king himself; without the hope of his return, they had little or no moral justification for continuing the fight.

However, despite the unenviable fact that the Scots were increasingly out on a political limb, a powerful patriotic instinct to continue despite everything is clear in the exhortations coming particularly from the Scottish delegation in Paris as late as 1303. This was most strongly associated with churchmen like Wishart and Lamberton; however, the lay élites, to whom such notions came less easily because personal lordship was their *raison-d'être*, could and did identify with it. The Scottish government did not therefore give up immediately after experiencing the chilly wind of their diplomatic isolation.

But many increasingly found that they could not square the dubiousness of their position with the world as they saw it. These were men, like the earl of Atholl, who had fought long and hard for an independent Scottish government and undoubtedly saw themselves now as standing between a rock and a very hard place. They came from all kinds of backgrounds; they presumably also came from all social classes, though we must be wary of speaking about those whose actions, let alone their motivations, remain almost completely hidden. The point is that there was now an evaporation of support not just from 'the middling sort' in southern Scotland, but also from those on whose shoulders government had rested for the last six years in areas which had not yet gone head to head with an English army. Once Edward had crossed the Forth *and* shown himself determined to maintain his war machine throughout the winter, the arguments for submitting – on good terms – must surely have become overwhelming.

If we let ourselves take a flight of fancy for a minute and imagine that a referendum had been the means of deciding whether or not to submit, the result might not have been much to the liking of many in our own times. The rather small 'No surrender' camp to which Wallace certainly belonged might make good cinema today, but it does not seem to have been much of a vote-winner from the winter of 1303 onwards. Again, class doesn't come into it: there are plenty of examples of obscure men, and sometimes boys, who pop up sporadically in the records because they have earned their reward for spying on their fellow countrymen. That was how Wallace and Fraser were caught at Happrew. Even gender doesn't wash as a measure of undiluted patriotism, as the examples of Eva of Stirling and Christina of Edinburgh, who each took advantage of local English garrisons to ply their trade, make clear. On the other hand, there were certainly those, like the men of Lennox (though who exactly they were is not clear), who disagreed with the decision made by their feudal superiors. We must all live with the consequences of the choices made by our predecessors, but we can never know that we would have chosen or acted differently. It is really very difficult, seven hundred years after the event, to justify the belief that we know better.

King Edward must have been very, very relieved. His last push was nothing short of monumental and it is not at all clear how he – and England – managed to sustain the campaign over 1303 and into 1304. Perhaps his subjects were prepared to throw everything into one last effort, so long as it really was the last. Although this war was never popular, the idea that the inferior Scots could prevail against the might of the English certainly stuck in many a southern throat.

Edward had also learned a few hard lessons. He would no doubt never have admitted it, nor have compromised on his right to do as he pleased with his reconquest. However, the leniency of the surrender terms, together with the presence of many former 'rebels' in the new administration, attests to the success of the Scottish government in keeping the great Plantagenet at bay for so long. This ability to learn, adapt and compromise – always with an eye on the main prize in the long run – was perhaps what defined Edward's greatness. On the other hand, although this was undoubtedly a defeat for the Scots in general, and the Comyns in particular, the political community does not seem to have experienced the sense of shame and bewilderment that afflicted it after Dunbar in 1296. It would be wrong to use hindsight at this point – the Scots did not submit because they knew that the earl of Carrick was going to seize the throne in a few years' time. Nevertheless, there was much to be proud of, even in defeat.

CHAPTER SEVEN

'EDWARD THE FAIR'? THE SETTLING OF SCOTLAND

Although the final arrangements for the future government of Scotland were not worked out until September 1305, some form of administrative structure was required in the meantime. Indeed, some officials – often Scots who had just changed sides – claimed to have successfully governed on Edward's behalf north of the Forth even before the king's arrival there.

According to an account made with him in 1305, one such recruit, Sir Alexander Abernethy, 'held the sheriffdoms of Kincardine, Forfar and Perth, with their clerks and constabularies and all others the king's servants there from [February 1303] till now ...' Abernethy can have submitted to Edward only comparatively recently since he had certainly been with the Scottish force in southern Scotland in 1301. He was rewarded with the wardenship of the land from the Forth to the Scottish mountains (the Grampians) with a force of sixty men-at-arms on 29 September 1303.[1] Another account gives the names of five sheriffs and two keepers of royal castles north of the Tay – all Scots – in regnal year 32 (20 November 1303–19 November 1304).[2]

Overall control of the north-east was given to John, earl of Atholl, previously the Scottish sheriff of Aberdeen, and 'warden and Justiciar of Scotland from the Forth to Orkney' from 29 March 1304. His deputy was the earl of Strathearn.[3] William, earl of Ross, released from English prison only in September 1303, was made warden beyond the Spey soon thereafter, since he accounted for the issues of Ross and the bishoprics of

Caithness and Sutherland in 1304. He was given the rather onerous task of trying to bring the western isles under effective crown
control, something his family had been trying to do for nearly a
century.[4]

Similar administrative overhauls were taking place in the
south even before the Scottish government submitted. Between
6 and 14 September 1303, the earl of Carrick and Sir John
Botetourt went on a tour of the sheriffdoms of Linlithgow,
Lanark and Peebles 'and elsewhere south of the Forth to ordain
and appoint sheriffs and other officials on the part of the king'.
Carrick, currently sheriff of Ayr and soon also of Lanark, clearly
occupied a prominent position in the English administrative
hierarchy. Although there does not seem to have been any question of his becoming Edward's chief representative in the south-
west, the younger Bruce worked closely with Botetourt until the
latter gave up his office on 30 April 1304 and there is no sign of
any dissatisfaction with the arrangement.[5] After April 1304, Sir
John Segrave, previously the royal lieutenant in the south-east,
became lieutenant south of the Forth (i.e. of all southern
Scotland) and justiciar of Lothian.[6] This suggests a desire on
Edward's part to keep the south in English hands, while he was
content to leave the north to the Scots to run. We could speculate
as to why that might have been – excluding Galloway and other
parts of the west, the south was culturally more like England in
that it was once Anglo-Saxon and the south-east was the first
part of Scotland to experience an influx of Normans under King
David I. North of the Forth (excluding the far west), though not
untouched by Norman innovation, was still heavily influenced by
Gaelic culture and customs.

Edward now also felt confident enough to despatch Sir James
Dalilegh, escheator south of the Forth, with two esquires and a
clerk, 'to value and assess the king's lands and to collect and
receive farms and escheats of the same'. This took almost six
months between November 1303 and May 1304. He was then
joined by Sir John Weston in order to make 'an extent of all the

king's lands in Scotland, both beyond the Scottish Sea [the Forth] towards Orkney and on this side in Galloway and elsewhere' until Christmas Day 1304. The two were provided with an escort of sixteen men-at-arms 'for more safely forwarding the king's business; inasmuch as during the war and the impending siege of Stirling castle, while the men of the parts beyond the Mounth and in Galloway and Carrick had not yet fully come to the king's peace, without such safe escort they could in no way have done the work'.

Additional numbers of men-at-arms joined their company at various stages. Local landowner Sir Reginald Cheyne provided a particularly large group, both mounted and unmounted, to escort them from Elgin to Inverness 'and staying with them there on account of the imminent peril of the enemies'. While in Elgin in June 1304, payment was made to twenty footsoldiers 'watching nightly, through fear of some enemies who had not yet come to the king's peace'. It is difficult, given what happened only two years later when Robert Bruce seized the Scottish throne, to avoid concluding that Scotland was far from pacified even after the submission of its leaders. Certainly, these examples hint at a landscape of resistance to English rule at the very moment of Edward's triumph that, at the very least, might be tapped into by any Scottish leader seeking to reverse it.[7]

As escheator south of the Forth, Dalilegh's accounts over this period make interesting reading. The sheriffdoms of Lanark, Peebles, Ayr and Dumfries brought in the very gratifying total of £668 4s. 34d. for the first year (1302–3); this was despite the fact that in Lanarkshire the barony of Cambusnethan and the farms of the burgh of Glasgow had apparently been laid waste by the ravenous Irish, the lands of Nemphlar and Cartland produced nothing because they were still in the hands of the Scots, and the barony of Rutherglen was granted a £10 rebate, 'on account of the inability of the tenants'. The total value of royal lands in these four sheriffdoms should have amounted to £1,037 16s. 4d.[8]

The total for the next year (1303–4), excluding Dumfries, was less than one third of the previous year's total at £206 3s. This surprising decrease was presumably caused partly by the fact that in the previous year Edward was able to draw the revenues of estates forfeited by their rebellious owners. In 1303–4, when most Scots had submitted, the escheator could only claim those issues which normally went to the king. However, this last figure also suggests that there had been a serious decline in revenue as a result of the war; given that Dumfries is missed out in the second account, these lands were now only worth between a quarter and a fifth of their pre-war value, a figure which is corroborated elsewhere.[9]

Segrave, Atholl and Ross, together with William Bevercotes, who became chancellor by December 1304, Sir John Sandale, appointed chamberlain by March 1305, and Dalilegh as escheator, ruled Scotland in Edward's name in the period leading up to the finalisation of Scotland's new constitution in September 1305.[10] The re-establishment of a viable administration was vital to the success of the reconquest and there is little doubt that, despite references to continuing unrest, most of the country was reintegrated under an effective national system by the end of 1304. By August of that year, for example, writs to various Scottish sheriffs were once more sent out *sub magno sigilo regis quo utitur in Scocia* [under the king's great seal used in Scotland]'.[11] It is undoubtedly no coincidence that the seal should have re-appeared at the same time as a Scottish chancery and exchequer were re-established at Berwick.

Repairs to most of the castles which had housed English garrisons over the previous years of war were now able to take place. The king also decided to build a castle at Tullibothwell (some three miles north-east of Stirling, near modern-day Menstrie[12]) but, 'not having a fit site', had to order the earl of Atholl, as royal lieutenant north of the Forth, and the chamberlain, Sir John Sandale, 'to buy or provide one by exchange in a good place beyond the Forth'. Another castle was to be built near

Polmaise, south-west of Stirling, where the lieutenant south of the Forth – Sir John Segrave – was also ordered to purchase or exchange the land. The importance of Stirling castle, controlling the river crossing and, therefore, both north–south and east–west routes, was clearly uppermost in Edward's mind; a network of fortifications were to provide sufficient protection for this vital strategic spot.[13]

Even by the summer of 1303, when the Scots still considered the military option to be viable, there is increasing evidence that the English administration was tightening its grip throughout southern Scotland. The holding of inquests into landholding is one such indication. The first of these took place at Lanark in January 1303, only a week after the death of Sir John Baird, whose lands were the subject of the jury's deliberations. The issue was still complicated by the fact that Baird's feudal superior, Sir Nicholas Bigger, was presumably not at Edward's peace since Sir John's barony of Strathaven was currently in the hands of Sir John Segrave, Edward's lieutenant. However, the fact that Alexander Baird, the heir, could instigate proceedings to gain entry to his inheritance so quickly must have been extremely heartening not only to Edward's officials, but also to those whose lives were regulated by the system.[14]

This is not meant to imply that the Scots had been unable to administer these areas successfully in the past; we really have very little idea whether they could or not south of the Forth, though we can presume – and there is some evidence – that north of it was governed just it had been under Alexander III. However, the fact that evidence for such inquests only appears from 1303 onwards suggests that Edward's officials had certainly not been able to.[15]

Further inquests followed in Fife in March 1303, in the presence of Sir John Cambo, lieutenant of the sheriff, Sir Richard Siward; in Lanark again in December, before Magnus of Strathearn and Nicholas Bannatyne, lieutenants of the earl of Carrick, the sheriff; at Roxburgh and Peebles in January 1304; at

Dumfries at some point in regnal year 32 (20 November 1303–19 November 1304); and at Stirling in February 1304, while the castle was still occupied by a Scottish garrison.[16] This last inquest produced the valuable information that the lands of Kilsyth and Callender (near Falkirk) had decreased in value from £40 to £8 6s. 8d., and from £60 to £12 respectively. At one fifth of their peacetime value, these support the figures that Dalilegh was accounting for around the same time in southern Scotland generally.

The competing jurisdictions which had split Scotland asunder over the past seven or eight years certainly posed some knotty problems for the inquest juries to solve. In February 1304, for example, it was necessary to establish the precise landholding relationship between Sir John Soules 'the fugitive' – and former guardian, currently in France – and Sir Ingram de Guines, who had served Edward as a royal officer in Eskdale.[17]

De Guines had leased Durisdeer castle and barony in Nithsdale to Soules in 1295, just before the outbreak of war, for a period of twelve years; Sir John subsequently transferred this lease to Sir William Conigesburgh of Lanarkshire. However, and despite the fact that the two main protagonists were now technically enemies, de Guines subsequently re-leased Durisdeer to Soules for a further twelve years in order to pay off a debt to a Dumfries burgess. Philipstoun, near Linlithgow, ultimately also owned by de Guines, was leased by Conigesburgh to Soules for five years from 21 May 1301.[18]

These transactions appear very dubious to modern eyes and no doubt Edward would not have approved of them either, though he presumably had no knowledge of them until after the reconquest. However, they may indicate that those who had long occupied the same social circles tended to view the war pragmatically; it would take more than a few years of conflict to persuade landowners that their political loyalties automatically meant cutting off all contact with friends, families and neighbours on the opposing side. English merchants were another group who felt the same way about the war, though for them the incentive was their natural desire to seize any opportunity to make money.[19]

These inquests also make it clear that Scottish juries fluctuated in numbers rather than comprising the 'twelve good men and true' beloved of the English system. Edward was also happy to allow the *probi homines* (good men) of each sheriffdom to fulfil their traditional function, however recently they had submitted. This had some ironic repercussions. In September 1304, the earl of Atholl presided over an investigation into one particular judicial decision made by the former Scottish government. Atholl and a number of the jurors, such as Sir Gilbert Hay and Sir David Wemyss, were ideally qualified to look into this case because they had themselves been part of the Scottish administration now under investigation.[20]

The biggest headache facing Edward during the process of resettlement was the restitution of lands to former 'rebels' whose estates had been granted out to others before the Scots submitted. Edward seems to have operated two different policies towards whatever fell into his hands through the adherence of their owners to the Scottish side. Lands and property in England were granted out extremely rarely, for the simple reason that their revenues, in contrast to those in Scotland, were easily forthcoming and Edward was presumably keen to use them himself to fund the war.[21]

Grants of the Scottish lands of these 'rebels' had been made almost immediately upon the resumption of war in 1297.[22] However, in many cases the award was effectively a means of encouraging commitment to the conquest of Scotland among Edward's supporters; any material benefit would only accrue if the recipient actually managed to recover his gift from the original proprietor. Unfortunately for him, he often became owner in more than name only in the last year or so of the war, which meant that he then had to watch his lands being handed back at the very point when he had just begun to recover some of his outlay.[23]

However, before we feel too sorry for Edward's loyal servants, there is no doubt that some were adept at profiting from the confused situation in Scotland, often at the expense of less experienced, or less powerful, colleagues. John Autry, a valet of the earl of Lincoln, discovered that he could not gain access to his gift of the manor of Duddingston because 'Archibald Livingston [the sheriff of Linlithgow] falsely persuaded the king that the manor was in [Edward's] hands, and procured a writ to the sheriff of Edinburgh to give him sasine and got it unfairly. When John came to the siege of Stirling with the earl ... Archibald kept him out of the manor'. It is to be doubted whether Autry would have been satisfied with the king's injunction to his lieutenant to 'hear the parties and do justice to both', especially since Thomas de Bois, whose lands he had originally been given, would now be getting them back,[24] thanks to the submission agreement.

Sir Nicholas Graham, who claimed in 1304 to have 'been long at the king's peace', found himself similarly dispossessed of his lands in Northumberland, seized by earl Patrick of Dunbar at the beginning of the war. Graham had spent the time since his submission suing 'the earl and the sheriff of Roxburgh for Halsington and other lands deforced by the earl, without success'. Most revealingly, he begged the king to give orders that Dunbar's influence would not prevent him from gaining redress.[25]

Perhaps those best placed to play the system were Scots at Edward's peace, often to the disadvantage of those innocents who were not used to Scottish legal procedures. John of Bristol, a royal serjeant, fought a long and losing battle against the resourceful William Penpont. Penpont claimed to be the heir of Alan of Dumfries, whose lands Bristol had been granted. However, he was initially caught out when he first made his claim because Alan was a bastard and thus could not pass on his property. Undeterred, Penpont came back again, claiming to be cousin and heir of William Hauwyse, who had held the lands over thirty years previously. Bristol petitioned the king, claiming that

Penpont was confusing a writ of sasine with a writ of mortancestor: the first, which the latter held, would only allow restitution of lands taken into the king's hands during the war; the second, which he did not have, was the usual legal procedure whereby distant relatives could inherit after many years.

Bristol was no fool, realising that 'the people of these parts dislike any English disinheritor among them by the king's gift'. He did not want to be accused of keeping Penpont from his inheritance, even if the latter was far from convincing in this new claim. He thus begged the king to regard the property as an 'escheat by reason of the bastardy of the last feoffee'. Edward agreed that the writ of sasine validated claims only to lands held by relatives at the beginning of the war, putting Penpont clearly in the wrong.

However, this did not stop the latter from claiming in 1305 that he had recovered sasine of his lands and property in Dumfries through an inquest but remained disinherited by Bristol's continued possession. Parliament ordained that a writ should be sent to the Scottish chancellor, ordering him to 'make remedy according to the customs of those parts', an edict which did not perhaps augur well for Bristol.[26] Penpont may not have been pushing his luck, but the fact that he took two attempts at establishing his claim to these lands makes it rather likely that he was.

Conflicting claims also arose among Edward's non-Scottish officers who had been granted lands by the king's gift, particularly when access to these lands was finally won. Sir John de St John, junior, was unhappy about his ability to enforce his rights of feudal superiority, as owner of John Balliol's Galloway lands, over those to whom the king had granted other parts of these estates. The important point here is that Balliol was not covered by Sir John Comyn's submission agreement and those to whom his lands were granted were allowed to keep them.

One such case involved the lands of Ardrossan, held from St John by Sir William Latimer until his death on 5 December 1304. According to St John, a 'stranger', Sir Thomas Latimer, who was in fact Sir William's second son, tried to gain entry to those lands, but was prevented by Sir John's bailiffs. Sir Thomas then went to court where he argued that Ardrossan was held directly from the king. However, St John's claims to hold these lands in chief were eventually upheld and Latimer was told to perform his homage and fealty to him 'according to the custom of these parts'.[27] Distance from the king (and hence access to him) was always crucial in the administration of property rights, and those in Scotland – both Scots and English officials serving there – were in a potentially vulnerable situation once Edward had gone home.

In general, the English chancery, which issued the writs of sasine activating a claimant's right to property, seems to have been distinctly unable to make impartial – and final – judgements based on a full appraisal of the facts. There was thus considerable scope for the pursuit of fraudulent claims, even if it is impossible now to prove that this was going on. There may even have been a belief among the Scots at Edward's peace that he took a favourable attitude to their land claims because the king was unwilling to risk accusations of injustice and oppression. Edward certainly seems to have gone to great lengths, often at the expense of his own supporters, to ensure that no Scot could complain of being unfairly dealt with.

This did not mean that the dispossessed necessarily took their removal meekly; there are certainly examples of vocal and even violent opposition to the return of property after the implementation of the submission agreements. Lady Alice Beauchamp, widow of Edward's steward, for example, petitioned the king for 'restitution of, or compensation for, her dower' from lands granted to her husband. However, it was explained firmly to her that even if Sir Walter had been alive, he could not retain the land-grant 'on account of the agreement between the king and John Comyn'. There was no mention of any liability for compensation.[28]

Edward was not entirely consistent, however. The earl of Norfolk, who had, rather unusually, been granted one of Sir

Edmund Comyn's English manors (Fakenham Aspes in Suffolk), was to be granted 'land or something else in lieu to the same amount' when Comyn reclaimed the manor after his submission. However, the earl was a political hot potato whom Edward was currently trying to placate and this response was the exception rather than the rule.

The earl of Ross found himself on the sharp end of a far more vigorous reaction to his submission and subsequent rehabilitation than a mere complaining petition. During the period when he remained in prison in England, refusing to accept Edward as his liege lord, his wife's inheritance in the sheriffdom of Edinburgh had been given to Sir Thomas Morham. Sir Thomas was most unwilling to relinquish these lands, which had been granted to him as a reward for his service to Edward, and continued to uplift their issues even after the earl had them restored to him in 1303. Morham also pulled down houses and caused other destruction. The sheriff of Edinburgh was ordered to stop him and make amends to Ross, but the incident illustrates the depth of feeling involved. The issue of disinherited in the Anglo-Scottish wars began a long time before the 1330s, when they caused the resumption of hostilities after a 'final' peace treaty in 1328.[29]

Some of the complaints which came before Edward in February 1305 stemmed from a basic ignorance of laws and customs peculiar to Scotland among those who were ultimately responsible for its government. This was a serious problem for the English king, since he was already aware of his newest subjects' sensitivity on this subject. At the same time, Edward seems to have been reluctant to place total reliance for the running of the judicial system on those who had so recently fought against him.

The Scots, probably heartened by the third clause of the submission document, were more than happy to provide information about usual practice on a wide range of issues. For example, Sir John Sulleye, an Englishman, informed the king that:

> The people of Scotland ... say ... that the king's chamber-
> lain does not have anything more than the robes of his
> office and half a mark which is owed for doing homage to
> the king, according to what he has had up till now, as was
> usual during the time of King Alexander ...

It is easy to imagine the howls of outrage among those faced with
demands for payment beyond what they were used to for an
unavoidable service; accusations of foreign oppression similar to
those voiced in 1297 were surely but a short step away if redress
was not swiftly forthcoming. Edward duly agreed that the chamberlain should 'inquire into the usual customs of these parts in
previous times', indicating the *de facto* reliance on native exper-
tise.[30] However, this also created a potential conflict since the
chamberlain doing the inquiring obviously had a vested interest
in the result, having perhaps imagined he had acquired a far more
lucrative office along English lines than actually turned out to be
the case (though half a mark for each homage surely amounted
to a tidy sum).

It is interesting also that, even though homage to the king was
performed only by certain sections of the landholding class
(though not exclusively the top level), the above petition was
ostensibly from 'the people of Scotland'. Doubtless the notion
that any people speaks with one voice was largely exaggerated,
but it may also indicate that the community of the realm – or
selected representatives – continued to act as arbiter and mouth-
piece of Scottish public opinion even after its surrender in 1304.
After all, Edward was himself doing much to encourage such
active participation, particularly through the ongoing consultation process prior to the final settlement. This was very different
indeed from 1296.

There was even a petition from Edward's new Scottish chancellor, the Englishman, William Bevercotes. He had discovered
'that other chancellors, his predecessors, who have been given the
office of chancellor of the land of Scotland have been given in

their office in the king's name all the hospitals which were vacant and in the king's gift in the land of Scotland'. Again, the king ordered an investigation 'as to what was usual in the times of the kings of Scots'.[31] It is amazing how quickly a sense of history can develop when the powers-that-be think it might serve a useful purpose in their own times.

However, as we might expect with Edward, there were limits to this apparent sensitivity. One of the first to experience it was none other than the earl of Carrick. On 31 August 1304 an inquest was held into 'the privileges claimed by Robert Bruce', following the death of his father in April.[32] The inquest jury's findings provided the king with a dilemma, since it was concluded that the earl had the following rights in Annandale:

> ... that no sheriff of Dumfries or other servant of the king or his ancestors may enter the bounds of Annandale to make attachments, summonses, or distraints, nor have they done so for time beyond memory; but that the king may choose a coroner from one of the earl's homagers in Annandale and issue writs to him direct, who shall represent and answer to the king and his justices of Lothian at Dumfries; that the earl has these liberties by the title of antiquity, that is, from the time of William, king of Scotland and all his successors uninterruptedly till this day.

On 26 October 1304 the result of this inquest, which was a fair interpretation of King William's original charter to the Bruces, was sent by Edward to John Langton, bishop of Chichester, the English chancellor. Langton, together with the rest of the royal council, was to peruse its contents and advise the king.[33] The almost vice-regal powers which the lords of Annandale had clearly long enjoyed were of great concern to Edward, who was always very careful to ensure that his own royal rights, as he perceived them, were not infringed. Just because Carrick and his ancestors had enjoyed such privileges under the kings of Scots did not mean they would necessarily be allowed to continue under English rule. Indeed, the whole point of Edward's famous *Quo Warranto* inquiries in England earlier in the reign was that 'tenure from time out of mind was not now adequate warrant for the exercise of rights of jurisdiction which properly belonged to the king'.[34]

The earl of Carrick petitioned Edward some ten days later, presumably wondering what was happening and pressing for a favourable judgement.[35] Unfortunately we do not know what that final judgement was and the length of time it took for Edward and his officials to think through the matter highlights both the king's resistance to allowing such extensive privileges and his awareness that getting rid of them in Scotland would do little to keep the natives from becoming restless. We know that Bruce had been canvassing for unspecified, but almost certainly treasonable, support from William Lamberton, bishop of St Andrews and perhaps other members of the Scottish élites as early as the siege of Stirling within weeks of his father's death and his own acquisition of his family's claim to the Scottish throne.[36] This questioning of his traditional liberties in Annandale cannot therefore have marked the beginning of the road towards Carrick's seizure of the crown. But it may have hardened his resolve.

Land was not the only issue which Scotland's new master had to address in the mopping-up period after the war. A petition was sent in from all the Scottish burghs, seeking the preservation of their traditional liberties from the meddling of sheriffs and other royal officials. They also requested that the burghs should maintain their monopoly of the holding of markets, 'as was usual before this time'. Then there was a complaint about the activities of the burgesses of Berwick and Roxburgh, who had allegedly imposed taxes on the merchandise from other burghs, contrary to their charters. This was almost certainly a thinly veiled criticism of the communities of English burgesses who lived permanently in both these towns.[37]

However, the burgesses of Roxburgh 'from the nation of England' had their own complaint to make, asserting that they were hindered from carrying out their business by the 'burgesses of that town from the nation of Scotland'. They rather fancied having a charter of privileges like the one granted to Berwick and confirmed in 1302.[38] Although there was certainly antagonism between Scots and English before the outbreak of war, this hostility had no doubt become far more entrenched, particularly along the border.

Burghs, like individual landowners, could and did take advantage of the unsettled state of Scotland during the period of conflict to advance their own interests. According to a petition from the burgesses of Perth, the burgesses of Dundee had 'attracted certain profits which belong by right to the town of Perth and are now endeavouring to harm them in other ways, as far as they can'.[39] Whatever the rights or wrongs of such cases, the overall impression is that neither Edward nor the guardians had previously been able to wield sufficient authority to prevent abuses occurring.

One petition presented to Edward in February 1305 stands out in marked contrast to the rest, which were usually concerned with re-establishing previous conditions: 'the king's husbandmen' in Scotland wished to improve their customary situation, whereby they could be 'removed from year to year', by being allowed to hold their lands in the same way as husbandmen in England, who could not. As usual, although an investigation as to 'what would be to the king's profit' was ordered, there is no record of the final result.[40] However, this is a truly remarkable petition, not least because of the collective approach, together with the fact that the situation in England was obviously known north of the border (though we should not preclude the possibility that the king had encouraged such a petition, having highlighted the differences between the two nations).

In his article 'Colonial Scotland: The English in Scotland under Edward I', Michael Prestwich has written about Edward's policy towards the granting of lands to his supporters. In contradicting the view of the chronicler, Pierre Langtoft, that the English king's lack of generosity in dispensing patronage during the Scottish wars was responsible for his inability to hold the northern kingdom, Prestwich states:

> Edward was much less ungenerous in the case of Scotland than he had been in Wales, and the danger in his policy was less that English magnates would be discontented at receiving inadequate rewards for service, than the alienation of the Scottish nobles whom the king was anxious to win over to his cause.[41]

This synopsis is certainly correct in theory. Edward's grants of Scottish lands to his supporters were indeed numerous as the fact that fifty-one of these grantees were required to provide men-at-arms for castleguard highlights. Unfortunately, as so many of these court cases indicate, many never actually gained access to their lands, or, if they did, were in possession for only a short space of time, certainly not long enough to recoup what many must have spent on campaigning in the north even if they were at the king's wages.

The Scots whose lands formed this potential patronage thus had little cause to feel alienated. The restoration of their property was a fundamental condition of their submissions, either as individuals, such as the earl of Carrick, or through the general agreement concluded by John Comyn, the guardian. Indeed, Edward's own supporters, who were forced to step aside in favour of those whom they had just spent six years fighting, had far more cause for resentment. In addition, the barrage of petitions for lands and offices addressed to the king after the second conquest of 1303–4 makes it quite clear that only then was Scotland regarded as an attractive source of preferment, presumably because only then was there a guarantee that the successful applicant would actually benefit. Any policy of colonialism before then, 'in a broad sense of conquest, expropriation, exploitation and settlement',[42] was restricted to the town-planning exercise at Berwick.

So, with the settlement of Scotland almost completed, this erstwhile Siberia of English office-holding seems to have become a land of opportunity. The men who now petitioned the king for offices and lands in Scotland might have had experience of working in the north, but others had done no more than go on campaign there.

Richard Vigrous, a burgess of Roxburgh and member of the garrison there since 1298, requested a grant of land for his services. Margaret of Hawick sought confirmation of lands conceded for the service of her father, probably Ralph of Hawick, who had also served in the Roxburgh garrison. Geoffrey Ampelford, another Roxburgh man and member of the royal household, requested the constabulary of Berwick or Dundee. John Cave, the royal clerk in charge of victuals at Glasgow and Kirkintilloch, petitioned the king for the lands of Dalile in Lanarkshire.[43]

Newcomers included John Perraunt, who requested the constabulary of Berwick castle, John Cunningham, who wanted to be coroner of Lothian, an office unfilled in the previous decade, and Thomas Cotingham, another member of the royal household, who sought 'possession of things pertaining to the custody of the gate of Stirling'.[44] Such offices brought in little or no salary – the fees and issues attached to them were the source of their value.

However, the line between 'making the most' of an office and downright corruption was a fine one and the Scots were not slow to make accusations of misconduct against royal officials now that they seemed to have the royal ear. Sir Matthew Redmayne, Edward's sheriff of Dumfries, was first on the list, with complaints arriving as early as April 1304. Led by a leading burgess, William Jargun,[45] several local men asserted that Redmayne extorted payments from them in order to regain possession of their lands after submitting to Edward. They also accused the sheriff and his officials of seeking 'to grieve and distress the poor people by tallages', though it should be noted that any tax which was not popular, no matter how lawful or customary, was described as a tallage. Redmayne had also allegedly acquired the lands of John Heytone and Matthew Terregles by various dubious methods, including 'champetry' (or bribery), another pejorative term.[46]

Some of these accusations, which included the taking of carts, corn and beasts for the use of the king himself, together with the 'tallages' which presumably Edward had also authorised, are reminiscent of the complaints levied against the king even by the English in 1297. It is impossible to establish whether these were completely novel demands made on the Scottish people, or whether the petition resulted from a general aversion to handing over anything to this re-established, but still perceptibly alien, central government. However, some of the other accusations, if true, do suggest that Redmayne had been abusing his position. The activities of such over-zealous officials were what had prompted the Scots to military action in 1297 and unless Edward could put a stop to it for good, his government would once more find itself unpopular, if not hated.

This was also true of the activities of such royal stalwarts as Dalilegh and Weston, whom we left peregrinating round Scotland assessing the extent of royal lands and revenues. The king could certainly not accuse them of lacking assiduousness on his behalf; however, those, such as the abbot of the convent of Jedburgh, and Sir Reginald Cheyne, who had suffered 'great injury and loss . . . by reason of his loyalty . . . to the king who now is', were not so happy about being deprived of their lands despite, in many cases, clear title.[47] Edward's officials do seem to have been very keen to prevent revenues, in particular, from being restored to their original owners. But again, this was not a situation that Edward could allow to continue unchecked.

Lucrative church lands and revenues certainly caused much litigation in the royal courts before they were completely restored to those who had held them in 1296. It is also clear that, in many cases, the war had taken a great toll on ecclesiastical property and many churchmen now welcomed the English king as their defender. Thus, when each church or religious house petitioned the king to be restored to their lands and revenues, they also asked Edward to take them into his protection and maintain them.[48] Their feelings may have been shared by many other inhabitants of Scotland, but that would surely change if they came to believe that he either could not or would not protect them.

The plethora of court cases which Edward was determined to consider before he turned his attention to the final settlement of Scotland indicates the extent to which the war had disrupted so much of normal life. Although many doubtless welcomed the fact that rents and taxes had been less easily collected by either government, at least as many suffered from the lack of a nationally competent authority to provide redress for all manner of grievances. Edward, whose enthusiasm for the law characterised his reign,[49] was doubtless keen to illustrate the benefits of his justice to his Scottish subjects and was certainly intent on modernising the more archaic aspects – in his eyes – of Scotland's judicial system. The former required the king's immediate and concentrated attention; the latter could wait until he was ready to put the finishing touches to the settlement of his new acquisition.

Most of the first category of judicial activity was completed in the parliament of February 1305. There was then one important outstanding piece of legal business to complete, although its resolution was by no means certain until the summer. According to the chronicler, Pierre Langtoft, William Wallace and Simon Fraser sought to come to Edward's peace some time in 1303 but did not turn up on the appointed day. At some point after Christmas 1303, Wallace again apparently sought to come to Edward's peace 'without surrendering into his hands body or head'; he also requested 'an honourable allowance of wood and cattle', a request which Edward angrily refused.[50]

Andrew Fisher, the best of Sir William's many biographers, has stated that 'the Wallace we read of here ... is neither the Wallace of history nor of tradition'. But it would surely do Sir William no dishonour to suggest that he might have offered to surrender – on terms – once it became perfectly clear that almost everyone else had submitted to Edward. Since we know so very little of 'the Wallace of history', and he is so easily confused with 'the Wallace of tradition', it would be rash to state categorically that the ex-guardian totally rejected the idea of honourable surrender when the odds were so clearly stacked against him. However, Edward's refusal to consider anything other than an abject and total submission would equally have given Wallace little choice but to remain a fugitive.

The declaration of outlawry at the St Andrews parliament of 1304 was almost certainly accompanied by the grant to someone described as the king's 'dear valet' of 'all goods and chattels of whatever kind he may gain from Sir William Wallace, the king's enemy'. The name of the beneficiary was originally Edward Bruce, the earl of Carrick's younger brother, but the surname was then deleted and that of Keith substituted. Edward Bruce was certainly a royal valet in the prince of Wales's household, while there is no evidence that Edward Keith, Sir Robert Keith's sibling, was similarly employed.[51] There is perhaps nothing sinister about the change of beneficiary of this grant – it could easily have been a scribal error in the first place. But it is perhaps fortunate for the reputation of the future patriotic hero, Robert Bruce, that his brother did not profit at the expense of William Wallace.

The last mention of Wallace before his capture was in September 1304, when members of the Dundee garrison under Thomas d'Umfraville gave chase to him 'beneath' Yrenside (Ironside), a hill behind Dundee.[52] He disappears for almost a year until 3 August 1305, when he was finally captured by men of the keeper of Dumbarton, Sir John Menteith, near Glasgow. A mere twenty days later, Wallace was brought to trial and executed at Smithfield. The charges brought against him – such as the holding of Scottish parliaments and the maintenance of the Franco-Scottish alliance – can be read just as easily as a list of his achievements.[53]

Edward's experiences in Scotland 'undoubtedly crystallized [his] theories and practices in dealing with treason'. Prior to Wallace's trial, a number of Scots had been charged with treacherous behaviour, but this was the first time that trial, sentence and execution had actually been carried out. Wallace, of course, denied the charge that he had betrayed his king, since he did not recognise Edward as such and accepted the other crimes attributed to him. Having been declared an outlaw at the St Andrews parliament, the record of the charges which Edward accused him of was regarded in the middle ages as proof in itself, and thus Wallace had no right to put himself on a jury; 'in such circumstances there was no proper trial but merely the passing of sentence and its execution'.[54]

In strictly legal terms, Edward's justification for the charge of treason – that Balliol's return to the English king's homage and fealty in 1296, which conceded that the latter's conquest of Scotland was 'by right', together with the homage and fealties gathered generally, made all Scots Edward's vassals – was probably more 'correct' than Wallace's assertion that the lack of a personal oath to the English king exonerated him from that charge. However, the law was by no means clear-cut and Edward was himself in the vanguard of attempts to refine such legal uncertainties to the advantage of crown and state. The only thing we can be absolutely sure of is that both protagonists passionately believed they were right; and that Wallace had absolutely no chance once he fell into Edward's hands.[55]

Similarly, the gruesome methods by which Sir William met his death were not thought up specially for him by the bloodthirsty English king. Each punishment corresponded to one of the crimes with which Wallace was charged and 'the process was akin in the sentence pronounced to the one which concerned

David ap Gruffydd', the Welsh prince executed by Edward in 1283. Nevertheless, it is hard not to agree that 'from the political view-point the trial and sentence were ill-judged and personal animosity may have clouded the king's vision'.[56] The clemency shown to the Scots in general contrasts sharply with the fate of William Wallace and stamps the trial and execution with a degree of vindictiveness which does Edward no credit.

It is not entirely clear why Wallace should have inspired such fury. The English king usually reacted violently only against those whom he regarded as having betrayed him personally in some way, as was evident both in the trial of David ap Gruffydd and the fines added to the submission terms of February 1304. Sir William's death may well have been witnessed by many of the Scots who were in London to attend the parliament of September 1305 in which the ordinances for the future government of Scotland were set out. Their silence at Wallace's fate does imply condonement, if not complicity. However, we must ask ourselves what they could have done when it was abundantly clear that the judgement was a foregone conclusion. They would have been on dangerous ground to plead clemency by virtue of Wallace's denial of the charge of treason – which completely contradicted Edward's claims to rule Scotland by right – and no-one, including Sir William himself, disputed the other charges. Nevertheless, the ferocity of this execution should not be forgotten when discussing Edward's statesmanlike behaviour during much of the period between 1304 and 1305.

The final settlement of Scotland was a far more protracted and considered process than it had been in 1296. In the Westminster parliament of February 1305, the bishop of Glasgow, the earl of Carrick and Sir John Moubray were ordered to advise the king as to how this settlement might best be achieved. This is a most remarkable trio: Carrick we might expect to be involved, but the inclusion of Moubray, Sir John Comyn's right-hand man, and Robert Wishart, whom Edward regarded as particularly seditious, attests to the king's desire to accommodate rather than alienate.[57] Nonetheless, Wishart's presence is striking for another reason; given that he and Carrick were close allies and could therefore 'out-vote' the one Comyn representative, this was a significant reversal in the balance of political power in Scotland among the Scots themselves.

Though it is not stated, the members of this triumvirate were almost certainly Edward's choices, because of what happened next. Having advised the king on Scottish procedure, including the need to hold a Scottish parliament in Scotland itself, the three were sent north to oversee the selection of those who would attend it. Edward had in fact decided that these delegates should come to London, not because he failed to appreciate Scottish sensitivities on this point but almost certainly because he was now seriously ill. (Indeed, this parliament would be postponed twice before finally meeting in September 1305.)

And it was back in Scotland at an assembly held at Scone or Perth in May 1305 that the earl of Carrick finally realised that having the English king's favour meant little when it came to persuading his colleagues in the Scottish political community that he – rather than John Comyn – was now its most influential member. Of the ten selected to attend the London parliament, almost all were Comyn adherents, with the exception of Bishop Lamberton of St Andrews, who was probably one of the few neutral figures. If – and there was surely no doubt on the matter – Robert Bruce harboured a burning desire to become king, then he was now faced with the uncomfortable realisation that a man of far more experience, influence and military prowess was intending to stand in his way. His rival was not the spent force in exile, John Balliol, but the latter's very present and highly motivated nephew, John Comyn of Badenoch.[58]

The ordinances promulgated in the September parliament with the advice of the ten Scottish representatives listed not only the offices which were to form the new administration, but also named those who were to hold them. Since the English administration had been up and running throughout much of Scotland since at least

1304, the changes instituted in September 1305 should be regarded as the end of the process of re-establishment, not the beginning.

In the first instance, the number of Scots holding the office of sheriff before and after the publication of the ordinances, as shown in Table 8,[59] is striking. In 1304, only four out of a total of seventeen sheriffs were English; equally, out of the thirteen Scottish sheriffs, only three – Sir Richard Siward, Sir Alexander Comyn, and Sir Archibald Livingston – had held office under King Edward after 1296. It is also possible, especially in the north-east, that many of the men installed by Edward as sheriffs in 1303 had held office under the guardians precisely because they were natural leaders in these areas. Even Alexander Pilche, leader of the burgesses of Inverness who had caused so much trouble in 1297, was allowed to keep control of Inverness castle, albeit temporarily. Heritable sheriffdoms, which Edward had previously completely ignored, were also reinstated, as was the attachment of the office of escheatry to the sheriff's functions 'as usual'.[60]

Table 8a: *Sheriffs in 1304*
Those whose names are in italics held the same
office both before and after the ordinances.

Aberdeen – Sir Alexander Comyn

Ayr – earl of Carrick

Aucterarder – *Sir Malcolm Innerpeffray*

Banff – Sir Duncan Frendraught

Clackmannan – Sir William Biset

Dumbarton – *Sir John Menteith*

Dumfries – Sir Matthew Redeman

Edinburgh – Sir Ebulo Mountz

Fife – Sir Richard Siward

Forfar – John Pollok/Henry Preston

Inverness (constable of castle) – Alexander Pilche

Lanark – earl of Carrick

Linlithgow – Sir Archibald Livingstone

Mearns (Kincardine) – *Sir Richard Dundemor*

Nairn (constable of castle) – Gervase the clerk

Peebles – *Robert Hastangs*

Perth – Sir Robert Harcars

Roxburgh – Sir Robert Hastangs

Stirling – Sir Archibald Livingston

Table 8b: *Sheriffs of the ordinances*[61]

Aberdeen – Sir Norman Leslie	Forfar – Sir William Airth
Ayr – Sir Godfrey Ros	Forres & Nairn – Alexander
Clackmannan & Aucterarder	Wiseman
– *Sir Malcolm Innerpeffray*	Kincardine (Mearns) – *Sir*
Cromarty – Sir William	*Richard Dundemor*
Mowat (heritable)	Kinross – the heritable sheriff
Dumbarton – *Sir John Menteith*	Lanark – Sir Henry Sinclair
Dumfries – Sir Richard Siward	Peebles – *Robert Hastangs*
Edinburgh, Haddington &	Perth – Sir John Inchmartin
Linlithgow – Sir Ivo Aldeburgh	Selkirk – the heritable sheriff
Elgin – William Wiseman	Stirling – William Bisset
Fife – Sir Constantine of	Wigtown – Thomas
Lochore	MacCullough

The sheriff of Berwick was to be named by the chamberlain of Scotland, who had the keeping of Berwick castle. The lieutenant of Scotland was to hold the castles of Roxburgh and Jedburgh, and could choose a sheriff at Roxburgh.[62]

In 1305 only two Englishmen were named as sheriffs – Sir Ivo Aldeburgh, who was to hold the reunited sheriffdoms of 'the three Lothians', Edinburgh, Haddington and Linlithgow, and Robert Hastangs, who continued as sheriff of Peebles. All these officers could be appointed or removed by the lieutenant or the chamberlain; they were also to be 'sufficient men and most profitable for the king and people, and the maintenance of peace'. With these last exceptions, it is likely that the Scottish delegates had a big say in these appointments, given that most of the appointees were local to the area in which they served.

To be fair, in 1296 Edward had conformed to Scottish practice with the appointment of justiciars of Lothian, Galloway and north of the Forth. This format was adapted slightly in the ordinances of 1305. Instead of three justiciars, there were now to be four 'pairs', one Englishman and one Scotsman. The extra pair was to have authority 'beyond the mountains' (the Grampians). The justiciars normally toured their area of jurisdiction hearing criminal cases previously prepared by the coroners. Edward clearly did not feel comfortable about giving sole responsibility for criminal justice to Scotsmen, but he also recognised that he could not do without them completely. All eight appointees – Sir John Lisle and Sir Adam Gordon for Lothian, Sir Walter Burghdon and Sir Roger Kirkpatrick for Galloway, Sir William Inge and Sir Robert Keith for north of the Forth, and Sir John Vaux and Sir Reginald Cheyne for beyond the mountains – were men of considerable, though varying, administrative experience.[63] The coroners themselves were to be appointed by the three main officers of state, if the present holders were found to be unfit, 'unless the latter hold by charter', in which case the king was to be consulted.

Doubtless the appointment which concerned the Scots most was the top job, that of lieutenant. John of Brittany, the king's favoured nephew and currently governor of Aquitaine,[64] was given that honour, with a company of sixty men-at-arms. His salary, which not only maintained him in office, but also paid for his retinue and the garrisons of the castles of Jedburgh and Roxburgh, was to be 2,000 marks per annum, to be received from the chamberlain from the issues of the land of Scotland. This was not overly generous, since Surrey had been given the same amount with only fifty in his retinue and without responsibility for Jedburgh and Roxburgh. Indeed, Brittany clearly felt it wasn't enough since it was increased to 3,000 marks on 15 October 1305, before he had even arrived in Scotland.[65] Presumably the appointment of a single royal lieutenant brought to an end the role of the earls of Atholl and Ross in the north, as well as Segrave in the south.

The earl was due to take up office on 2 February 1306. In the meantime, Sir Brian FitzAlan and the bishop of St Andrews were to act as guardians of Scotland. In the event, Brittany was unable to leave Gascony until at least 17 April 1306 and Lamberton, Sir John Sandale, the chamberlain, Sir Robert Keith and Sir John Kingston were all ordered on 16 February to act on his behalf until his arrival.[66]

Twenty-one Scots – four bishops, four abbots, five earls and eight barons – were to form the lieutenant's council, along with the chancellor and the chamberlain, the justiciars and other royal officials. Again, this included some of the most prominent members of the former patriotic cause, such as the bishops of St Andrews and Dunkeld, the earls of Buchan, Atholl and Carrick, Sir John Moubray, Sir Alastair of Argyll, Sir Robert Keith and Sir Adam Gordon. This was rehabilitation on a grand scale. Robert Bruce might have felt pleased to be on this council, along with his ally, the earl of Atholl, but again the extent to which Comyn friends and relatives dominated this group is telling. Scotland could not be governed without them, a fact that Edward seems to have effectively recognised.

The king, mindful of his promises in the submission agreement but with his own personal agenda in mind, was keen to tackle the thorny subject of Scottish law and custom. There was no compromising on one issue: the ancient '*usage* of Scots and Brets' was banned from henceforth. However, the lieutenant, when he finally arrived, was also to assemble 'the good people of Scotland in a convenient place, and there the laws of King David, and amendments and additions by other kings shall be rehearsed'. Brittany could then, 'with the aid which he shall have there of both English and Scots men ... amend such of these laws and usages which are plainly against the king'. It was clear, therefore, what should take priority and it wasn't Scottish law and custom. Those matters requiring Edward's attention were to be sent to him in writing, along with the amendments already agreed, all before 12 May 1306. There was certainly to be a serious overhaul of the Scottish legal system by means of public consultation, but the king had the final say.

The parliament of September 1305, which could be regarded as an exemplary piece of statesmanship, must be placed within a wider context. During the eighteen months preceding the promulgation of the ordinance for Scotland's future government, and with the brutal example of Wallace still fresh in their minds, the Scottish élites already knew that Edward considered that the 'despites, trespasses, outrages and disobediences' which they had perpetrated during the war were so great that they could never make sufficient amends. However, the king was still keen that they should endure some form of punishment to allow him to forgive them, even if he might never forget their previous treachery. He was also gracious enough to intimate that because the Scots had 'borne themselves well and loyally' since his return from Scotland, and in anticipation of their future good behaviour, he would allow the terms of their submission to stand with regard to the saving of life and limb, and the quittance of imprisonment and disinheritance. It's hard to imagine that Edward would go back on his promises, but clearly he was feeling the pain of the years of war, in his own body as well as his treasury.

The only clear-cut exception when it came to magnanimity was King John, whose lands were again forfeited, meaning that Edward could permanently dispose of them as he wished. They were to be treated as separate 'from the demesnes pertaining to the *roiaute* [kingship/crown] of Scotland', which could not be given away. Balliol was effectively being treated like any other landowner (except that he had lost his lands) rather than as a king; equally, and despite the use here of the word *roiaute*, Scotland was now consistently described as a 'land' and not a 'kingdom'. That was one highly significant deterioration since 1296, though Edward never did make any formal pronouncement on the constitutional status of his northern-most possession.

And finally, in order to satisfy his apparent twin desire to punish and be merciful, Edward devised a scheme in October 1305 under which the Scottish nobility would pay over the annual value of their lands for a varying number of years. This also satisfied his far greater need to improve his finances, which the original plan for exile would have done nothing to alleviate.

The money thus paid over by Sir John Comyn and the rest was to be used 'for the work of the castles that we are having built in the said land of Scotland for the security of the said land and keeping the peace, or to be put to another use, as we see should be done'.[67] Perhaps Edward did see the irony of having the Scottish nobility pay for new fortifications which could be used against them should they harbour any thoughts of rebellion.

It could be argued that the Scots were buying their lands back, but it is perhaps more helpful to look at this as a system of fines, prompted primarily by Edward's desire, after so many years of major expenditure, to have Scotland pay, at least a little, for the emptying of his coffers. In return the sentences of exile were dropped. Those Scots who had submitted to Edward before Comyn were to pay the value of their rents for two years instead of three, except if they could show that they were completely free of this burden by the king's special command. The Scottish clergy, apart from the bishop of Glasgow, were to pay over the value of one year's rents. Wishart, still correctly identified as a – perhaps the – driving force behind the maintenance of Scottish resistance, was to pay three years' rents. Sir Ingram d'Umfraville, who had only recently returned from France to submit, was to be punished accordingly for his 'cowardliness' with the payment of the value of five years' rents.[68] Two knights who had returned with him, Sir William Balliol and Sir John Wishart, were each to pay four years' rents.

In order to facilitate the payment of these fines, the lieutenant and chamberlain of Scotland, 'when they have come', were ordered to make an assessment of the relevant lands. Their owners would then hand over half of the annual revenue each year until the total had been paid, thoughtfully giving them something to live on. It was also made quite clear that these conditions were in no way to apply to those Scots who had been imprisoned or who had not yet submitted.[69] Given that many Scottish estates must have been in a state of some disorder after the war, Edward may have been rather optimistic in expecting much of a return in the immediate future. Still, he wasn't to know that another rebellion was just around the corner.

This, then, was Scotland's future, carefully mapped out by its new king with at least some help from its political community. It is pointless to ask if it was a fair settlement, given that the key question was still whether Edward had any right to rule the northern kingdom. What was important was the extent to which all this careful planning and painstaking balancing of competing needs and desires would actually work in keeping the peace. Geoffrey Barrow has asserted that

> ... despite the conversion of old enemies into new advisers, the real power was to be vested in the lieutenant, chancellor and chamberlain ... To say therefore that the official element was derived 'mainly from Scotland' is true only in the rather unreal numerical sense. There was no escaping the fact that Scotland was once more what she had been in 1296, a conquered country, occupied by foreign garrisons and governed by the foreign officials of a foreign king.[70]

There is a large degree of truth in this, especially for those living in the south-east, where the sheriffs were all English and the centre of Edwardian government resided. There is also no getting around the fact that this was indeed a reconquest, despite all the consultation. But there is a danger in over-emphasising this point or seeing it as the only way of looking at this revolution in Scottish affairs. For most people living far from Berwick, the local officer was still a familiar face, and the rules and regulations which he was there to enforce were also – so far – easily recognisable. The new administration was therefore far less obviously novel and intrusive than it had been in 1296; indeed, all this care was taken precisely to foster consensus and acquiescence at all levels of society. Edward had learned his lesson well.

Of course, many might still have harboured the suspicion that the leopard could not really change his spots. Edward's arrogant assumption that aspects of Scots law would require amendment if it offended 'God and reason' might well have set off just such alarm bells. It was also the case that the two issues which had ostensibly sparked off many of the revolts in 1297 – taxation and overseas military service – were in no sense addressed by any of the king's edicts during the settlement of Scotland. In the short term, these issues were unlikely to trouble relations between Edward and his newest subjects since there was no other war on the horizon. In the long term, however, there was nothing to stop Scotland from being hit by the kind of intensive government which they were quite unaccustomed to, and which contrasted greatly, with a touch of rose-tinted nostalgia, with life under the kings of Scots.[71] As it turned out, there was no time for the relationship between Edward and the Scots to turn sour in this respect. But that does not mean either that such an antagonism was not a very real possibility, or that the deep-seated animosity which this war had already fostered just fizzled away in a new dawn of fellowship and mutual respect.

CHAPTER EIGHT

LESSONS IN CONQUEST

The ordinances of 1305 set the seal on Edward's second conquest of Scotland. There was no longer either a Scottish king or, this time, a kingdom – merely a land. There is no doubt that there was much on which Edward would not compromise – notably the desire to maintain senior authority within the Scottish government in the hands of those he trusted (i.e. not Scots), to keep south-east Scotland entirely within English control, and his own ultimate right to alter anything deemed derogatory to his own sovereignty. However, the second settlement of Scotland, which took a year and a half to perfect, was a quite different affair from that of 1296, which was done and dusted within a single parliament.

There is only one real explanation for this change of attitude; the years of war had taught Edward I that, in contrast to the conquest of Wales and indeed to his first conquest of 1296, it was extremely unwise to treat Scotland in a way that might prompt its people to resist. The English king therefore sought to adhere as much as possible to Scotland's distinctive governmental system and to accord its political leaders a degree of respect that had been markedly lacking the first time round.

In the distant past, when chiefs, then kings, subjected others to their rule, they were not interested in interfering in the way things were done in the subordinate territory. What they wanted was regular tribute (in cash or, more likely, goods) and perhaps a pleasing and appropriate acknowledgement of their own superior status. But conquest had moved on in the last century or so, reflecting increasingly sophisticated governmental structures and developing concepts of kingship and sovereignty. And there were few more sophisticated and centralised systems of government than that of England, refined to a peak of (comparative) intrusiveness by the Norman practices introduced by William the Conqueror but building on the Anglo-Saxon structures already in place.

In seeking to apply English customs and habits to a greater or lesser extent across his domains (though Gascony was a rather different case), Edward was not alone in seeing them as best practice. King John of Scotland's government had, after all, sought to establish sheriffdoms – Anglo-Saxon in origin and introduced to the rest of Scotland 150 years earlier – in the newly acquired north-west Highlands and Hebrides where Norse and earlier practices presumably already existed. But with attempts to assimilate as well as dominate, it should come as no surprise that identities strengthened as a reaction to challenges to the way it was believed things had always been done (within kingdoms as much as between them), even as, in more peaceful circumstances, they might also strengthen in time around rulers intent on focusing more and more government on themselves.

Nevertheless, the ability of the Scots to elicit even such a tacit acknowledgement of the strength of their resistance from Edward I, despite its ultimate failure, is extremely important to our understanding of this war. Good and bad luck played their part, as ever. The Scots were perhaps fortunate, for example, that the conquest of Wales had already stretched English resources, even if it also provided Edward with a valuable learning experience; on the other hand, they were unlucky that the battle of Courtrai happened at the very moment when the return of their king with French aid was considered a distinct possibility. But unforeseen events have a habit of occurring and it is only their nature that is unexpected.

Equally, England's response to the conflict was fundamental to its pursuit. Edward was very fortunate to have chosen to prosecute a war against an inferior nation (from the English point of view) into which he could divert the considerable and understandable resentment at the constant demands he made of his subjects away from himself (even if that war naturally created fresh demands). However, though the English certainly didn't like the thought of being bested by the Scots, their basic lack of interest in the conquest of the northern kingdom, once it became clear that the war would provide very little opportunity for glory, riches and honour, soon turned into downright apathy, if not antipathy. Even English patriotism had its limits when there was little or no scope for individuals to pick up anything other than the promise of lands or offices and increased debt. Edward certainly seems to have been extremely concerned about the state of his war machine, judging by the increasingly frenzied letters to royal officials in 1303 particularly. The earl of Ulster, for one, would never again believe the promises made to persuade him to serve in Edward's army after that year's campaign proved as unforthcoming in pay as the one in 1296.

Though it is important to understand how Scotland came to be taken over by Edward I at the beginning of these wars, the more interesting questions surely arrive after the fact of conquest, as England attempted to make that conquest stick and Scotland attempted to be rid of it. The administration set up in 1296 was not particularly well thought out, primarily because Edward I was more concerned with getting back to his war with France. This, unfortunately, did nothing to give the new administration a good, or even acceptable, start. On the one hand, enthusiastic and competent officers, such as Cressingham and Ormesby, proved far too adept at extracting an unprecedented level of revenue, to the complete bewilderment of the generally untaxed Scottish population; on the other hand, the lack of interest shown by both Surrey and Percy in the judicial aspect of their offices particularly ensured that the Scots felt unable to seek redress for their grievances.

From the Scottish point of view, therefore, the regime was bound to be regarded as oppressive from day one, even if the kingdom was not treated any differently from the rest of Edward's dominions, including England (after the initial pointed snubs to Scottish sovereignty). It is also highly unlikely that the king meant for his regime to be quite as heavy-handed or lopsided in the way it was administered, but without his eye on his officials, they were always far more likely to err on the side of Edward's needs – and their own – rather than those of the Scots. The depth of feeling within the conquered nation is illustrated by the fact that no-one waited for a coordinated or official response; local communities throughout the kingdom voted with their feet and sought to expel the offending representatives of Edwardian government, presumably without worrying too much about the consequences. The full extent of such activities is almost certainly lost through the lack of evidence. However, William Wallace's rising in Lanarkshire is surely a good example of local men taking events into their own hands, even if, in this instance, its leader became remarkably and unusually famous.

Indeed, Scotland's very lack of centralisation probably gave the kingdom an advantage in this war of survival, not least because of the ability of local leaders to function with some semblance of normality even when the central (Scottish) government was either impotent or seriously handicapped. As with Wales under Owain Glyn Dŵr a century later, this meant it was far harder for the English to bring about a piecemeal reconquest, because revolt could continue to break out anywhere at any time. However, Scotland had an advantage over Wales in that there was less danger 'of rash actions by individual groups'[1] because, beyond certain restricted geographical areas, there was still enough of a governmental superstructure to maintain a degree of co-ordination from 1297 onwards.

The inability of Edward's officials to act effectively against these impromptu revolts in 1297 perhaps panicked the king into the early release of Scots, like MacDougall of Argyll and the

Comyns of Badenoch and Buchan, who had experience of dealing with the individual localities involved. Doubtless Edward
realised he was taking a huge risk – these were, after all, key
members of the former government who had gone to war against
him. Presumably he believed that the crushing military defeat at
Dunbar and the oaths which they had subsequently sworn to
him would be sufficient to check any rebellious instincts, spurred
on by his desire to see Scotland as effectively settled by his even
greater desire to recover his duchy of Gascony. If so, he was
deluding himself. The actions of Scotland's most powerful family,
the Comyns, in particular – reckoned by English contemporaries
to have been duplicitous – underline the importance of Andrew
Murray and William Wallace in showing the Scottish élites the
'how', rather than the 'why', of effective rebellion. Confidence is
everything when going to war, especially if the opposition is so
much more powerful.

During the period between 1296 and September 1297, the
English government, both north and south of the border, continued to treat Scotland as finished business, albeit with a few loose
ends to tidy up. The battle of Stirling Bridge changed all that –
from then on it was proper war. The campaign leading up to the
battle of Falkirk in 1298 was intended to restore Edward's
authority in Scotland with an overwhelming show of force. But,
despite involving one of the most impressive armies in western
Europe, this campaign exposed the weaknesses of the English
war machine. The battle itself, though certainly an English
victory, was perhaps more of a close-run thing than Edward
would have cared to admit. Equally, it did not lead to the collapse
of the Scottish government but instead finally convinced the
guardians that they should refrain from engaging the enemy
directly in battle.

That changed everything, contributing directly to the length
of the war and the dire effects on English finances. There is no
doubt that the length of the English supply line was vastly more
overstretched in Scotland than it had been in Wales. While it

would be foolish to assert that, after 1298 (and to an extent before then), this became a conflict the Scots could sustain far more easily (not least because we have almost no evidence for the workings of the Scottish government and military machine), it was certainly one that proved that a small nation could put up an effective fight. And, eventually, under Robert Bruce the Scots would prove to be the military power in the British Isles, even if they didn't enjoy that supremacy for long.

To be fair, Edward was a quick learner. He was perfectly aware of the difficulties exposed in 1298 and made great efforts to remedy them, overhauling the fleet and issuing even more specific guidelines for the most efficient purchase and conveyance of food supplies, for example. However, his understanding of what needed to be done did not quite square with either his subjects' diminishing enthusiasm for the war or their ability to pay for it. The spiralling nature of the debt incurred by the English crown from the various component parts of the war machine was not immediately obvious, but by 1301 Edward was forced to choose to whom he would postpone payment; this in turn unleashed the law of diminishing returns as the losers had even less reason to trust royal promises in the future. In the end, the English king presided over a system of making war that was already antiquated, however much he might tweak it to make it more efficient.

The problem with the lack of suitable personnel has been mentioned many times already. In south-east Scotland, where the English were most secure, the war effort – not to mention the effort to maintain a successful peace – was hampered by constant changes of royal officers and the lack of consistent overall command. In the south-west, where the English struggled to do more than hold on to isolated and ineffective castles, the significance of Sir John de St John as warden should not be underestimated, not least because his appointment in 1300 brought more consistent and effective pressure to bear on the Scots of that region, pressure that helped to persuade many communities to change side. Sir John Segrave perhaps also brought a degree of coherence to the English military presence in the south-east, but only from 1301.

Problems of personnel were compounded by the fact that, even though the seat of English government was moved from London to York (York being equidistant from London and Edinburgh), it was still a considerable distance from the administrative and military operations it was attempting to coordinate. This problem was exacerbated by the fact that the officers on the ground were often unable to attend meetings at York because they were constantly needed at their posts. This placed a greater reliance on messengers, which rendered the whole operation correspondingly more vulnerable.

However, while the situation was certainly made more difficult by the lack of enthusiasm for office in Scotland among the English élites, we should not forget the experiences of the foot-soldiers who also served in both the armies and the garrisons. It would be overstating the case to suggest that there was a general lack of concern on the part of royal officials whether these foot-soldiers stayed or went. Nevertheless, their place at the bottom of the pecking order surely meant that they must, at the very least, have felt extremely vulnerable. The general role of infantry was about to undergo a significant transformation, but as yet the archer in particular was not given the respect which he would be accorded later in the fourteenth century.[2]

There is no doubt that this had serious implications for the success of Edward's military operations; time and again the lack of wages and supplies meant that the footsoldiers, who bore first and hardest the brunt of any shortfall, took the pragmatic decision to return home in large numbers. The army could not continue to function without them and it effectively disintegrated. Despite occasional attempts at bribery,[3] the footsoldiers were not fooled. Pride will only go so far if it is undermined by personal privation, and the lack of booty and excitement once the Scots stopped fighting battles can have provided very little incentive for a prolonged march through an alien landscape.

All of these significant difficulties, coupled with the fact that the Scots showed little sign of being able to defeat the English militarily, meant that the conflict quickly degenerated into a war of attrition. If one wanted to place a bet, then England clearly had the ability to sit it out the longest; but perhaps only just. The will to fight among the wider population, and the consequences of continuing to do so, played a vital role in deciding the contest. Enthusiasm in England, which was never very high, had reached an all-time low by 1303; though we will never know how close it came to vanishing altogether, we should not forget that the English had already nearly launched a civil war in this reign. The unpopularity of Edward II within a year of taking the throne, though partly his own fault, is perhaps also an indication of what his father might have faced if the war had gone on much longer.

The contradictory sentiments of patriotism and war-weariness come across clearly in the political songs remaining from the period. In the bluntly titled *Song against the King's Taxes*, it was lamented that:

> Now goes in England from year to year
> The fifteenth penny, to do thus a common harm.
> And it makes them go down, who used to sit upon a
> bench;
> And it obliges the common people to sell both cows
> vessels and clothes
> It does not please thus to pay the fifteenth to the last
> penny.[4]

While this song indicates the difficulties caused further down the social ladder, there is little reason to presume that the élites were much more enamoured with the war, since it had so little to offer them in terms of their traditional rewards. Even Edward admitted that the siege of Stirling would provide an unusual

opportunity for new knights to 'gain their shoes or their boots'.[5]
If the enemy refused to engage, then campaigning was little more
than a lengthy horse-ride, redeemed only by the odd skirmish;
even the sieges tended to be a triumph for the engineers. Heroic,
chivalric, glorious – this war was none of these things.
Nevertheless, we cannot ignore the fact that Edward's own military reputation, which was certainly boosted by comparison with
his unenthusiastic son, remained intact after his death (though it
was perhaps easier to celebrate him once he was no longer around
to demand still more from his English subjects):

> Of England he was lord
> and a king who knew much of war;
> In no book can we read
> Of a king who sustained better his land.
> All the things which he would do,
> wisely he brought them to an end.
> Now his body lies in the earth;
> and the world is going to ruin.[6]

The fact that a nation could criticise its king for the burdens
which his ambition placed upon it one day, and then eulogise
him for having done so the next is an entirely human reaction to
the end of an era. Edward's final, devastating failure to bring
Scotland to heel was glossed over by the belief, which he would
certainly have shared, that he could have succeeded if death had
not intervened. Edward II, on the other hand, showed neither
the inclination nor the ability to allow the English any pride in
their dealings with Scotland during his reign, however much he
believed in his own rights to rule there.

But while Edward I still lived, there were two sides to this
coin. While the Scottish élites remained fairly solidly behind the
war effort between 1297 and 1304, there were many others who,
for all number of reasons, could not sustain their active support,
particularly if they lived in close proximity to an English garrison

or the regular path of an English army. Scotland's geography played a fundamental role in giving King John's government a heartland from which it could operate in relative safety; however, retreating into the 'normality' of Scotland north of the Forth was not an option for the lesser folk of the south. Again, a comparison with rebellion in Wales is instructive; according to Professor Rees Davies, 'It was exhaustion and military frustration which eventually defeated Glyn Dŵr'.[7] This was just as true for the Scots a century earlier, even if the English may not have been far behind them.

What is remarkable is the extent to which these military enterprises took up so many months of the year, either in the planning or the execution. This was at least as true for the Scots, who often managed to keep raiding parties together over the winter months. Sir John Comyn's exertions immediately before the battle of Roslin in February 1303 involved criss-crossing the strenuous hills and dales of east central Scotland, sometimes overnight. The Scottish military machine – opaque though its workings certainly are – was by then a quite different beast from the one that so boldly and ineffectively took on the English at Dunbar seven years earlier. From 1301, however, increasing English garrison activity outwith the campaigning season made it very difficult for the Scots to compensate for the gains made in the previous months by English armies. The lack of siege engines also worked against them since they no longer had enough time to coax an English garrison into submission, as they had at Stirling and Bothwell a few years earlier.

But there were pauses in the conflict too, interludes that sometimes reflect Scottish success in persuading Philip of France or the pope to pressurise Edward, though this was not always entirely unhelpful to the English war effort. By 1300, the English king attempted to compensate for his inability to keep his army together over the winter by granting the Scots truces. However, these were most certainly a means to an end and even the truce of Asnières, which allowed for the French to play a direct role in

Scotland, was surely regarded as a disagreeable option to stave off a worse alternative. At least new garrisons were given some time to establish themselves, even if they might still be in danger thanks to perennial supply problems.

Equally, the references to administration of a more 'normal' kind within the English zone from 1300 onwards is one of the best indicators of increasing success. The taking of castles is one thing, but they served little purpose (not least given their costs to maintain) if their recapture was not translated into increasing acceptance, and therefore authority, within their own hinterland. The deliberate targeting of the 'middling sort' was part and parcel of this development and was one whose success the Scottish government could only prevent by direct intimidation. And that meant that a Scottish force of sufficient strength needed to venture into English-held territory and persuade the inhabitants there that they would be 'better off' without Edward's peace. This was certainly employed, but as English administrative achievement became more widespread and more stable, it proved impossible to dam the tide of acceptance of Edward's regime. Subjection is a two-way relationship.

This is not meant to imply that Scottish resistance was either uncommitted or ineffective; it does no discredit to the losing side to point out the huge odds it was up against, nor that the risk of severe economic disruption was sufficient, at both an individual and a community level, to prompt a change of allegiance, willingly or otherwise. Given the deteriorating climate, which led to poor or very bad harvests in the late 1290s, this might well have been a matter of life and death and who are we to question those in the past for decisions that may well have involved preventing their children from starving?

However, any discussion of positive and negative factors working for each side in any conflict, though necessary, is unlikely to illuminate what this war must have looked like to contemporaries. In the first place, each point of view would depend on a variety of factors other than being Scottish or English. While hindsight can allow us to glimpse certain trends which explain success or failure, such insights were generally not available to those involved at the time. Unfortunately, the writing of history demands both a coherent structure and the drawing of conclusions, eliding over the likelihood that at any given point there were a number of outcomes that in turn would have had very different consequences. This problem has already been highlighted most eloquently by Professor Rees Davies:

> Hindsight is the besetting sin of the historian. Nowhere is it, perhaps, more pernicious in its impact than when discussing a war or a revolt. Chaos is turned into order at the stroke of the historian's pen; isolated and unrelated episodes are arranged into neat causal patterns; lines of development and crucial turning-points are perceived with a clarity and confidence denied to contemporaries.[8]

History will continue, for the moment anyway, to be written in terms of a progression from A to B. Nevertheless, historians must, at the very least, admit the problems posed by the presumption that they should not merely take the past apart and leave it like that, despite the fact that a disordered muddle might better reflect the situation at the time, even if it might not do much to illuminate in the present.[9]

It is certainly possible to understand why the Scots surrendered to Edward I in 1304, with the important caveat that their eventual capitulation was by no means inevitable and, for most of the period, remained highly unlikely. Even in 1303, especially after the surprise Scottish 'victory' at Roslin, the permanent English forces in Scotland could appear demoralised and ineffectual. And this is the crux of the matter, the double-edged sword under which both sides operated.

For the English, their very success in extending control over more and more of Scotland also made them correspondingly vulnerable as resources were further stretched, often to near breaking point. The total number of permanent troops stationed in Scotland did not increase dramatically as more garrisons were installed. While this could reflect increasing confidence, it might also highlight dire necessity and certainly meant that Selkirk castle, for example, could be captured by the Scots as late as 1303, despite lying deep within the English-held south-east. For the Scots, English vulnerability was exploited to great effect even up until September 1303, when some nobles considered submitting but changed their minds when they saw the state of the Irish footsoldiers. However, as English garrisons – and with them, English justice – became an increasingly permanent fixture throughout more of the country, it must have been far harder for the Scottish government to convince the war-weary population at large to give up the chance to live their lives (more) normally.

Looking at the situation from this perspective alone, an English victory becomes the most likely outcome, not least because Edward would never have given up except in extraordinary circumstances and he still, despite the difficulties, had access to far greater resources than the Scottish government. But there were many other factors, some foreseeable and others quite unexpected, which could push the advantage to one side or the other. Courtrai was one such unlikely event that had serious repercussions for the Scots. If it had not happened, Comyn and his advisers might have decided to sit the contest out even once the English had moved north of the Forth, in the hope that the French king would influence events in their favour, as the delegation sent to Paris in October 1302 still hoped against hope he might do. While there is no point in engaging in 'what ifs', it is only right to look at what alternatives, if any, they had when assessing why people did what they did.

It is particularly hard to avoid hindsight when it comes to Edward's second conquest of Scotland since *we* know that Robert Bruce was going to kill John Comyn, seize the throne and start

the whole ball rolling again less than six months after the publication of the ordinances for Scotland's government under English
rule. But, of course, contemporaries did not, even if a number of
important Scots probably had an inkling that either Comyn or
Bruce would aim for the throne eventually.[10] It is important,
therefore, to regard this settlement as genuine; certainly the
English expected it to last, and surely most of those Scots who
had recently sworn solemn oaths of loyalty were prepared to
abide by them until the death of Edward I rendered them void
and they could revisit their decision. At the very least Scotland
needed a period of recuperation, as indeed did England.

However, even before the settlement of Scotland had been
agreed, there were signs that all was not well, for the same old
reasons of lack of finance, never mind the pockets of resistance to
English rule that have already been noted. In July 1305, John,
earl of Atholl, still warden north of the Forth, petitioned the king
for a more effective source of his fee of 1,200 marks since he had
only received £540 so far and most of that had been spent on
repairing castles and retaining soldiers. A further £800 was
allowed to him for his expenses since 29 March 1304, presumably the date on which he took up office.

Sir Alexander Abernethy experienced similar problems,
prompting his own request to the king in August 1305 for
payment for himself, his retinue of sixty men-at-arms and various officials under his jurisdiction. William, earl of Ross, as
Edward's warden beyond the Spey, had also 'not yet had any
allowance for himself or his servants'.[11] Edward would have to do
rather better than this if he was to be regarded as a credible source
of patronage by the Scottish nobility, one of his many roles as
king, but probably the most important in the eyes of his most
exalted subjects. It was obviously still hard to get some parts of
Scotland to pay dues, perhaps because there was now a climate of
tax avoidance; the re-establishment of a national administration
which could pay for itself was taking rather longer than any of
Edward's officials might have wished.

Over time, the new regime would surely have dealt with these problems, so long as it continued in the vein in which it had begun, so as not to give the Scots cause for impotent resentment through heavy-handedness. But time was no longer on England's – or, more importantly, Edward's – side, though the future was still as unpredictable as the outcome of the war had once been. On the other hand, having proved that they could indeed exercise power successfully in defiance of the English king, the Scots now only needed a leader to act as a catalyst for revolt. The legitimacy of that leader – who now had to assume the empty throne to justify the continuing struggle – would not be beyond all doubt, since only John Balliol (in retirement in France) or his son Edward (still held in England) could lay claim to the kingship unequivocally; for obvious practical reasons their race was run, for the moment at least. The main obstacle to the success of Robert Bruce would not be the English but the Comyn family and their allies who, after all, dominated that very part of Scotland which had so effectively resisted Edward I. As King John's nephew, leader of Scottish resistance before 1304 and head of Scotland's most important family, John Comyn of Badenoch had far more credentials to rule than the man who killed him. Indeed, given the extent to which Carrick had been cold-shouldered by the Scottish political community after 1300, his eventual success as king was one of the more unlikely directions that history could have taken.

The first phase of the attempted conquest of Scotland by England cannot be regarded as a blueprint for success or failure in military affairs; the role of the unexpected, combined with the more predictable, makes every war unique. Nevertheless, one small, northern European nation's struggle against an overmighty neighbour and, equally, a dynamic and ambitious kingdom's attempt to extend its boundaries, as most contemporary states (including Scotland) sought to do, can tell us much about the realities of making war and the fine line between success and failure. To that extent, the history of warfare is both individual and universal.

The Anglo-Scottish wars also took place at a crucial juncture in the evolution of western European military strategy; now commanders found less use for the mighty charge of mounted knights and looked instead to strategies focused on footsoldiers, particularly archers. The English learned much from the Scots – directly, in terms of imaginative and effective use of infantry, and indirectly, as they were forced to adapt to the terrain now being exploited by their enemies, and which might itself become a weapon of war. These insights – used first by veterans of the Scottish wars against Edward II's internal enemies and then built upon by Edward III – were put to great effect by the English against the French from the middle of the fourteenth century.

But the Anglo-Scottish wars were never just about battles and logistics. Leaders on both sides relied on propaganda and the white heat of xenophobia to fuel their often-creaking military machines, a habit that led even the English to believe they were fighting a defensive war against the Scots and the French, who were intent on destroying 'England from Tweed into Kent.'[12] Atrocities committed by both sides (if no doubt exaggerated by the other) provided a pill bitter enough to make losing unbearable, whatever the cost of fighting on. And there can be little doubt that the histories of Scotland and England have been conditioned to a greater and lesser extent by the events precipitated by Alexander III's dramatic early death, even if it is the Scots who tend to pay more attention to the details now. Cicero certainly had a point when he said that 'Freedom suppressed and again regained bites with keener fangs than freedom never endangered.'

However, the significance of this war does not lie in who did what to whom and how terrible it was; the regularity with which neighbour has fought with neighbour throughout history makes that form of analysis mundane. Rather, it informs our understanding of warfare in general, together with the state-building processes of which it is a symptom, just as much as the higher profile conflicts between the 'great nations' of England and

France. An embarrassment of evidence, which has given the history of these 'great nations' undue prominence, is not an indication of superiority *per se*, but neither is its scarcity – something medieval Scottish history will always have to contend with – an excuse for filling the gaps with wishful thinking. War is, and no doubt always will be, expensive, tedious, horrifying, but, above all, complex.

ENDNOTES

Introduction: In Praise of Fact and Fiction

1 *Wyntoun*, ii, p. 279.
2 See F. Watson, 'The Enigmatic Lion: Scotland, kingship and national identity', in D. Broun, R. J. Finlay & M. Lynch (eds.), *Image and Identity: The Making and Remaking of Scotland* (Edinburgh, 1988), pp. 20, 32; C. Kidd, *Subverting Scotland's Past* (Cambridge, 1993), pp. 16–7.
3 From the sixteenth century painted inscription on Edward's tomb in Westminster Abbey: RCAHM, London, I, *Westminster Abbey*, p. 29.
4 The best examples in each category are Barrow's *Robert Bruce and the Community of the Realm of Scotland*, and the biography of Edward I by Prestwich.

1 The Lion and the Leopard

1 Quoted in Michael Brown, *The Wars of Scotland, 1214–1371*, Edinburgh University Press, 2004, p. 32.
2 *Ibid.* p.59.
3 T. Wright, *Political Poems and Songs relating to English History* (London, 1839), pp. 160–81.
4 R. Frame, *The Political Development of the British Isles, 1100–1500* (Oxford, 1995), p. 7.
5 *Ibid.*, p. 59.
6 *Ibid.*, p. 130.
7 For the history of Anglo-Scottish relations generally and the overlordship question in particular, see *ibid.*, pp. 14–18, 33–4, 47–9; A.A.M. Duncan, *Scotland: The Making of the Kingdom* (Edinburgh, 1992), Chapter 9; M. Powicke, *The Thirteenth Century* (Oxford, 1991), pp. 585–596.

8 See, for example, Frame, *The Political Development of the British Isles*, pp. 162–4; M. Prestwich, *Edward I* (London, 1988), pp. 356–8; N. Reid, 'The kingless kingdom: the Scottish guardian-ship of 1286–1306', *SHR*, ixi (1982), pp. 105–29; A. Young, *Robert the Bruce's Rivals: The Comyns, 1212–1314* (East Linton, 1997), Chapter 5.

9 See Prestwich, *Edward I*, Chapters 7 to 9.

10 See A. Young, 'Noble Families and Political Factions in the Reign of Alexander III', in N. Reid (ed.), *Scotland in the Reign of Alexander III, 1249–1286* (Edinburgh, 1990) pp. 1–30, esp. p. 7; Frame, *The Political Development of the British Isles*, pp. 62–3.

11 See Prestwich, *Edward I*, p. 359.

12 The Isle of Man and the Western Isles were ceded by Norway to the Scottish Crown in 1266.

13 The following discussion is based on A.A.M. Duncan, 'The Process of Norham, 1291', in P.R. Coss and S.D. Lloyd (eds.), *Thirteenth Century England V* (Woodbridge, 1995), pp. 207–29.

14 These were Bruce himself, Count Florence and John Hastings, together with four 'no-hopers' of illegitimate descent, Patrick, earl of March, William de Ros, William de Vescy and Nicholas de Soulis. Another no-hoper, Robert de Pinkeny, was probably not yet present at Norham, while King Eric of Norway, Roger de Mandeville and Patrick Golightly also put in claims at a later date. We will come to Balliol and Comyn shortly.

15 Duncan, 'The Process of Norham', p. 220.

16 Ibid., p. 224.

17 Ibid., p. 222; Barrow, *Bruce*, p. 31. See also Duncan, *Kingship of the Scots*, p.248 onwards for a discussion of the doctoring of the Great Roll and the implications for our understanding of this tortuous process.

18 W. Ullman, *The Growth of Papal Government in the Middle Ages*, 3rd edition (London, 1969), p. 177.

19 The special daughter status 'no-one between' was granted to Bishop Jocelyn of Glasgow by Pope Alexander III in April 1175 during the ongoing quarrel with the archbishops of York over the relationship between the latter and the Scottish church: Duncan, *Scotland: The Making of the Kingdom*, p. 263.

20 Duncan, 'The Process of Norham', p. 229.

21 The following discussion on the Great Cause is based on Barrow, *Bruce*, pp. 39–53 and R. Nicholson, *Scotland: The Later Middle Ages*, pp. 38–43.

22 Barrow, *Bruce*, p. 40.

23 Duncan, 'The Process of Norham', pp. 214–5.

24 Barrow, *Bruce*, pp. 43–8.

25 *Rot. Scot*, vol. i, p. 3.

26 Nicholson, *Scotland: The Later Middle Ages*, p. 41.

27 Balliol would have sworn homage and fealty to Edward for his English lands when he inherited them; these second ceremonies were thus exclusively related to the kingdom of Scotland.

28 *APS*, i, p. 447; see R. A. MacDonald, *The Kingdom of the Isles: Scotland's Western Seaboard, c. 1100–c. 1336* (East Linton, 1997), p. 163, n. 14.

29 Bower, *Scotichronicon*, volume VI, p. 41.

30 Nicholson, *Scotland: The Later Middle Ages*, p. 44, also quoting from A.A.M. Duncan, 'The early parliaments of Scotland', *SHR*, xlv (1966), pp. 40–3, 46. For general discussions of the reign of King John and the lead-up to the outbreak of war see Nicholson, *Scotland: The Later Middle Ages*, Chapter 3 and Barrow, *Bruce*, Chapter 4.

31 F. Watson, 'The enigmatic lion: Scotland, kingship, and national identity in the wars of independence', p. 20. See also M. Brown, *The wars of Scotland*, p.171.

32 Cf. MacDonald, *The Kingdom of the Isles*, Chapter 5.

33 RPS 1293 2/20.

34 Amanda Beam, *The Balliol Dynasty, 1210–1364*, John Donald, 2008, p. 85.

35 The New Year in the middle ages began on 25 March (nine months – the period of conception – before Christmas). January 1293 was thus still technically January 1292, but the modern dating has been used throughout to avoid clumsiness or confusion.

36 See Barrow, *Bruce*, pp. 51–2; Nicholson, *Scotland: The Later Middle Ages*, pp. 45–6.

37 Barrow, *Bruce*, p. 55.

38 Prestwich, *Edward I*, pp. 219–232.

39 Barrow, *Robert Bruce*, p.83.

40 Barrow, *Bruce*, pp. 66–7.

41 Prestwich, *Edward I*, pp. 469–70.

42 P. Coss, *The Knight in Medieval England* (Stroud, 1995), p. 100.

43 *Ibid.*, pp. 83–4.

44 P. Contamine, *War in the Middle Ages* (Oxford, 1986), p. 80. *Servitium debitum* is, literally, service owed.

45 Coss, *The Knight in Medieval England*, pp. 100–1; also Barrow, *Bruce*, p. 68.

46 Hugh Cressingham served as one in Norfolk during the Welsh uprising.

47 Prestwich, *Edward I*, p. 407; see also Contamine, *War in the Middle Ages*, p. 151.

48 See A. Grant, *Independence and Nationhood: Scotland 1306–1469* (London, 1984), pp. 72–3.

49 Haakon's successor, King Magnus, decided to cede the western highlands and islands to the king of Scots in the Treaty of Perth (1266).

50 Barrow, *Bruce*, p. 24; Frame, *The Political Development of the British Isles*, p. 162.

51 F. Watson, 'Adapting tradition?: the earldom of Strathearn, 1114–1296', in R. Oram and G. Stell (eds.), *Lordship and Architecture in Medieval and Renaissance Scotland* (Glasgow, 1998); also F. Watson, 'Expressions of power: thirteenth-century Scottish castles', in S.Foster, A.Macinnes and R.Macinnes (eds.), *Scottish Power-centres*. Earl Malise was acknowledging that the military service required in these traumatic times was unprecedented and that its performance was at the goodwill of his tenant, rather than as an obligation owed to him as lord. However, these grants might also provide evidence of the fact that any form of military service was highly unusual in the more settled times of the later thirteenth century.

52 F. Watson, 'Adapting tradition?: the earldom of Strathearn' in *Lordship and Architecture in Medieval and Renaissance Scotland*, eds. G. Stell and R. Oram (Edinburgh, 2005), 26–43. Blench-ferme was the payment to the lord of a token, such as a pair of spurs at Christmas, and was certainly part of the development of feudalism; feu-ferme was a money rent and was unusual in this period. Money rents were, however, the norm in burghs.

53 Barrow, *Bruce*, p. 67, G.W.S. Barrow, 'The Army in Alexander III's Scotland' in N. Reid, *Scotland in the reign of Alexander III, 1249–1286* (Edinburgh, 1990) pp. 133–4.

54 See Prestwich, *Edward I*, pp. 470–6 and Barrow, *Bruce*, pp. 69–79 for accounts of the conquest of 1296.

55 Though John Comyn of Badenoch, junior, the future guardian, was captured in Dunbar castle: *CDS*, ii, no. 742. See also M. Brown, *The Wars of Scotland*, pp.176–7 for a discussion of the more pragmatic reaction to the conquest from those who might

be termed part of the Bruce faction in Scottish politics, as well as reflections on the symbolism used by Edward I to underline Scotland's new status.

56 See Duncan, *Kingship of Scots*, p. 323 for the assertion that discovery of the treaty hardened Edward's attitude towards King John.

57 *Lanercost*, pp. 150-1.

58 F. Watson, 'Settling the Stalemate: Edward I's Peace in Scotland, 1303–1305' in M. Prestwich, R. Britnell & R. Frame (eds.), *Thirteenth Century England VI* (Woodbridge, 1997), p. 129.

59 *Scalachronica*, p.17.

60 See Fiona Watson, *Traitor, Outlaw, King Part One: The Making of Robert Bruce* (2018) p. 78 for details of what the Bruces were doing at this crucial juncture.

2 The Resistible Rise of Edwardian Government

1 Though only John Comyn the younger of Badenoch participated in the battle at Dunbar from that most powerful family, the earl of Buchan had certainly been one of the leaders of the Scottish army in the north of England and they were still undoubtedly directing events: see A. Young, *Robert the Bruce's Rivals: The Comyns, 1212–1314* (East Linton, 1997), p. 257.

2 *CDS*, iv, p. 448; *CDS*, ii, p. 177; *CDS*, ii, no. 1326; E101/364/13; *CDS*, ii, no. 1403.

3 See above, Chapter One for the process of Norham. *Guisborough*, p. 284; Stevenson, *Documents*, ii, pp. 31–2; Barrow, *Bruce*, p. 75. See Duncan, 'The Process of Norham', *passim* and F. Watson, 'Settling the Stalemate: Edward I's peace in Scotland, 1303–5', *passim*, for discussions of the efforts made to bestow legality on Edward's activities vis-à-vis Scotland before 1296.

4 One mark (merk in Scotland) was equal to three-quarters of a pound.

5 *Foedera*, i, p. 731; *CDS.*, ii, no. 928; *CPR, 1292–1301*, p. 205.

6 *Rot. Scot.*, i, p. 35.

7 *CDS*, ii, no. 496; *Rot. Scot.*, i, p. 35.

8 The revenues brought in for the use of the seal on, for example, grants of charters.

9 *CDS*, ii, no. 853; Bateson, 'The Scottish King's Household', in *Miscellany*, ii (SHS, 1904) p. 38; *CPR, 1292–1301*, p. 148.

10 *CDS*, ii, no. 835; no. 876.

11 Bateson, 'The Scottish King's Household', pp. 18–19; *Rot. Scot.*, i, p. 37.

12 The office of justiciar was revived in England in 1258, at the instigation of the Montfortians, after a lapse of twenty-four years. However, this was not a permanent revival and the main judicial officers under Edward I were the justices: Prestwich, *Edward I*, pp. 25; 289–92.

13 *CDS*, ii, no. 853; *Rot. Scot.*, i, p. 27, 30; Bateson, 'The Scottish King's Household', p. 42.

14 Two of King John's creations of 1293, Skye and Lorne, disappeared; Rutherglen seems to have taken on shrieval status independent of Lanark, although there is only one piece of evidence for this arrangement, suggesting that it was short-lived: *Rot. Scot.*, i, pp. 24–28.

15 *Ibid.*, p. 23.

16 *CDS*, ii, p. 264; *Rot. Scot.*, i, p. 36.

17 *CDS*, ii, no. 824 (4); Barrow, *Bruce*, p. 83; *Rot. Scot.*, i, pp. 41, 42.

18 Cruggleton had been inherited, after the death of Roger de Quincy, earl of Winchester, by the Comyns of Buchan. However, John Comyn of Buchan subsequently resigned some of his lands in Galloway to King John in return for others in the north-east; Cruggleton almost certainly formed part of this package and thus escheated to King Edward along with the rest of Balliol's lands: *SP*, ii, pp. 254–5; Stevenson, *Documents*, i, p. 329; R.C. Reid, 'Cruggleton Castle', *TDGAS*, xxxi (1962) pp. 153–4; *CDS*, ii, no. 1541.

19 *Rot. Scot.*, i, p. 31.

20 *Ibid.*, p. 22.

21 *Ibid.*, pp. 31–2. See R A MacDonald, *The Kingdom of the Isles*, (East Linton, 1997), pp. 107, 113, 143 for the Stewart earls of Menteith's interests in the north-west.

22 *Rot. Scot.*, i, p. 36; *CPR*, *1292–1301*, p. 198.

23 Some were described indiscriminately as both keepers and constables, though this usually applied to royal castles, whose owner was ultimately the king. In private castles, the keeper – the owner – was often non-resident and a constable was therefore required to lead the garrison.

24 *Rot. Scot.*, i, pp. 34, 36, 37. The Trinity and Michaelmas terms are the eighth Sunday after Easter to 8 July and 6 October to 25 November respectively. It is interesting to note that these are the English names for these terms. The Scottish equivalents are Whitsun and Martinmas.

25 T.F. Tout, 'Medieval Town-planning', in *The Collected Papers of Thomas Frederick Tout* (Manchester, 1934), iii, pp. 79–80, 84–5.

26 *Ibid.*, p. 23; *CDS*, ii, no. 824 (1), (6). Sir Reginald was perhaps a member of the Bruce contingent which defected to the English side in March 1296 and the office of sheriff of Ayr was thus his reward: see Barrow, *Bruce*, p. 146 and *Rot. Scot.*, i, p. 23, for Crawford's association with the Bruces. Twynham is less easy to place. He was named as co-heir to Helewisa Levintone, wife of Eustace Balliol, who was probably King John's uncle (*CDS*, ii, no. 35; *CDS*, i, nos. 1098, 2665); however, it is highly unlikely that a 'Balliol man' was given office in a sheriffdom which had formed part of King John's demesne lands.

27 The extent of Gaelic-speaking among the Scottish élites cannot be ascertained. It seems highly likely, however, that men such as the earl of Carrick, whose mother came from an ancient Celtic family, and James the Steward, who moved in Gaelic-speaking circles, were able to communicate in that language. We can presume, however, that the Edwardian sheriffs generally could not.

28 Prestwich, *Edward 1*, pp. 258–266.

29 *Ibid.* pp. 553–4.

30 Fordun, pp. 303–4.

31 *Rot. Scot.*, p. 40; A.A.M. Duncan and A.L. Brown, 'Argyll and the Isles in the earlier Middle Ages', *PSAS*, xc (1956–7), pp. 216–7.

32 Stevenson, *Documents*, ii, pp. 187–8; *CDS*, ii, p. 195; *Rot. Scot.*, i, pp. 31, 40; Stevenson, *Documents*, ii, p. 190. Despite the fact that the two letters from Alasdair Macdonald of Islay to Edward I have been putatively placed by Stevenson in June 1297, the only date mentioned in either was the reference to Alasdair's army going to the Isles after Palm Sunday (7 April 1297). This proves that the rebellion was underway long before Alasdair Macdougall of Argyll was released. The first letter was thus probably written earlier than the second, which indicates that though the latter was not initially involved, he quickly joined the rebellion.

33 *Rot. Scot.*, i, p. 40.

34 It is not clear why he held Glassary, which lies within the sheriffdom of Lorne once held by Alasdair of Argyll: *APS*, i, p. 447. Perhaps the action taken by MacDonald against MacDougall led the Steward to assume that office, as well as trying to hold on to his own office of sheriff of Kintyre.

35   Stevenson, *Documents*, ii, pp. 189–90.

36   *Rot. Scot.*, i, p. 40; Stevenson, *Documents*, ii, p. 187. Cf. MacDonald, *The Kingdom of the Isles*, pp. 163–7.

37   MacDonald, *The Kingdom of the Isles*, p. 167; Young, *Robert the Bruce's Rivals: The Comyns*, pp. 72, 85; 165 Barrow, *Bruce*, p. 56.

38   Prestwich, *Documents*, p. 73.

39   *Wyntoun*, ii, p. 342; *CDS*, ii, no. 1597; *Hary's Wallace*, i, pp. 34, 39.

40   *CDS.*, ii, no. 894.

41   *Ibid.*, pp. 198, 210.

42   *Guisborough*, pp. 294, 295–6; Stevenson, *Documents*, ii, p. 192; Barrow, *Bruce*, pp. 81–2.

43   Stevenson, *Documents*, ii, p. 198; *Parl. Writs.*, i, pp. 294–5.

44   *CPR, 1292–1301*, p. 251; *CDS*, ii, p. 235.

45   *Guisborough*, p. 299.

46   *Ibid.*, p. 294.

47   *Rot. Scot.*, i, p. 40; see Prestwich, *Edward I*, pp. 414–435, for a full account of English opposition to Edward I in 1297; *Memo. de Parl.*, nos. 280, 302.

48   See F. Watson, 'Edward I in Scotland, 1296–1305', unpublished Ph.D. thesis (Glasgow, 1991), p. 245.

49   A Young, *Robert the Bruce's Rivals: The Comyns*, pp. 163–5.

50   Stevenson, *Documents*, ii, pp. 175, 210.

51   *Guisborough*, p. 297; Stevenson, *Documents*, ii, pp. 212, 227.

52   *CDS*, ii, p. xxx; *CDS*, iv, no. 1835.

53   *CDS*, ii, no. 1737.

54   Stevenson, *Documents*, ii, pp. 217–8.

55   See Barrow, *Bruce*, p. 86.

56   *Rot. Scot.*, i, 41; Prestwich, *Documents*, p. 100.

57   Stevenson, *Documents*, ii, pp. 195–6, 227.

58   Stevenson, *Documents*, ii, p. 227; *CDS*, iv, p. 464; p. 484.

59   Prestwich, *Documents*, 23. In 1264 the chamberlain's account brought in approximately £5500 as the entire Scottish royal revenue for that year: Duncan, *Scotland: The Making of the Kingdom*, p. 599. Bar is in modern-day Lorraine, on France's eastern border during this period.

60   *Guisborough*, pp. 294, 303.

61   Prestwich, *Documents*, p. 104.

62   A. Fisher, *William Wallace* (Edinburgh, 1986), p. 40.

63   *Rot. Scot.*, i, p. 42; Stevenson, *Documents*, ii, pp. 222, 226; *CCR, 1296–1301*, p. 42; Gough, *Scotland in 1298*, p. 55; Stevenson, *Documents*, ii, pp. 369–70.

64 *Guisborough*, p. 294.
65 Stevenson, *Documents*, ii, pp. 183–4.
66 *Ibid.*, pp. 200–3.
67 *Ibid.*, pp. 221–2.
68 Barrow, *Bruce*, p. 35; *CDS*, ii, no. 499; Stevenson, *Documents*, ii, pp. 194–5.
69 *Ibid.*, pp. 222–4.
70 *Ibid.*, pp. 225–6.
71 See *Patent Rolls, 1292–1301*, pp.232–3 for Henry Percy's presence among the regency council still in England.
72 *CDS*, ii, no. 941; *Foedera*, i, p. 793; *CPR, 1292–1301*, pp. 306–7.
73 *CDS*, v, no. 1168; E159/71, m.102.
74 *CDS*, ii, no. 945.
75 Stevenson, *Documents*, ii, pp. 206–7.
76 Stevenson, *Documents*, ii, pp. 195–6.
77 *Ibid.*, pp. 201–2; 218; *CCR, 1296–1302*, p. 67; *CDS*, ii, nos. 1054–5; Stevenson, *Documents*, p. 221.
78 *Wyntoun*, ii, pp. 343–4.
79 *CCR, 1296–1302*, p. 63.
80 *Guisborough*, p. 301.
81 *Ibid.*, p. 300; *Lanercost*, pp. 190–1;
82 *Rot. Scot.*, i, pp. 49–50; *CCR, 1296–1302*, p. 132.
83 Stevenson, *Documents*, pp. 102, 195–6.
84 E159/71, m.108.
85 *CDS*, ii. no.876.
86 Wallace was first described as 'keeper of the kingdom and leader of the army, in the name of the prince, Lord John, king of Scots, by consent of the community' on 29 March 1298 [Stevenson, *Wallace Papers* no. xvi]; Wallace and Murray described themselves as 'leaders of the army of the kingdom of Scotland and the community of the same kingdom' in the letter to the German towns.
87 Stevenson, *Wallace Papers.*, no. xv.
88 Prestwich, *Edward I*, p. 479; Stevenson, *Documents*, ii, p. 232; *CDS*, iv., no. 1835.
89 E101/6/30, m.3; *Guisborough*, pp. 304–7.
90 E101/6/30, m.1.
91 *Lanercost*, pp. 193, 192. Lanercost priory is only about twelve miles from Carlisle and twenty from the border.
92 *CPR, 1292–1301*, p. 314.
93 E101/6/35, mm.11, 4.

94 Prestwich, *Edward I*, pp. 424, 478–9; Stevenson, *Documents*, ii, pp. 255–6; Gough, *Scotland in 1298*, pp. 64–6.

95 E159/71, m.24; Gough, *Scotland in 1298*, pp. 79, 82.

96 E159/71, m.108.

97 E101/6/35, m.7.

98 E101/6/35, m.9; *Guisborough*, pp. 313–5; Prestwich, *Edward I*, p. 479.

99 Prestwich, *Edward I*, chapter 15; J. Favier, *Philippe le Bel* (Paris, 1978) chapter 8.

100 M. Kervyn de Lettenhove, ed., Études sur l'histoire du XIIIe siècle (Brussels, 1854, pp. 53–4. I am most grateful to David Pilling for alerting me to this bizarre episode in the convoluted history of Flanders, Philip IV and Edward I.

101 *Ibid.*, pp. 421–2, 427; *CCR, 1296–1302*, p. 77; *Parl. Writs*, i, p. 306.

102 The regnal year, by which most official documents are dated, begins on the day on which the king in question ascended the throne. In Edward I's case, this was 20 November 1272. Thus regnal year 26, the one in question here, ran from 20 November 1297 to 19 November 1298.

103 Stevenson, *Documents*, ii, p. 239; E101/6/35, m.7; Gough, *Scotland in 1298*, pp. 1–5.

104 E159/71, m.108; E101/6/30, m.3.

105 E159/71, m.108; E101/6/30, m.2.

106 E101/6/33, m.1.

107 E101/6/35, m.17.

108 *Ibid.*, ii, p. 260.

3 A KINGDOM DIVIDED

1 E101/6/30, m. 1; *Itin.*, p. 119; *CCR, 1296–1302*, p. 201.

2 *Parl. Writs*, i, pp. 312–6.

3 E101/12/17; C47/2/20; Prestwich, *Edward I*, p. 429.

4 *Parl. Writs*, i, pp. 309–312; Gough, *Scotland in 1298*, pp. 124–5.

5 *CPR, 1292–1301*, p. 335.

6 E101/6/33, m.5.

7 E101/552/2.

8 J. Lydon, 'The Years of Crisis, 1254–1315', in *A New History of Ireland: Medieval Ireland, 1169–1534*, ed. A. Cosgrave (Oxford, 1987), p. 199.

9 Gough, *Scotland in 1298*, p. 124.

10 *Ibid.*, pp. 125–6; E159/71, m.46.

11 C47/2/117.

12 *Guisborough*, p. 326; Gough, *Scotland in 1298*, p. 25.

13 Given that the lowest wage paid to those in the king's service was 2d. per day, let us presume that half of that sum was spent on bread, which constituted a large part of the staple diet of most of the medieval population. If we also presume that the wheat, once it had arrived in Scotland, was sold to the English soldiers at the 15s. per quarter that Amersham paid for it, then it is possible to calculate approximately how much was needed to feed the army per day. Since there are one hundred and eighty pennies in fifteen shillings, one hundred and eighty footsoldiers would therefore consume one quarter of wheat or, to put it another way, one hundred and twelve quarters of wheat per day were needed, roughly speaking, to feed twenty thousand footsoldiers.

14 Stevenson, *Documents*, ii, p. 334.

15 Gough, *Scotland in 1298*, pp. 102, 107.

16 *Parl. Writs*, i, pp. 310–1.

17 *Guisborough*, p. 323; Edward is placed at Roxburgh on 3 July, having been at Chillingham the day before. Roxburgh is ten miles east of Coldstream, which in turn is twenty miles north of Chillingham [*Itin.*, p.167].

18 *Rishanger*, p. 186.

19 *Guisborough*, p. 326.

20 E101/12/17; E101/7/9; C47/2/17; E101/597/3; Gough, *Scotland in 1298*, pp. 98–9.

21 *Ibid.*, p. 129.

22 See *Guisborough*, pp. 325–7 and *Lanercost*, p. 191 for contemporary descriptions of the battle.

23 *Ibid.*, p. 192.

24 E101/12/17; C47/2/20.

25 *Wyntoun*, p. 348.

26 Stevenson, *Documents*, ii, pp. 301–4; *Itin.*, p. 125.

27 *Rishanger*, p. 188; *Guisborough*, pp. 328–9; *Lib. Quot.*, p. 101; *Itin.*, p. 126; *CDS*, ii, no. 1005; *CDS*, iv., Appendix 1, no. 7. See also Brown, *The Wars of Scotland*, p. 187 for a shift in Robert Bruce, earl of Carrick's attitude towards adherence to the Scottish side and the potential for new leadership after Wallace's defeat at Falkirk.

28 Guisborough calls him Sir Thomas but no such person appears in the records for this period while Sir Hugh Bisset was certainly active in Edward's service.

29 *Guisborough*, p. 329.

30 Prestwich, 'Colonial Scotland: The English in Scotland under Edward I', in R. Mason (ed.), *Scotland and England, 1286–1815* (Edinburgh, 1987), p. 8; Prestwich, *Edward I*, P. 483; *CDS*, ii, no. 1009; Barrow, *Bruce*, p. 104.

31 Stevenson, *Documents*, ii, pp. 313–4; E101/554/8/23.

32 Stevenson, *Documents*, ii, p. 332; E101/7/1, m.6.

33 R.R. Davies, *The Revolt of Owain Glyn Dŵr* (Oxford, 1995), pp. 251–2.

34 The figures for these graphs came from a variety of sources. They do not include other members of the garrisons, such as masons, carpenters, bakers etc. It has also not been considered worthwhile to present graphs of those garrisons, such as Lochmaben and Dumfries, for which information is insufficiently full. They should be used, therefore, only to give a rough comparison of the numbers in each and the variations over time.

35 *Wyntoun*, p. 348

36 *CPR, 1292–1301*, p. 351; Stevenson, *Documents*, ii, pp. 329–30.

37 *CPR, 1292–1301*, p. 387; Stevenson, *Documents*, ii, pp. 336.

38 *Ibid.*, p. 331; *CDS*, ii, no. 1026.

39 E159/72, m. 12.

40 *CPR, 1292–1301*, p. 387.

41 *CDS*, iv, no. 1773, p. 361.

42 Stevenson, *Documents*, ii, p. 339.

43 *Ibid.*, pp. 343–9.

44 E101/7/9.

45 E372/144.

46 *Facsimiles of the National Manuscripts of Scotland*, ed. W. Gibson-Clark (London, 1867–71), part 1, p. xiv; *Highland Papers*, ed. J.R.N. Macphail (SHS, 1914–34), ii, p. 131; Stevenson, *Wallace Docs.*, no. xv.

47 Barrow, *Bruce*, p. 95; Favier, *Philippe le Bel*, pp. 227–31.

48 E101/362/18/64.

49 *CPR, 1292–1301*, p. 418.

50 F.M. Powicke, *The Thirteenth Century, 1216–1307*, p. 630.

51 Stevenson, *Documents*, ii, pp. 350–355.

52 Sir Nicholas Harris Nicolas, *A History of the Royal Navy from the earliest time to the wars of the French Revolution* (London, 1847), i, pp. 294–5.

53 A portion of land comprising a dwelling-house and its associated buildings.

54 E101/7/24.

55 *Highland Papers*, ii, p. 131.

56 Barrow, *Bruce*, p. 105; *CPR, 1292–1301*, p. 466; *CDS*, ii, nos. 1066, 1108; *CDS*, ii, no. 1949. 22 April, when Patrick, earl of Dunbar, Edward I's captain of the south-eastern garrisons, and Sir John Kingston, constable of Edinburgh castle, were ordered to investigate Sir Herbert's activities, presumably soon after his capture, is one of the few dates we have to give some kind of timescale for the Scottish siege of Stirling and the truce, which Morham organised.

57 This is not a theme explored in, for example, Professor Contamine's seminal work, *War in the Middle Ages*, compared with Professor Rhys Davies's *The Revolt of Owen Glyn Dwr*, where the situation in Wales clearly provides parallels with Scotland.

58 See p. 288, n. 59.

59 E152/72, m. 8.

60 R.A. Brown, H.M. Colvin & A.J. Taylor (eds.), *The History of the King's Works in Scotland*, volume i *The Middle Ages* (1963), p. 563; *Guisborough*, p. 294.

61 E152/72, m. 21.

62 Stevenson, *Documents*, ii, pp. 375–6.

63 *CDS*, ii, no. 1057.

64 Stevenson, *Documents*, ii, pp. 333–5.

65 *Ibid.*, ii. pp. 329–30; *CPR, 1292–1301*, p. 387.

66 Stevenson, *Documents*, ii, p. 331; *CDS*, ii. no. 1026; *CPR, 1292–1301*, p. 409.

67 *CDS*, ii, no. 1064. A hobelar was so-called because of the small sturdy pony, known as a hobby horse, on which he rode. Edward I had been impressed by their use on the rough terrain which was injurious to the finely-bred warhorses on which the English cavalry generally rode: see Prestwich, *Edward I*, pp. 513–4.

68 E101/7/23/19.

69 E101/7/20, m. 8; m. 3.

70 E101/7/23, m. 19.

71 E101/7/23/19; *CDS*, ii, no. 1088; E159/72, m. 102; *CPR, 1292–1301*, p. 387.

72 Barrow, *Robert Bruce*, p.125

73 Barrow, *Bruce*, p. 95; *The Gascon Calendar of 1322*, ed. G.P. Cuttino, Camden Third Series, vol. ixv, (London, 1949), no. 131.

74 Barrow, *Bruce*, p. 106; *SP*, vii, pp. 420–2.

75 Stevenson, *Documents*, ii, pp. 301–3.

76 *Ibid.*, ii, p. 302, footnote 1.

77 E159/72, m. 102.

78 The document, which is faded in several parts, reads 'on Thursday next ... past', which has to be 'on Thursday next *before* the assumption of our Lady past', that is, 13 August, otherwise the events which Hastangs goes on to describe would have taken place after his letter was written.

79 Despite fading in the manuscript the remaining letters 'le' make it clear that Atholl was the name obscured: see Barrow, *Bruce*, 106, n.99. Comyn is described as 'the son,' though there is no reference to his father after 1298, implying that he was incapacitated in some way.

80 Watson, *Traitor, Outlaw, King*, pp. 105–7.

81 *Facsimile of the National Manuscripts of Scotland*, ii, no. viii.

82 *CDS*, ii, no. 1949.

83 E101/7/20, m. 3.

84 *CPR, 1292–1301*, p. 484.

85 E101/7/20, mm. 3–4; *CDS*, ii, no. 1101.

86 E101/7/20, m. 1.

87 *CDS* ii, no. 1005; *CPR, 1293–1301*, p. 455; *CCR, 1296–1302*, p. 288.

88 See, for example, Stevenson, *Documents*, ii, pp. 375–6.

89 *Ibid.*, ii, pp. 365–6.

90 References to women are, unsurprisingly, rather scarce.

91 *Lib. Quot.*, pp. 117–119.

92 *CPR, 1292–1301*, p. 389; E101/7/20, m. 4.

93 E101/7/20, mm. 3–4; E101/7/20, m. 8.

94 This is Robert Bruce (VI), son of the Competitor and father of the earl of Carrick.

95 E159/72, mm. 16, 78, 82.

96 *CPR, 1292–1301*, p. 438.

97 *Parl. Writs*, i, pp. 323–5; *CDS*, ii, no. 1092.

98 *CCR, 1292–1302*, pp. 372–4.

99 *Lib. Quot.*, p. 208.

100 *Ibid.*, p. 55.

101 Prestwich, *Edward I*, pp. 183–4; *Lib. Quot.*, p. 114.

102 Prestwich, *Edward I*, pp. 483–4; *Guisborough*, p. 324; *Itin.*, p. 149.

103 This is a rather curious arrangement since it rendered three south-eastern castles dependent on the unreliable shipment of victuals up the Forth, not to mention the fact that Roxburgh and Jedburgh were a considerable land journey away from Edinburgh. In practice, however, the evidence suggests that both garrisons continued to be supplied direct from Berwick.

104 *Lib. Quot.*, pp. 145–8.

105 Stevenson, *Documents*, ii, pp. 401–2.

106 *APS*, i, p. 454; *CDS*, ii, no. 1109.

107 *Lib. Quot.*, pp. 143–4.

108 *Ibid.*, p. 147; Prestwich, *Edward I*, p. 502; *CDS*, ii, no. 1949; Barrow, *Bruce*, p. 105.

109 A.Z. Freeman, 'Wall-breakers and river-bridgers; military engineers in the Scottish Wars of Edward I', *Journal of British Studies*, 10 (Chicago, 1971), pp. 3–4, quoted in M.A. Haskell, 'The Scottish Campaign of Edward I, 1303–4', M.A. thesis, University of Durham (Durham, 1991), p. 13.

4 STALEMATE

1 *CDS*, ii, no. 1867.

2 *Ibid.*, no. 1169.

3 *Lib. Quot.*, p. 183.

4 Prestwich, *Edward I*, pp. 381–5; J.E. Morris, *The Welsh Wars of Edward I* (Stroud, 1996), p. 291.

5 *Guisborough*, p. 245.

6 Stevenson, *Documents*, ii, pp. 407–8.

7 I.e., with the correct gear.

8 *CPR 1292–1301*, p. 484.

9 *Lib. Quot.*, p. 28.

10 *CPR, 1292–1301*, p. 490; Prestwich, *Edward I*, pp. 513–4.

11 Stevenson, *Documents*, ii, pp. 409–10.

12 *CPR, 1292–1301*, p. 491.

13 *Lib. Quot.*, p. 31; Stevenson, *Documents*, ii, pp. 360–5; *Itin.*, p. 152; *CCR, 1296–1302*, p. 334; *Lib. Quot.*, pp. 160, 161.

14 *Ibid.*, p. 129.

15 Stevenson, *Documents*, ii, pp. 410–12.

16 E159/73, m. 26; *Lib. Quot.*, pp. 139; 145–8.

17 Ibid, pp. 151–152, 178–79.

18 See p. 141 for a discussion of the capabilities of the Scottish government.

19 *CDS*, v, no. 220; G.O. Sayles, 'The Guardians of Scotland and a parliament at Rutherglen in 1300', *SHR*, xxiv (1927), pp. 246–50.

20 Barrow, *Bruce*, pp. 111–2.

21 *CDS*, ii, no. 1128; *Lib. Quot.*, pp. 106–114; 130–1.

22 *Ibid.*, pp. 105–6; 127–8; 135–6.

23 *Parl. Writs* i. p. 327.

24 Prestwich, *Edward I*, pp. 484–6; E159/73, m. 16.

25 J. Lydon, 'The Years of Crisis, 1254–1315', p. 199; J. Lydon, 'Irish levies in the Scottish Wars, 1296–1302', *Irish Sword*, v (1962), p. 208.

26 Morris, *The Welsh Wars of Edward I*, p. 296.

27 Murray, *The Constitutional History of the Cinque Ports*, p. 242. The original Cinque Ports were Hastings, Romney, Hythe, Dover and Sandwich on the south-east coast of England. Their obligations and privileges were then extended to a number of others, the most important of which were Winchelsea and Rye: *Ibid.*, p. 1.

28 Nicolas, *A History of the Royal Navy*, i, pp. 294–5.

29 *CPR, 1296–1302*, p. 523.

30 Prestwich, *Edward I, pp. 522–5*.

31 *Itin.*, p. 158.

32 *Lib. Quot.*, pp. 223, 231; *CDS*, v, no. 272 (Jedburgh); *Lib. Quot.*, 140–151, 220–223, 243 (Roxburgh); 221, 230, 251, 148; 255, 257; 146–7 (Berwick town); 231–2, 247–256; 140 (Lochmaben).

33 T. Wright (ed.), *The Roll of Caerlaverock* (London, 1864), p. 26.

34 *Ibid.*, pp. 2, 6, 9, 18.

35 *Ibid.*, pp. 2, 11, 14–15, 18, 25.

36 *Ibid.*, pp. 27–35.

37 *Rishanger*, pp. 440–1; *Lib. Quot.*, pp. 175, 177–9, 186.

38 *Ibid.*, pp. 76–7; *CDS*, ii, nos. 1147, 1148, 1159.

39 *Rishanger*, p. 442; Barrow, *Bruce*, p. 113.

40 *Itin.*, pp. 161–3.

41 *CPR, 1292–1301*, pp. 536; 537–8. 1,000 marks per annum seems an awfully high value of land even for the whole of Galloway.

42 Stevenson, *Documents*, ii, pp. 296–8.

43 *CDS*, ii, no. 1144; *Lib. Quot.*, pp. 115–119.

44 Stevenson, *Documents*, ii, pp. 296–8.

45 *Lib. Quot.*, pp. 147–8.

46 *CDS*, v, no. 234; see below, p. 152.

47 *Lib. Quot.*, 9, 12, 99.

48 *Ibid.*, pp. 8–13, 136.

49 M. Prestwich, *War, Politics and Finance under Edward I* (London, 1972), p. 175.

50 *Foedera*, 1, p. 924; *CPR, 1292–1301*, p. 541; Prestwich, *Edward I*, pp. 489–90.

51 *The Gascon Calendar of 1322*, ed. G.P. Cuttino, Camden Third Series, vol. ixv (London, 1949), no. 513; see also Prestwich, *Edward I*, p. 490.

52 *Lib. Quot.*, p. 121.

53 *Ibid.*, pp. 73, 82.

54 *Ibid.*, pp. 153–4, 13, 150–2.; E101/9/25, m. 6.

55 *Guisborough*, p. 294.

56 *CPR, 1292–1301*, p. 580; *CDS*, ii, no. 1244.

57 *Ibid.*, no. 1193; *CDS*, v, no. 247; *CCR, 1296–1302*, p. 480.

58 *CDS*, ii, nos. 1194, 1244.

59 *CPR, 1292–1301*, p. 428.

60 *CDS*, ii, no. 1115.

61 *Liber S. Thome de Aberbrothoc* (Bannatyne Club, 1848–56), i, no. 231; Watson, 'The Engimatic Lion: Scotland, kingship and national identity in the wars of independence' p. 26 *CDS*, ii, no. 1592; *Memo. de Parl.*, no. 296; The cases are undated but probably took place between 1300 and 1303; the bishop of St Andrews, Sir Ingram d'Umfraville and even Sir John Soules were all guardians at some point during that period.

62 *CPR, 1292–1301*, p. 592.

63 *CDS*, ii, no. 1244; *CPR, 1292–1301*, 585, 592, 595. Audley was first described as keeper of Selkirk Forest in August 1301: E101/9/15, dorso.

64 Stevenson, *Documents*, ii, pp. 429–30.

65 E101/9/3.

66 See Prestwich, *Edward I*, pp. 220–4; also, Davies, *Owain Glyn Dŵr*, p. 236.

67 *CCR, 1296–1302*, p. 480; *CPR, 1292–1301*, p. 578.

68 *CDS*, ii, no. 1192; *CCR, 1296–1302*, pp. 489–90; *CDS*, ii, no. 1193.

69 *CPR, 1292–1301*, p. 589.

70 Lydon, 'Irish levies in the Scottish wars, 1296–1302', pp. 209–214.

71 *CDS*, v, no. 247; Stevenson, *Documents*, ii, pp. 429–30; *CCR, 1296–1302*, p. 487.

72 *CCR, 1292–1302*, pp. 482–3.

73 *CDS*, ii, no. 1190; *Itin.*, p. 177.

74 *CDS*, ii, no. 1191.

75 *Itin.*, p. 178; E101/358/6.

76 *The Gascon Calendar of 1322*, no. 1148.

77 *CDS*, ii, no. 1236; E101/7/24, m. 1; *Lib. Quot.*, pp. 141, 145.

78 *CDS*, iv, no. 1829.

79 E101/364/13; E101/358/6; *CDS*, iv, p. 451. Stevenson, *Documents*, ii, pp. 432–3; *CDS*, ii, no. 1220.

80 *Itin.*, 178; *CDS*, ii, no. 1178.

81 *CDS*, ii, no. 1304.

82 Barrow, *Bruce*, pp. 114–5; N.H. Reid, 'The Political Role of the monarchy in Scotland, 1249–1329', unpublished Ph.D. thesis (Edinburgh, 1984) pp. 180–8. Both Barrow and Reid believe Comyn was ousted as guardian and the issue is certainly far from clear. But I find it hard to believe he did relinquish the guardianship when there was no-one left in Scotland to gainsay his family's – and his own – obvious power and thirst for leadership.

83 *CDS*, iv, pp. 450–1; *CDS*, ii, no. 1317; Barrow, *Bruce*, p. 121, n.80; *CDS*, iv, p. 454; E101/9/15, dorso.

84 *C.P.R., 1292–1391*, p. 585; See above, p. 114.

85 Stevenson; *Documents*, ii, pp. 431–3.

86 *CDS*, ii, no. 1233.

87 Sir Thomas Paignel, one of St John's knights, had certainly been with the prince at Ayr: *CDS*, ii, no. 1326; E101/364/13.

88 *CDS*, ii, no. 1224; *CDS*, iv, p. 446.

89 Stevenson, *Documents*, ii, pp. 434–5.

90 *CDS*, ii, pp. 199, 264; *Lib. Quot.*, p. 146; *CDS*, v, no. 201; E101/358/6.

91 *CDS*, ii, no. 1225.

92 *CDS*, v, no. 257.

93 *CCR, 1296–1302*, p. 498.

94 *CDS*, ii, no. 1223.

95 *CDS*, ii, no. 1228. The proffer was the lay fifteenth and the clerical ninth – a form of property tax on landowners and the church – agreed at the Lincoln parliament of January 1301: *Parl. Writs*, i, p. 105.

96 This was the father of the Sir Thomas Grey of Heton who later wrote the *Scalacronica*, a chronicle account of the Anglo-Scottish wars composed in the 1350s, after a spell as a prisoner in Edinburgh castle [see *Scalachronica*, pp. iii, xv].

97 *CDS*, ii, no. 1230.

98 *Ibid.*, no. 1218.
99 *CDS*, v, no. 264.
100 *Itin.*, p. 179.
101 *CDS*, ii, nos. 1224, 1235, 1290; E101/10/15; G.W.S. Barrow &
    A. Royan, 'James Fifth Stewart of Scotland, 1260(?)–1309', in K.
    Stringer (ed.), *Essays on the Nobility of Medieval Scotland*
    (Edinburgh, 1985), p. 179; Barrow, *Bruce*, p. 121; Prestwich,
    Edward I, p. 494; see p. 153.
102 *Itin.*, p. 180.
103 *CDS*, ii, nos. 1230, 1237.
104 *CDS*, iv, p. 453.
105 *CDS*, ii, no. 1190.
106 *CDS*, v, no. 260.
107 *Ibid.*, no. 261; *CPR, 1292–1301*, pp. 608–9; *CPR, 1302–7*, p. 2.
108 *CDS*, v, no. 262.
109 E159/75, m. 10.
110 Warrants issued to those going about royal business to prove that
    they were entitled to do so.
111 *CCR, 1296–1302*, pp. 574–5.
112 *CDS*, v, no. 263.
113 E159/75, mm. 68, 69.
114 *Ibid.*, m. 14.
115 *CDS*, v, no. 259.

5 TURNING THE SCREW

1 *Foedera*, ii, p. 892.
2 *CPR, 1292–1301*, p. 616.
3 *CDS*, ii, no. 1121.
4 *CDS*, iv, p. 454.
5 See p. 165.
6 *CDS*, ii, nos. 1234, 1236, 1293. Confirmation of the raising of the
   siege at Ayr, in line with the truce of Asnières which began on 26
   January 1302, is to be found in a letter of 23 January 1302 from
   Walter Beauchamp, the steward of Edward's household, to James
   Dalilegh as 'warden of the stores at Newcastle-on-Ayr',
   commanding him to deliver flour for Beauchamp's own use. The
   steward was writing from Irvine, ten miles north of Ayr, and such
   a request would clearly not have been feasible if the Scots were
   still mounting a blockade [*CDS*, ii, no.1281].

7 E101/9/18, m. 2; *CDS*, ii, no. 1190.

8 *CDS*, iv, p. 450; E101/68/1, m. 16; *CDS*, ii, no. 1598.

9 *Ibid.*, no. 1257.

10 S. Cruden, *The Scottish Castle* (Edinburgh, 1960), p. 70.

11 *Kelso Liber* (Bannatyne Club, 1846), i, no. 193.

12 E101/9/16, m. 1 dorso.

13 E101/13/17, m. 26.

14 E101/364/13; E101/684/46, m. 5.

15 *CDS*, ii, no. 1264.

16 E101/9/2.

17 Barrow, *Bruce*, pp. 119–120; see also RRSV, p. 200.

18 Palgrave, *Documents*, i, pp. 243–4.

19 *CDS*, ii, no. 1247; *Itin.*, p. 178.

20 R.J. Goldstein, 'The Scottish Mission to Boniface VIII in 1301', *SHR*, lxx (1991), pp. 1–16; Barrow, *Bruce*, pp. 116–9; Prestwich, *Edward I*, p. 495; Stones, *Relations*, no. 32. John Balliol's son, Edward, was still in custody in England, but, as with the Scottish king, if the pope demanded his release, there would be little, other than engaging in delaying tactics, that Edward could do to stop it.

21 Prestwich, *Edward I*, p. 494.

22 See Michael Penman, *Robert the Bruce, King of the Scots* (Yale, 2014) p. 69 for a discussion of the pope's relationship to Balliol's release and its implications.

23 There is no evidence to suggest that Bruce of Annandale, now permanently resident in England, was in receipt of any of the issues of his lordship, nor, indeed, had anything to do with Annandale at all; on the other hand, the English exchequer certainly received money from the lordship in 1300: see p. 140.

24 Trivet, *Annales*, p. 397, n. 7; E101/371/21/32; *CDS*, ii, no. 1657.

25 *Itin.*, p. 182; E101/10/18, part 2, m. 170.

26 Barrow, *Bruce*, pp. 122–3; A.A.M. Duncan, 'The Community of the Realm of Scotland and Robert Bruce', *SHR*, xlv (1966), pp. 195–8; Prestwich, *Edward I*, pp. 496–7.

27 E159/75, m. 16.

28 E101/68/1, mm. 14–25d; E159/75, m. 17.

29 Sir Archibald Livingstone was also sheriff of Stirling, in name at least, prior to the capture of Stirling castle from the Scots in 1304: *CDS*, ii, no. 1457.

30 E101/68/1, m. 23; A.J. Taylor, 'Thomas de Houghton', *The Antiquaries Journal*, xxx (1950), p. 31.

31 Stevenson, *Documents*, ii, pp. 394–7; Taylor, 'Thomas de Houghton', p. 30.

32 A.J. Taylor, 'Master James of St George', *EHR*, lx (1950), pp. 449–50; Brown, Colvin & Taylor, *The History of the King's Works in Scotland*, i, p. 413.

33 *CDS*, ii, no. 1324.

34 *Ibid.*, no. 1412.

35 RCAMS, *Selkirkshire*, fifteenth report (HMSO, 1957), pp. 4, 11; A.T. Simpson and S. Stevenson, *Historic Selkirk: the archaeological implications of development* (Scottish Burgh Survey, 1981), pp. 1, 4.

36 RCAHMS, *Selkirkshire*, pp. 4, 46; Simpson & Stevenson, *Historic Selkirk*, pp. 1, 4–5.

37 *CDS*, ii, no. 1288.

38 Ibid., no. 1324; RCAHMS, *Selkirkshire*, p. 48.

39 E159/75, m. 7; E159/76, m. 68.

40 *APS*, i, p. 454.

41 See Barrow, *Bruce*, p. 124; *Melrose Liber*, i, no. 351.

42 *CCR, 1296–1302*, 548; *CDS*, ii, no. 1319; *CDS*, ii, no. 1229.

43 See, for example, C. McNamee, *The Wars of the Bruces: Scotland, England and Ireland, 1306–1328* (East Linton, 1997), Chapter 3.

44 Barrow, *Bruce*, p. 124.

45 *CDS*, v, no. 287.

46 *CDS*, ii, no. 1313.

47 C.M. Fraser (ed.), *Northern Petitions, Berwick, Cumbria and Durham*, vol. 144 (Surtees Society, 1981), no. 13.

48 Duncan, *Scotland: The Making of the Kingdom*, pp. 494–6.

49 Stevenson, *Documents*, ii, pp. 443–4; *CPR, 1301–1307*, pp. 60–61; *CDS*, ii, no. 1314.

50 *CPR, 1301–1307*, p. 78.

51 *CDS*, ii, nos. 526, 832, 853; *CCR, 1296–1302*, p. 545.

52 *CDS*, ii, no. 1321 (6).

53 Barrow, *Bruce*, p. 105; *CDS*, ii, no. 1608. Despite the appointment of an escheator, Edward's officials continued to use English terminology – Martinmas and Pentecost.

54 *Ibid.*, no. 1227.

55 Stevenson, *Documents*, ii, pp. 393–8.

56 E159/75, mm. 10, 20.

57 Ibid., mm. 16, 74.

58 E101/68/1, m. 19.

59 *CPR, 1301–1307*, p. 35.

60 Castleguard was a traditional duty required of landholders.

61 E101/10/5; E101/10/10; M. Prestwich, 'Colonial Scotland: The English in Scotland under Edward I', p. 9.

62 See Nicolas, *A History of the Royal Navy*, i, p. 280, for an account of the violent and costly quarrel between the Cinque Ports and Yarmouth.

63 *CPR, 1301–1307*, pp. 52–3.

64 *CCR, 1296–1302*, p. 564.

65 E101/13/34, m. 18; E101/10/15.

66 E101/9/13, mm. 1–2; E101/9/30, mm. 16–29.

6 CHECKMATE

1 *CCR, 1296–1302*, p. 599.

2 Stevenson, *Documents*, ii, pp. 446–7.

3 *CDS*, v, no. 292; *CDS*, ii, nos. 1325, 1331.

4 *CDS*, v, no. 297. The earl was leaving rather late for the parliament of 14 October.

5 Stevenson, *Documents*, ii, p. 448.

6 *CCR, 1296–1302*, pp. 611–2; *CPR, 1301–1307*, pp. 74–5.

7 *Ibid.*, p. 98.

8 *CCR, 1296–1302*, p. 612; *CPR, 1301–1307*, p. 75.

9 *CCR, 1302–1307*, pp. 65–6.

10 *Parl. Writs*, i, pp. 368–9.

11 E101/11/19, m. 3.

12 Ibid., mm. 3, 4, 6.

13 *CDS*, ii, no. 1341; *CPR, 1301–1307*, p. 105; *CCR, 1302–1307*, p. 71.

14 *CPR., 1301–1307*, p. 111; *CCR, 1302–1307*, pp. 71, 20; *CDS*, ii, no. 1649.

15 *CDS*, iv, p. 456; *CPR, 1301–1307*, p. 109.

16 *CPR, 1292–1301*, pp. 60–61.

17 *Guisborough*, pp. 351–2.

18 E159/76, m. 68.

19 *Ibid.*, mm. 12, 15; *Parl. Writs*, i, p. 132.

20 *CCR, 1302–1307*, p. 80.

21 *CDS*, v, no. 321; *CPR, 1301–1307*, p. 129.

22 *CCR, 1302–1307*, p. 76; *CPR. 1301–1307*, p. 131.

23 *Ibid.*, p. 187.

24 *Parl. Writs*, i, p. 370–1; J. Lydon, 'The Years of Crisis, 1254–1315', p. 200.

25 E101/364/13, mm. 4–22, mm.99–100.
26 E101/365/6, mm. 2, 17; E101/684/53, mm. 11–13; E101/11/20, m.10; E101/13/36, part 3, m. 187; E101/364/13, m. 32.
27 Prestwich, *Edward I*, p. 498: Prestwich, *War, Politics and Finance*, pp. 80, 97–8; E101/612/11.
28 *CDS*, ii. nos. 1356, 1385; Stevenson, *Documents*, ii, pp. 178–9 (wrongly calendared under 1297).
29 *CDS*, ii, no. 1375; *Itin.*, p. 210.
30 E101/364/13, mm. 65–102.
31 *Ibid.*, m. 5.
32 *CCR, 1302–1307*, p. 91.
33 *CPR, 1301–1307*, pp. 146–7.
34 *CDS*, v, no. 331 E101/11/19, m. 5.
35 E159/76, m. 18.
36 *Ibid.*, m. 20.
37 *APS*, i, pp. 454–5; Palgrave *Documents*, p. 333; Barrow, *Bruce*, pp. 127–8.
38 Stevenson, *Documents*, ii, pp. 449–50
39 *CDS*, ii, no. 1389.
40 E159/76, m. 74.
41 *Ibid.*, m. 70; E101/364/13, m. 12.
42 *CDS*, ii, no. 1386.
43 Haskell (1991) *The Scottish Campaign of Edward I*, pp. 26-7
44 E101/364/13, m. 93; Haskell, *The Scottish Campaign of Edward I, 1303–4*, p. 27; E101/364/6, m. 3.
45 E101/364/13, m. 100; E159/76, m. 74.
46 Haskell, *The Scottish Campaign of Edward I, 1303–4*, p. 28.
47 Barrow, *Bruce*, p. 127.
48 E159/76, m. 21; J. Lydon, 'The Years of Crisis, 1254–1315', pp. 200–1; see below, p. 216.
49 E.M. Barron, *The Scottish War of Independence* (Inverness, 1934), p. 193; Haskell, *The Scottish Campaign of Edward I, 1303–4*, pp. 31–3; E101/364/13, m. 100.
50 E101/11/21, mm. 55–59; *CDS*, ii, no. 1390.
51 *Ibid.*, nos. 1392–3.
52 Stevenson, *Documents*, ii, p. 453.
53 *CDS*, ii, no. 1405. It's not clear which direction Comyn was travelling in but, given that the Forth peters out to the north of Drymen, it seems most likely that he was coming south. Certainly, the guardian is not mentioned as a leader of any of the Scottish contingents operating in the south-west over the

summer of 1303, which suggests that he had command of forces ineffectually shadowing the English army in the north-east.

54 Barrow, *Bruce*, pp. 183, 325.

55 E101/10/18; mm. 1,193.

56 *CDS*, ii, pp. 392–3; C47/22/3, m. 33.

57 *CDS*, ii, no. 1432.

58 *Ibid.*, no. 1437; *CDS*, iv, p. 481.

59 *CDS*, ii, no. 1465; Stevenson, *Documents*, ii, pp. 467–70.

60 *CDS*, iv, p. 475. Wallace is here denied his knighthood in the English sources, though he was accorded it earlier in the year [e.g. E159/76, m. 18].

61 *CDS*, v, no. 346. The brackets in this document indicate illegible parts of the manuscript and their most likely contents.

62 See Penman, *Robert the Bruce*, p.49 onwards for a discussion of the career of Robert Wishart and the role of the Scottish church more generally in the wars with England.

63 Palgrave, *Documents*, i, pp. 286–8; 278–9; 280; 278–9; 279–82; 283; 283–5; 288–291, 334; E159/79, m. 30; *The Gascon Calendar of 1322*, no. 437.

64 E159/79, m., 30; *CDS*, ii, no. 1691.

65 See Watson, 'Settling the Stalemate: Edward I's peace in Scotland, 1303–5, pp. 127–143, for a fuller discussion of the context, conditions and aftermath of the Scottish submissions of 1304.

66 Haskell, *The Scottish Campaign of Edward I. 1303–4*, p. 38.

67 H.G. Richards and G. Sayles. 'The Scottish Parliaments of Edward I', *SHR*, xxv (1925), p. 311; Palgrave, *Documents*, i, pp. 194–7, 299–301, 345–6.

68 *CDS*, ii, nos. 1471, 1489, 1462–3.

69 *Ibid.*, nos. 1515, 1561.

70 *Ibid.*, no. 1457; *CDS*, v, no. 353.

71 See above n. 29.

72 *Ibid.*, no. 363; *CDS*, ii, no. 1519.

73 *CDS*, iv, p. 475.

74 *Itin.*, pp. 225–6; Prestwich, *Edward I*, pp. 501–2; Barrow, *Bruce*, pp. 128–30; *Foedera*, i, p. 969; *CDS*, ii, no. 1564.

75 This is presumably Sir John's uncle, rather than the other Sir Alexander, his cousin, brother of Comyn of Buchan, who had remained, technically at least, on Edward's side.

76 Palgrave, *Documents*, i, pp. 274, 276.

7 'EDWARD THE FAIR'? THE SETTLING OF SCOTLAND

1 *CDS*, ii, no. 1694.
2 *Ibid.*, no. 1646.
3 *Ibid.*, nos. 1592, 1682, 1689.
4 *Ibid.*, no. 1403; pp. 438–9; no. 1669; Duncan, *Scotland: The Making of the Kingdom*, p. 197; *CCR, 1302–1307*, p. 336.
5 E101/11/19, m. 4; *CDS*, ii, nos. 1657, 1658, 1420: E101/101/15.
6 *CCR, 1302–1307*, p. 25; *CDS*, ii, nos. 1659, 1707.
7 E101/19/11, m. 11 (dorso); *CDS*, ii, no. 1646, p. 443.
8 Bateson, 'The Scottish King's Household', p. 25.
9 *CDS*, ii, no. 1608.
10 *CDS*, ii, no. 1611, p. 442, nos. 1520, 1689, 1654–6, 1658.
11 *CDS*, iv, p. 484.
12 See *Registrum Monasterii de Cambuskenneth 1147–1535* (Grampian Club, 1872), p. 41, for a reference to the lands of Tulybethwyne.
13 *CDS*, ii, no. 1722.
14 *Ibid.*, ii, no. 1420.
15 Inquests were held at both Berwick and Roxburgh in 1299, but this was as a prelude to the granting out of 'rebel' lands and so was not part of usual peacetime procedure: *CPR, 1292–1301*, p. 428.
16 *CDS*, ii, p. 198, nos. 1420, 1435, 1436, 1619, 1457.
17 Stevenson, *Documents*, ii, p. 331.
18 *CDS*, ii, p. 203, no. 1452.
19 See, for example, W. Stanford Reid, 'Trade, Traders, and Scottish Independence', in *Speculum*, no.xxix (1954), p. 213.
20 *CDS*, ii, no. 1592.
21 See *CPR, 1292–1301*, p. 560; *CDS*, ii, nos. 982, 992, for these few examples.
22 See p. 81.
23 See, for example, *CDS*, ii, no. 1621.
24 *Ibid.*, no. 1613.
25 *CDS*, iv, no. 1804.
26 *CDS*, ii, no. 1423; *Memo. de Parl.*, no. 403.
27 *Guisborough*, p. 363; *CDS*, ii, no. 1615; Rev. C. Moor (ed.), *The Knights of Edward I* (Harleian Society, volume 80, 1930) iii, p. 20.
28 *CDS*, ii, no. 1621.
29 *CDS*, v, no. 365. See R. Nicholson, *Edward III and the Scots* (London, 1965), for the role of the Disinherited in the period after the death of Robert Bruce.

30 *Memo. de Parl.*, no. 384.

31 *Ibid.*, no. 323.

32 *CDS*, ii, no. 1493.

33 *Ibid.*, ii, no. 1589; *RRS*, ii, no. 80, pp. 178–9.

34 Prestwich, *Edward I*, pp. 346–7.

35 *CDS*, ii, no. 1604.

36 See Barrow, *Bruce*, p. 131.

37 *Memo. de Parl.*, nos. 333, 383.

38 *Ibid.*, no. 319.

39 *Ibid.*, no. 310.

40 *Ibid.*, no. 400. Husbandmen were peasants who had their own holdings but also worked their lord's lands (in this case, the king's).

41 Prestwich, 'Colonial Scotland: The English in Scotland under Edward I', pp. 7–8.

42 *Ibid.*, p. 6.

43 *Memo. de Parl.*, nos. 294, 349, 337; *CDS*, ii, nos. 1686, 1921.

44 *Memo. de Parl.*, nos. 338, 339, 372.

45 Jargun was actually the Dumfries burgess to whom Sir Ingram de Guines had owed money: see above, p. 238.

46 *CDS*, ii, no. 1526.

47 *Ibid.*, no. 1724; *Memo. de Parl.*, nos. 382, 385, 305; see *RRS*, i, no. 195, pp. 231–2 for Jedburgh's claim to Restenneth.

48 *Memo. de Parl.*, nos. 280, 283, 303, 362, 398.

49 See, Prestwich, *Edward I*, Chapter 10.

50 *Langtoft*, ii, p. 353.

51 *CDS*, ii, no. 1424; E101/364/13, m. 9. The date and place of this document is obscured at the end, but enough remains to suggest that it was issued at St Andrews.

52 *CDS*, iv, no. 477. Professor Barrow has suggested that 'Yrenside' is Earnside: Barrow, *Bruce*, p. 136. However, the presence of the constable of Dundee, together with the fact that a 'Y' is more likely to have turned into an 'I', rather than an 'Ea', makes Ironside near Dundee far more likely.

53 Barrow, *Bruce*, pp. 136–7.

54 J.G. Bellamy, *The Law of Treason in England in the later Middle Ages* (Cambridge, 1970), pp. 31–2, 35.

55 *Ibid.*, pp. 37–8; Barrow, *Bruce*, p. 137, n. 39.

56 Bellamy, *The Law of Treason in England in the later Middle Ages*, pp. 38–9.

57 *Memo. de Parl.*, nos. 14, 293; *APS*, i, pp. 119–120; Barrow, *Bruce*, p. 134.

58 Penman makes the point on p.37 of *Robert the Bruce* that in 1292 John Comyn effectively became his uncle King John's heir presumptive because the latter's son, Edward, was only nine at the time.

59 Most, if not all, of these sheriffs were actually appointed in 1303.

60 *CDS*, ii, no. 1691, p. 457; Bateson, 'The Scottish King's Household', p. 42.

61 All references to the ordinances are *CDS*, ii, no. 1691.

62 Ibid., p. 457; Palgrave, *Documents*, i, p. 292.

63 *CDS*, ii, nos. 678, 715; *Feodera*, i, p. 925; *CDS*, ii, no. 546, p. 443.

64 See Prestwich, *Edward I*, p. 132.

65 Stevenson, *Documents*, ii, p. 225; *Rot. Scot.*, i, p. 34.

66 *CPR, 1301–1307*, p. 415. This was, in fact, six days after the murder of Sir John Comyn at Dumfries.

67 These were presumably the castles of Tullibothwell and Polmaise or their alternative sites.

68 The order restoring Sir Ingram's lands in England was issued as late as 8 October 1305: *CCR, 1302–1307*, p. 291.

69 *Rot. Parl.*, i, pp. 211–2.

70 Barrow, *Bruce*, p. 135, also quoting from F. M. Powicke, *The Thirteenth Century*, p. 711.

71 See p. 1.

8 Lessons in Conquest

1 See Davies, *Owain Glyn Dŵr*, p. 233.

2 See, for example, Contamine, *War in the Middle Ages*, pp. 132–7, 151–65.

3 See p. 113.

4 Wright, *Political Songs*, p. 183.

5 Haskell, *The Scottish Campaign of Edward I, 1303–4*, p. 38.

6 Wright, *Political Songs*, p. 242.

7 Davies, *Owain Glyn Dŵr*, p. 237.

8 *Ibid.*, p. 263.

9 The authors of *1066 and all that* were perhaps perfectly aware that many a true word is spoken in jest.

10 See Watson, *Traitor, Outlaw, King*, pp.136-8 for a fuller discussion of John Comyn's credentials to be king and the possibility

that he was seeking support for it, not least with the dissemination of the Comyn claim to the throne, put aside for Balliol in 1291 but found in a contemporary chronicle.

11 *CDS*, ii, nos. 1696, 1631, 1395.
12 Langtoft, Chronicle, p. 254.

BIBLIOGRAPHY

I UNPUBLISHED PRIMARY SOURCES

Public Record Office, London
Chancery Miscellanea, C47
Exchequer, King's Remembrancer's Memoranda Rolls, E159
Exchequer, Queen's Remembrancer, Various accounts, E101

British Library, London
Additional MSS. 28024
Cotton MSS. Cleopatra Diii

II PUBLISHED PRIMARY SOURCES

The Acts of the Parliaments of Scotland, eds. T. Thomson and C. Innes, vol. i (Edinburgh, 1844)

Anglo-Scottish Relations, 1174–1328: Some Selected Documents, ed. E.L.G. Stones, 2nd edition (Oxford, 1970)

Annales Nicholai Triveti, ed. T. Hog (London, 1845)

[BLIND HARRY], THE WALLACE, ed. M.P. McDiarmid (STS, 1968)

Calendar of Close Rolls, ed. H.C. Maxwell-Lyte (London, 1906–8)

Calendar of Documents relating to Scotland, ed. J. Bain *et al* (London, 1881–1986)

Calendar of Patent Rolls, ed. H.C. Maxwell-Lyte (London, 1906–8)

The Chronicle of Walter of Guisborough, ed. H. Rothwell, Camden Society, 3rd Series, lxxxix (1957)

Chronicon de Lanercost, 1201–1346, ed. J. Stevenson (Maitland Club, 1839)

Documents and Records illustrating the History of Scotland, ed. F. Palgrave (London, 1837)

Documents Illustrative of the Crisis of 1297–8 in England, ed. M. Prestwich, Camden Society, 4th ser. (London, 1980)

Documents Illustrative of the History of Scotland, 1286–1306, ed. J. Stevenson (Edinburgh, 1870)

Documents Illustrative of Sir William Wallace, His Life and Times, ed. J. Stevenson (Maitland Club, 1841)

Edward I and the throne of Scotland, 1290–1296, eds. E.L.G. Stones & G.G. Simpson (Oxford, 1978)

Études sur l'histoire du XIIIe siècle, ed., M Kervyn de Lettenhove (Brussels, 1854)

Facsimiles of the National Manuscripts of Scotland, ed. W. Gibson-Clark (London, 1867–71)

Foedera, Conventiones, Litterae et Cuiuscunque Generis Acta publica, ed. T. Rymer, Record Commission Edition (London, 1816–69)

The Gascon Calendar of 1322, ed. G.P. Cuttino, Camden Third Series, vol. lxv (London, 1949)

Highland Papers, ed. J.R.N. Macphail, volume ii (SHS, 1914–34)

Liber de Calchou (Bannatyne Club, 1846)

Liber Quotidianus Contrarotulatoris Garderobae, 1299–1300, ed. J. Topham *et al* (1787)

Liber Sancte Marie de Melros (Bannatyne Club, 1837)

Liber Sancte Thome de Aberbrothoc (Bannatyne Club, 1848–56)

Memorandum de Parliamento, 1305, ed. F.W. Maitland (Rolls Series, 1893)

Northern Petitions, Berwick, Cumbria and Durham, ed. C.M. Fraser vol. 144 (Surtees Society, 1981)

Parliamentary Writs and Writs of Military Summons, ed. F. Palgrave (Record Commission, 1827–33)

Regesta Regum Scottorum, ed. G.W.S. Barrow, vol. ii (Edinburgh, 1960)

Regesta Regum Scottorum, ed. A.A.M. Duncan, vol. v (Edinburgh, 1988)

Registrum Monasterii de Cambuskenneth, 1147–1535, ed. W. Fraser (Grampian Club, 1872)

The Roll of Caerlaverock, ed. T. Wright (London, 1864)

Rotuli Scotiae in Turri Londinensi et in Domo Capitulari Westmonasteriensi Asservati, ed. D. Macpherson *et al* (London, 1814)

The Scalachronica by Sir Thomas Grey of Heton, Knight, ed. J. Stevenson (Maitland Club, 1836)

Scotland in 1298: Documents relating to the campaign of Edward the First in that year, and especially to the Battle of Falkirk, ed. H. Gough (Paisley, 1888)

'The Scottish King's Household', ed. M. Bateson, in *Miscellany of the Scottish History Society*, volume ii (SHS, 1904)

The Sheriff Court Book of Fife, 1515–22, ed. W.C. Dickinson, (SHS, 1928)

Willelmi Rishanger, Chronica et Annales, ed. H.T. Riley (Rolls Series, 1865)

WYNTOUN, ANDREW OF, *The Orygynale Cronykil of Scotland*, ed. D. Laing (Edinburgh, 1872–9)

III   REFERENCE WORKS

An Inventory of the Historical Monuments in London, volume i, Westminister Abbey (RCAHM, 1924)

Itinerary of Edward I, Part ii: 1291–1307 ed. E.W. Stafford, List and Index Society, vol. 132 (London, 1976)

The Knights of Edward I, Rev. C. Moor, ed. (Harleian Society, volume 80, 1930)

RCAHMS, Inventory of *East Lothian* (1924), *Peeblesshire*, seventeenth report (HMSO, 1967) Inventory of *Roxburghshire*, fourteenth report (HMSO, 1956), Inventory of *Selkirkshire*, fifteenth report (HMSO, 1957)

The Scots' Peerage, 9 vols., ed. Sir J. Balfour Paul (Edinburgh, 1904–14)

IV   SECONDARY SOURCES

BARRON, E.M., THE SCOTTISH WAR OF INDEPENDENCE (Inverness, 1934)

BARROW, G.W.S., ROBERT BRUCE AND THE COMMUNITY OF THE REALM OF SCOTLAND, 3rd edition (Edinburgh, 1992)

—, 'James Fifth Stewart of Scotland, 1260(?)–1309', in K. Stringer, ed., *Essays on the Scottish Nobility* (Edinburgh, 1985)

—, 'The Army of Alexander III's Scotland, in N. Reid., ed., *Scotland in the reign of Alexander III, 1249–1286* (Edinburgh, 1990)

BELLAMY, J.G., THE LAW OF TREASON IN ENGLAND IN THE LATER MIDDLE AGES (Cambridge, 1970)

BROWN, M, THE WARS OF SCOTLAND, 1214–1371, (Edinburgh, 2004)

BROWN, R.A., COLVIN, H.M., & TAYLOR, A.J., EDS., THE HISTORY OF THE KING'S WORKS, volume i The Middle Ages (London, 1963)

CONTAMINE, P., WAR IN THE MIDDLE AGES (Oxford, 1986)

COSS, P., THE KNIGHT IN MEDIEVAL ENGLAND (Stroud, 1995)

CRUDEN, S., THE SCOTTISH CASTLE (Edinburgh, 1960)

DAVIES, R.R., THE REVOLT OF OWAIN GLYN DŴR, (Oxford, 1995)

DUNCAN, A.A.M., SCOTLAND: THE MAKING OF THE KINGDOM (Edinburgh, 1992)

—, THE KINGSHIP OF THE SCOTS (Edinburgh, 2002)

—, 'The Community of the Realm of Scotland and Robert Bruce', *SHR*, xlv (1966)

—, 'The Process of Norham, 1291', in P.R. Coss and S.D. Lloyd, eds., *Thirteenth Century England V* (Woodbridge, 1995)

DUNCAN, A.A.M. & BROWN, A.L., 'ARGYLL AND THE ISLES IN THE EARLIER MIDDLE AGES', PSAS, xc (1956–7)

FAVIER, J., PHILIPPE LE BEL (Paris, 1978)

FISHER, A., WILLIAM WALLACE (Edinburgh, 1986)

FRAME, R., THE POLITICAL DEVELOPMENT OF THE BRITISH ISLES, 1100–1500 (Oxford, 1995)

GOLDSTEIN, R.J., 'THE SCOTTISH MISSION TO BONIFACE VIII IN 1301', SHR, lxx (1991)

GRANT, A., INDEPENDENCE AND NATIONHOOD: SCOTLAND 1306–1469 (London, 1984)

HASKELL, M.A., THE SCOTTISH CAMPAIGN OF EDWARD I, 1303–4, M.A. thesis, University of Durham (Durham, 1991)

KIDD, C., SUBVERTING SCOTLAND'S PAST, (Cambridge, 1993)

LYDON, J., 'THE YEARS OF CRISIS, 1254–1315', IN A. COSGRAVE, ED., A NEW HISTORY OF IRELAND: MEDIEVAL IRELAND, 1169–1534 (Oxford, 1987)

—, 'Irish levies in the Scottish Wars, 1296–1302', *Irish Sword*, v (1962)

MACDONALD, R.A., THE KINGDOM OF THE ISLES: SCOTLAND'S WESTERN SEABOARD, c.1100–c.1336 (East Linton, 1997)

MACNAMEE, C., THE WARS OF THE BRUCES: SCOTLAND, ENGLAND AND IRELAND, 1306–1328, (East Linton, 1997)

MORRIS, J.E., THE WELSH WARS OF EDWARD I (Stroud, 1996)

MURRAY, K.M.E., THE CONSTITUTIONAL HISTORY OF THE CINQUE PORTS (Manchester, 1935)

NICHOLSON, R., EDWARD III AND THE SCOTS (London, 1965)

—, *Scotland: The Later Middle Ages* (Edinburgh, 1978)

NICOLAS, SIR NICHOLAS HARRIS, A HISTORY OF THE ROYAL NAVY FROM THE EARLIEST TIME TO THE WARS OF THE FRENCH REVOLUTION (London, 1847)

PENMAN, M. A., ROBERT THE BRUCE. KING OF THE SCOTS (Yale, 2014)

POWICKE, M.F., THE THIRTEENTH CENTURY (Oxford, 1991)

PRESTWICH, M.C., WAR, POLITICS AND FINANCE UNDER EDWARD I (London, 1972)

—, *Edward I* (London, 1988)

—, 'Colonial Scotland: The English in Scotland under Edward I' in R. Mason, ed., *Scotland and England, 1286–1815* (Edinburgh, 1987)

REID, N., 'THE KINGLESS KINGDOM: THE SCOTTISH GUARDIANSHIP OF 1286–1306', SHR, lxi (1982)

—, 'The Political Role of the Monarchy in Scotland, 1249–1329', unpublished Ph.D. thesis (Edinburgh, 1984)

—, Scotland in the reign of Alexander III, 1249–1286 (Edinburgh, 1990)

REID, R.C., 'CRUGGLETON CASTLE', TDGAS, Third Series, xxxi (Dumfries, 1931)

RICHARDS, H.G. & SAYLES, G., 'THE SCOTTISH PARLIAMENTS OF EDWARD I', SHR, xxv (1925)

SAYLES, G.O., 'THE GUARDIANS OF SCOTLAND AND A PARLIAMENT AT RUTHERGLEN IN 1300, SHR, xxiv (1927)

SIMPSON, A.T. & STEVENSON, S., HISTORIC SELKIRK: THE ARCHAEOLOGICAL IMPLICATIONS OF DEVELOPMENT (Scottish Burgh Survey, 1981)

STANFORD REID, W., 'TRADE, TRADERS, AND SCOTTISH INDEPENDENCE', IN SPECULUM, no. xxix (1954)

TAYLOR, A.J., 'MASTER JAMES OF ST GEORGE', EHR, lx (1950)

—, 'Thomas de Houghton', *The Antiquaries Journal*, xxx (1950)

TOUT, T.F., 'MEDIEVAL TOWN-PLANNING' IN THE COLLECTED PAPERS OF THOMAS FREDERICK TOUT, volume iii (Manchester, 1934)

ULLMAN, W., THE GROWTH OF PAPAL GOVERNMENT IN THE MIDDLE AGES, 3rd edition (London, 1969)

WATSON, F.J., 'SETTLING THE STALEMATE: EDWARD I's PEACE IN SCOTLAND, 1303–1305' IN M. PRESTWICH, R. BRITNELL & R. FRAME, EDS., THIRTEENTH CENTURY ENGLAND VI (Woodbridge, 1997)

—, *Edward I in Scotland, 1296–1305*, unpublished Ph.D. thesis (Glasgow, 1991)

—, 'The Enigmatic Lion: Scotland, kingship and national identity', in D. Broun, R. J. Finlay & M. Lynch, eds., *Image and Identity: The Making and Remaking of Scotland* (Edinburgh, 1988)

—, 'Adapting tradition?: the earldom of Strathearn, 1114–1296', in R. Oram and G. Stell eds., *Lordship and Architecture in Medieval and Renaissance Scotland* (Edinburgh, 2005)

—, 'Expressions of power: thirteenth-century Scottish castles, in S. Foster, A. Macinnes and R. Macinnes, eds., *Scottish Power-centres* (Glasgow, 1998)

WRIGHT, T., POLITICAL POEMS AND SONGS RELATING TO ENGLISH HISTORY (London, 1839)

YOUNG, A, ROBERT THE BRUCE'S RIVALS: THE COMYNS, 1212–1314 (East Linton, 1997)

—, Noble Families and Political Factions in the Reign of Alexander III' in N. Reid, ed., *Scotland in the Reign of Alexander III, 1249–1286* (Edinburgh, 1990)

INDEX